Garden Neighborhoods
of San Francisco

Garden Neighborhoods
of San Francisco

The Development of Residence Parks, 1905–1924

RICHARD BRANDI

McFarland & Company, Inc., Publishers
Jefferson, North Carolina

ISBN (print) 978-1-4766-7408-7
ISBN (ebook) 978-1-4766-4148-5

LIBRARY OF CONGRESS AND BRITISH LIBRARY
CATALOGUING DATA ARE AVAILABLE

Library of Congress Control Number 2021011945

On the cover: Balboa Terrace's pedestrian entrance off
Junipero Serra Boulevard. The transit shelter was used by streetcars
until 1929 when the tracks were relocated to a private right of way
in the center of the street. Photo by author, 2020.

Printed in the United States of America

*McFarland & Company, Inc., Publishers
Box 611, Jefferson, North Carolina 28640
www.mcfarlandpub.com*

Table of Contents

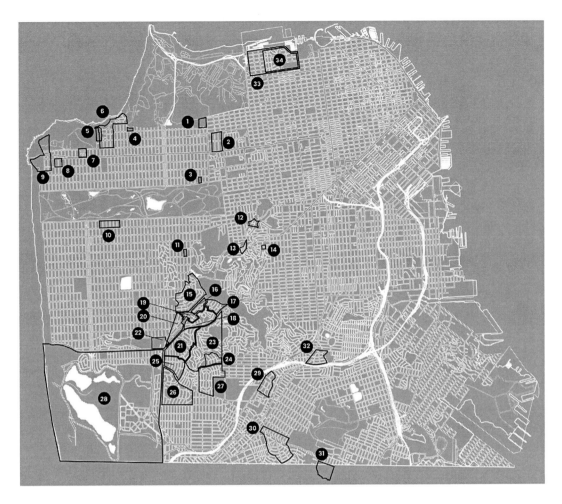

SAN FRANCISCO—Key map for all tracts: planned, built or advertised

Preface

Residence parks were built with picturesque streets, landscaping, detached houses, setbacks, and land use controls to convey the feeling of living in a park. The term was used during the first quarter of the twentieth century when developers were experimenting with how to create attractively designed residential developments using property deed restrictions that allowed them to control land use before the advent of zoning and other governmental regulations.

I became interested in residence parks several years ago as a result of my work with the Western Neighborhoods Project (WNP). I wrote a short book about three residence parks, and the St. Francis Wood Homes Association asked me to write a history for its centennial.[1] Later, I teamed up with Woody LaBounty of WNP to study eight residence parks for the San Francisco Office of Economic and Workforce Development (OEWD) and the Historic Preservation Fund Committee.

Interest in residence parks has grown over the last few years. The late Patrick McGrew published a book about one San Francisco residence park, *Historic Houses of Presidio Terrace*.[2] He followed the book with a survey of ten residence parks.[3] In 2001 Carolyn S. Loeb looked at the Westwood Highlands residence park.[4] More recently, other writers have explored San Francisco's residence parks: Ingleside Terraces (Woody LaBounty); Balboa Terrace (Jacquie Proctor); Westwood Park (Kathleen Beitiks); and Parkway Terrace (Inge Horton).[5]

But many other residence parks—at least thirty-six—were proposed or built between 1905 and 1924. This book explains how the developers went about the business of building residence parks over time, on different sites and for different markets. Also, how they conceived and planned them; how they modified their operations in light of war, recession, and inflation; the relationships developers had with one another and with city leaders; and how those relationships shaped residence parks. This book is not a social history or a survey of domestic architecture.

The book's first two chapters lay out the historical context in San Francisco and the reasons why residence parks came about when and where they did. Chapter 3 talks about the building of residence parks. Chapter 4 is a discussion of the people who lived in residence parks, the prohibition of Blacks and Asians, and others who were displaced by residence parks. Chapters 5 through 12 cover the work of the developers and the residence parks they built. Each chapter proceeds more or less chronologically. Chapter 13 details the work of Mark Daniels, landscape architect or engineer (he used both terms at different times), who was involved in many residence-park projects. Finally, Chapter 14 outlines the accomplishments of residence parks and how recent trends might presage their future.

Most residence park developers were individuals, partnerships, or small companies, and their business and personal records have not survived. Published biographies of the developers do not exist. Similarly, the biographical information available about leading public figures, such as Mayor James Rolph or Chief Engineer Michael O'Shaughnessy, barely touch on residential development, let alone residential parks. Information about the architects who worked for the developers of residence parks is also limited.

Fortunately, developers left a trail to follow in the newspapers. The *San Francisco Call* (1890–1913) and *San Francisco Chronicle* (1865–present) are fully searchable online, and their real estate sections covered developments in detail. These searches produced hundreds of articles and advertisements directly about or related to residence parks. This research was complemented by articles from the *San Francisco Examiner,* which became searchable online as this book was being written. It is possible to glean the intentions of and the decisions made by the developers and builders through advertisements or articles, although the veracity of some of the ads suffer from marketing hype and some of the articles are thinly disguised boosterism.

A note about the price of houses. It is not readily possible to come up with meaningful conversions of historical costs into today's dollars for a host of reasons.[6] But for a sense of what things cost, in 1915 the national average income was $1,267, a new car cost $390, and a new house $3,395.[7]

Additional archival research was conducted at the San Francisco History Center at the San Francisco Public Library (my thanks to Thomas Carey); California Historical Society; University of California, Berkeley, Environmental Design Archives; the Bancroft Library at the University of California, Berkeley; California State Library in Sacramento; the Archives of the Archdiocese of San Francisco; and San Francisco Heritage. Many of the illustrations in this book come from the Western Neighborhoods Project's OpenSF-History website, where thousands of digitized images are available. I thank David Gallagher for providing these illustrations.

I also wish to thank Nicole Meldahl for scouring the Internet for biographical information about the developers, engineers, landscapers, and architects involved with residence parks. I am indebted to Kashal Lachhwani for creating the maps of the residence parks and for enhancing the quality of some of the historic newspaper illustrations. Denise Bradley taught me about cultural landscapes of the residence parks. Evelyn Rose provided information about Glen Park. Carolyn S. Loeb kindly provided an illustration of Woodcrest. I tried to locate all copyright holders and would appreciate hearing from any I may have missed. My thanks to Richard Longstreth, Richard Walker, Woody LaBounty, David Parry, Christopher Pollock, Angus Macfarlane, James Russiello, John Freeman, and Inge Horton for their comments. Austin Yu and Lorri Ungaretti substantially improved my prose. I appreciate their help.

The maps show the approximate boundaries of the residence parks with north pointing up unless stated otherwise. Buildings and landscape features mentioned in this book generally can be viewed from the public right of way. Please respect private property and do not venture up driveways or entrances.

Introduction

One sunny fall day, I led a group of urban studies students on a tour of the Forest Hill neighborhood of San Francisco. Exiting the underground streetcar station, the students found themselves in a quiet, lush landscape. Narrow tree-lined streets wandered up and down the hilly site. We passed two large flower urns, each as big as a car, and saw an enormous concrete staircase climbing up a hill. Stopping in front of what looked like an English pub, the students discovered it was actually a clubhouse for the residents. We walked along streets free from traffic and saw stately houses surrounded by lawns and gardens. A few residents were tending their gardens or sweeping leaves from the sidewalks. The solitude was in stark contrast to the city the students knew. They had no idea where they were.

Their reaction is not surprising. During the first quarter of the twentieth century, a handful of real estate developers created something unusual for San Francisco: spacious and aesthetically designed subdivisions on curvilinear streets with detached houses surrounded by trees, lawns, and landscaping. These subdivisions are not conventional suburbs or typical speculative tracts. They are different and make up a large component of the city's residential fabric.

The subdivisions were called *residence parks* to emphasize the park-like setting. Residence parks were designed to bring together the best of town and country living. Houses had generously sized gardens sited on curving roads and were places where people could raise families in peace and safety. Names often included "Park" or "Terrace" to evoke a suburban or country feeling. The remoteness set residence parks apart from the city and presented an opportunity to create a living-in-a-park feeling. But the remoteness posed the risk that buyers might shy away. To counter this apprehension, developers provided entry gates, public sculptures, ceremonial stairs, or fountains (such as the urns and stairs in Forest Hill) to create an identity and impression of stability and permanence.

Although new to San Francisco in 1905, residence parks were part of an international movement that had captivated people's imagination. During the late nineteenth and early twentieth centuries, hundreds of garden suburbs were built. Some were self-contained villages; others were suburban subdivisions far from the city. In San Francisco, they were located within the city limits but in outlying districts, where electric streetcars would take the new residents downtown for employment, professional services, department stores, and entertainment. Grocery stores, schools, and churches were eventually built near the residence parks to meet everyday needs.

Residence parks were popular. Home buyers liked the spacious lots, landscaping, and high-quality houses designed by architects. Residence parks offered amenities and a degree of privacy that people could not otherwise achieve unless they were wealthy, in stark contrast to the typical pattern of building in San Francisco.

Many developers got into the act—even those with little or no real estate experience—with varying degrees of success. Creating a residence park required many skills: a developer who acquired the land and set the goals, an engineer who designed the streets while respecting the topography, architects who designed artistic houses, a landscape designer who created the park-like environment, a real estate broker who marketed and sold the lots, and someone to arrange financing before federally-backed mortgages were available.

Not all developers were willing or able to do all these things. They were businessmen, foremost, who hoped to turn a profit on what were speculative developments. Each developer had to weigh the costs of artistic improvements considering the time, resources, and expected financial gain. Others hoped to cash in on the popularity of residence parks by applying the term *residence park* to subdivisions with few or no residence park attributes.

San Francisco was slow to embrace residence parks during the long economic expansion of the late 1890s and early 1900s. The rollout of residence parks stalled during the rebuilding after the 1906 earthquake and fire. Then suddenly, residence parks flooded the market, just as the economy nosedived during World War I. Some projects failed or dropped amenities, but others held on, finally to be saved by the 1920s housing boom. Most of the houses in residence parks were constructed in the 1920s; by the late 1930s, residence parks had been substantially completed.

None of the people responsible for residence parks are household names, and the students on the tour had never heard of the tracts, the developers, or the architects. But the achievements are impressive and proved to be durable.

In this book, I look at thirty-six residence parks that were planned or launched in San Francisco between 1905 and 1924, the heyday of the residence-park phenomenon. Almost all the residence parks are located on the west side of San Francisco, where vacant land was available during the early twentieth century.

A Note About Maps

Some of the historical maps are based on archival sources and may have features that are illegible or labeling that is too small to read. Although efforts were made to increase the resolution, these maps are not readable in the normal way. Nonetheless they illustrate important points and are offered in that spirit.

1

The Allure of Garden Suburbs

For millennia, people have tried to get away from the crowds, dirt, and unhealthy conditions that characterized cities. Suburbs are as old as civilization; the word *suburb* comes from Latin *suburbium*. From ancient times, the wealthy took refuge in villas or hunting grounds in forests, mountains or near the sea, especially during the hot summer months, while everyone else endured as best they could.

During the nineteenth century the growing number of England's prosperous merchants were looking for a suburban escape, but they were not wealthy enough for country houses. The English began experimenting with planned garden suburbs for the well-to-do, combining the advantages of city life and country life, while minimizing the disadvantages of both.[1] In 1811, John Nash laid out one of the first garden suburbs in Blaise Hamlet, north of Bristol, England, where he laid out ten freestanding cottages around a green with a sundial. Nash and others designed many English garden suburbs that became widely known in America.

Andrew Jackson Downing's writings during the 1840s popularized the idea of living in the country. He collaborated with Alexander Jackson Davis, the "father" of American landscape design, on a highly influential pattern book of houses, *Cottage Residences,* which mixed romantic architecture with the English picturesque countryside. Many garden suburbs were constructed in the second half of the 1800s in the U.S. and a few became known as archetypes.

In 1853, Llewellyn Haskell launched one of the first garden suburbs, Llewellyn Park, in New Jersey, twelve miles west of Manhattan. It featured curvilinear roads and a park, called the "Ramble," that was influenced by Andrew Jackson Downing's writings, as well as by Frederick Law Olmsted and Calvert Vaux's plans for Central Park. Llewellyn Park became one of the best known and most highly emulated examples of suburban design after it appeared in a supplement to the Sixth Edition of Downing's *Theory and Practice* (1859).[2]

In 1869, Olmsted teamed with Vaux to create the railroad garden suburb, Riverside, forty miles outside Chicago. It earned a reputation as the archetypal example of the curvilinear American-planned suburb. Located on the banks of the Des Plaines River, along the route of a steam railroad, Olmsted's plan provided urban amenities and homes that provided privacy in a park-like setting by following three design principles that set the ideal for the spacious, curvilinear subdivision for generations to come: a tranquil site with mature trees, broad lawns, and variations in the topography; roads laid out in graceful curves to suggest tranquility; and irregularly shaped lots.

In the 1860s, a different type of garden suburb similar to San Francisco's residence parks was begun in the city of St. Louis. Called "private places," these residence parks were built within the city limits. They were exclusive residential subdivisions within the

Kingsbury Place (1902), one of twenty-two private places built in St Louis between 1850 and 1920. The private nature was confirmed when the author and a St. Louis native were chased out by a security guard (photograph by author, 2015).

street grid, featuring gates, private streets, and landscaped medians. They are called private because the streets are private property; they are not open to the public.

Garden suburbs proliferated around the country soon after the introduction of the electric streetcar in 1880s. Compared to older modes of transportation (horse cars, cable cars, and steam railroads), streetcar lines were cheaper to construct and operate, as well as faster and more comfortable, than horse and cable lines. The electric streetcar opened up areas for all kinds of development, including residence parks.

Two streetcar garden suburbs that became models for other developers were Chevy Chase and Roland Park, both in Maryland. In 1890, Francis Newlands announced the formation of the Chevy Chase Land Company on 1,700 acres of farmland in Maryland with his intention to create a suburban town and connect it with a streetcar line to Washington, D.C. The plan filed in 1892 used a grid overlaid with curving boulevards lined with trees.[3]

Also during the 1890s, Edward H. Bouton started Baltimore's Roland Park. City Beautiful designer George E. Kessler planned the eastern portion of the development in 1891, while Olmsted's son, Frederick Law Olmsted, Jr., laid out the western portion in 1897. The layout abandoned the city grid, and streets followed the natural crests and turns of the topography. When possible, mature trees remained in place. Roland Park was considered one of the leading residential subdivisions, a reputation known to developers of San Francisco's residence parks.[4]

Part of the appeal of garden suburbs was due to the changes brought about by the rapid industrialization after the Civil War. A huge increase in national wealth, economic output, and technological innovation was accompanied by rapid urbanization, pollution, labor unrest, and mass immigration. American cities suffered with overcrowding, congestion, tenements, and social strife. Cities grew without the benefit of additional parks that could have ameliorated dismal living conditions. Mingling with immigrants from unfamiliar countries, with different religions and social customs—and seeing once fashionable neighborhoods losing their cachet as cities densified—gave rise to a desire for social exclusivity on the part of the merchant and professional classes.

A Bleak Natural Environment

San Francisco didn't suffer as much as other cities from industrial pollution, mass immigration, or civil strife (except toward the Chinese) during the nineteenth century. Although there was a considerable manufacturing base that employed one-third of the city's workforce, industry was concentrated along the shore of San Francisco Bay, where westerly winds blew smoke across the bay, while wastes were dumped into the bay, not into drinking water supplies.[5] Early San Francisco suffered from many fires, overcrowding, substandard housing, and the kinds of morals that might be expected in a Gold Rush town filled with mostly young males far from home. As San Francisco grew, conditions in the Chinatown District rivaled those of the worst tenements in the East, and the South of Market area comingled dense worker housing with factories. As the city matured, white working-class men could build or afford to buy their own houses in the Mission or Western Addition District, and thousands did so. The more wealthy built large houses or mansions on relatively small lots compared to the Midwest or East Coast.

From the very beginning, there were attempts to create garden suburbs in the San Francisco Bay Area. The motivations had more to do with a desire for social exclusivity and to escape the bleak natural environment than with the perils of industrialization.

The bleak landscape as it appeared to Frederick Law Olmsted in 1856. Looking west from Russian Hill, Washerwoman's Lagoon (now Cow Hollow) in the middle ground, a treeless Presidio in the distance (OpenSFHistory wnp26.627).

It's difficult to imagine today, but San Francisco's natural environment appeared dreary and bleak to newcomers from the East Coast. Its average annual rainfall was half of Boston's. Droughts were common and trees were rare. After the short winter rainy season, the grasses and herbs quickly became dry, leaving the hills yellowish-brown for most of the year. The native plants tolerated long dry spells, but they appeared foreign and ugly to the new inhabitants. The western half of San Francisco was even more forbidding: a harsh environment of shifting sand dunes, where only coastal scrub and grasses survived.

Travelers found San Francisco desolate and forbidding. Arriving in 1835, Massachusetts native Richard Henry Dana, author of *Two Years Before the Mast,* described the site as "dreary sand hills, with little grass to be seen, and few trees, and beyond them higher hills, steep and barren, their sides gullied by the rains." When Frederick Law Olmsted, who was familiar with diverse vegetation around the world, visited in 1863 he described the hills as "perfectly bare of trees or shrubs—and almost awfully bleak."[6]

The harsh-looking natural environment was not softened by parks or green spaces. Residents did not plant ornamental vegetation, street trees, shrubs, gardens, or yards that might have lessened the severe look. Every inch of land was given over to residential or commercial uses with nothing left for parks, squares, or gardens. Frank Soulé noted the lack of parks early on:

> There seems to be no provision made ... for a public park—the true lungs of a large city. The existing plaza, or Portsmouth Square, and the other two or three diminutive squares ... seem the only breathing

Hyde Street, looking north from McAllister, 1891. Every inch was covered with buildings or streets with nothing left for parks, squares, or gardens (OpenSFHistory wnp37.03591).

holes intended for the future population of hundreds of thousands. This is a strange mistake, and can be only attributed to the jealous avarice of the city projects in turning every square vara [Spanish measurement of about a yard] … to an available building lot.… Not only is there no public park or garden, but there is not even a circus, oval, open terrace, broad avenue, or any ornamental line of street or building or verdant space of any kind other than three or four small squares alluded to; and which every resident knows are by no means verdant, except in patches where stagnant water collects and ditch weeds grow.[7]

Soulé's observation in 1855 remained valid throughout the nineteenth century. The lack of parks was due to several factors: squatters occupied many lots, and getting clear title was a perennial problem. Land speculation was a primary means of making money; the City of San Francisco earned most of its revenue from the sale of lots, so it had a financial disincentive to create parks. The city was limited from issuing debt to acquire and develop parks. In addition, many newcomers viewed their time in San Francisco as a chance to earn as much as they could before they returned home, so they saw no need to beautify the place. Even if gardens and parks were desired, the cost and paucity of water supplies and the periodic droughts made it difficult to maintain verdant areas.

The desire to live away from the rowdy residents and to be with others who had achieved wealth and respectability led to San Francisco's first garden suburb, South Park. Later attempts were made in Berkeley and San Mateo County, where the weather was better and there was room for large lots. These early projects were not well known outside the Bay Area, and all failed to develop; however, they reveal a theme that would replay in the twentieth century.

South Park—Social Exclusivity

In 1852, three years after the Gold Rush, San Francisco had a population of about 36,000, some sleeping in tents and shanties or on sand dunes and abandoned ships. George Gordon, an English immigrant and entrepreneur, started buying property for what he named *South Park*. He picked a location that was then on the outskirts of town—between Second and Third streets and Bryant and Brannan streets in the south of Market Street area—in order to escape the frequent fires, drunkenness, prostitution, and vice that characterized San Francisco. South Park was a compact oval tract with a private park in the style of the fashionable squares and ovals found in London and New York City. The park was fenced, and each property owner was given a key to the park. This was the first housing project in San Francisco to incorporate landscaping.

Gordon hired another Englishman, architect George H. Goddard, with experience in similar designs in London, to lay out attached two-story brick residences, clad with stucco and set around the oval park. The first houses were built in 1854. Each had an "English" basement, plus a kitchen, dining room, and servants' quarters. First floors contained the parlors and second floors the bedrooms. A separate building in the rear of each residence held a stable and coachman's quarters. The lots were narrow, even for San Francisco, with most being 21 feet wide, and relatively deep at 97 or 137½ feet. South Park introduced the row house to San Francisco; before South Park, houses were free standing, although crowded together.[8]

Although South Park was densely built, it had many of the elements that would characterize twentieth-century residence parks: a location away from the congestion of downtown (one mile), yet close enough to public transportation to reach it (the North

Horse car on Third Street on its way downtown in the 1860s. South Park's oval park in the distance. Public transportation was key, as South Park was located on the outskirts of the town (OpenSFHistory wnp27.0852).

Beach horse car line ran every ten minutes); an empty site on which to build (Gordon bought and assembled the parcels); a planned development with a tract architect; a private park; architectural controls; and deed restrictions banning stores, warehouses, and saloons. Because of the many fires in San Francisco, wood buildings were banned in the central commercial district, but they were the rule elsewhere.[9] However, all houses in South Park were to be of brick or stone construction. Gordon tried to enforce architectural controls, even with the rich and powerful. For example, when Andrew Shrader, a member of the board of supervisors, built a wood-frame house instead of brick in South Park, Gordon sued for breach of contract.[10] Gordon lost the suit, and then many wood buildings were built. Later twentieth-century residence tracts had more legally enforceable restrictions.

South Park captivated San Francisco's political and business elite. The townhouse designs evoked an upper-class London ambiance.[11] South Park got off to a good start, and by the early 1860s, it and nearby Rincon Hill were the fashionable places to reside for the social, artistic, political, and business elites. Isaac Friedlander, who had amassed a fortune in wheat and flour, lived at 30 South Park, where he hosted famous seventeen-course dinners for the socially prominent.[12]

However, South Park was not the financial success Gordon had hoped for. He paid a steep price for the parcels necessary to create a relatively large site. A banking panic slowed sales, and by the end of 1855 only the oval park and the northeast section had been built. Gordon lost interest and established the first sugar refinery in California; by 1860 it had become one of San Francisco's most important businesses. South Park lost its allure, as prominent families decamped to Nob Hill, made accessible by the invention of the cable car in 1873. Even before that, though, some wealthy residents chafed at the high density of South Park and left for more spacious areas.

Robert B. Woodward, a wealthy hotel proprietor, felt South Park was becoming too crowded and bought a two-block tract at 14th and Mission streets, even farther away from downtown. His estate later became the popular resort, Woodward's Gardens.[13] Others also left South Park, including Friedlander, who in 1866 built a mansion at 438 Bryant Street. Gradually, industry, manufacturing, warehousing, and ship's chandler activities surrounded South Park; by 1900, it was a working-class neighborhood. The 1906 earthquake and fire wiped it out, although the park oval survives to the present day.

Berkeley—Retreat from City Life

In 1865, at the peak of South Park's popularity, Frederick Law Olmsted designed a residential subdivision across San Francisco Bay in Berkeley at the behest of the Trustees of the College of California, a private school that merged in 1868 with the University of California. Called the *Berkeley Property* tract, it featured curvilinear parkways, a landscaped median, and a large garden. It stood on Piedmont Avenue between College Avenue, Prospect Street, Dwight Way, and Strawberry Creek and was intended to be a retreat from the congested life in the city. The late Susan Dinkelspiel Cerny wrote:

> The Berkeley Property tract was Olmsted's first fully developed landscape plan for a residential subdivision, and he accompanied it with an extensive written report outlining the social and healthful benefits of his physical layout. Olmsted's ideas for this residential neighborhood were based on the English garden suburb. Olmsted believed that "large domestic houses, on ample lots with garden setbacks, enhanced by sidewalk boulevards and plantings that would become luxuriant and graceful to shelter the visitor from the sun [would] express the manifestations of a refined domestic life." The neighborhood was to serve as a retreat from the congested life in the city.[14]

But being remote and lacking public transportation, the Berkeley property tract languished for many years.

Redwood City—Exclusivity with Nature

In 1888, two decades after Olmsted laid out a tract in Berkeley, an attempt was made to create a garden suburb in Redwood City, thirty-five miles south of San Francisco. Although it was the county seat of San Mateo County, Redwood City had fewer than 1,500 residents. A socially exclusive enclave called Wellesley Park was sited close to the San Francisco and San Jose railroad (later Southern Pacific), which ran to San Francisco. The streets of Wellesley Park followed a curving creek bed, and with the help of landscape gardener William Brown, the residence park had a picturesque quality. The developer Daniel O'Connell, a founder of the Bohemian Club, assured buyers of unmatched exclusivity when he wrote:

> In order to effectually protect the interest and comfort of those who make their homes in Wellesley Park, the name of each intending purchaser is submitted to a committee of gentlemen selected from the share-holders, who pass upon his desirability as a resident. Should he be deemed an unwelcome addition, the price of a Wellesley homestead is set so far beyond his reach that the hint is conclusively positive.[15]

Such snobbery was seldom admitted in other residence parks. But Wellesley Park attracted few buyers, due in part to the financial panic from 1893 to 1897. George C. Ross took over the project after O'Connell's death in 1899. Sales increased after the 1906 San Francisco earthquake and fire, although construction did not begin in earnest until the 1920s.[16]

Burlingame Park—Country Club Living

In 1893 Francis Newlands, who was also building Chevy Chase, Maryland, launched Burlingame Park in San Mateo County, promising it would "combine the charms of the country with the conveniences of the city." The site was closer to San Francisco than was Redwood City, and also near the railroad, but it too did not live up to expectations.

Newlands was a San Francisco attorney who married Cara Sharon, the daughter of Comstock mining and banking magnate William Sharon, one of the richest men in the West. According to historian Alan Hynding, "Newlands epitomized San Francisco's young men of wealth—bored, rich and eager to break from the stilted conventions of the city's old cliques by moving into a pseudo-rustic countryside."[17] The noted architect A. Page Brown designed five cottages with a rustic flavor, and John McLaren (the future superintendent of Golden Gate Park) did the landscaping. McLaren had worked earlier on George Henry Howard's San Mateo estate, *El Cerrito*, from about 1876 to 1887. (McLaren also planted the trees lining El Camino Real in Burlingame.)[18] The plat with curving roads was designed by engineer Richard P. Hammond, Jr., of Hammond and Baldwin, a predecessor to Baldwin & Howell a firm that was instrumental in creating residence parks in San Francisco. Richard was a cousin of William Hammond Hall, original designer and former superintendent of Golden Gate Park.

Hammond and Baldwin advertised Burlingame Park as having "piped water and sanitary drainage," great advantages at a time when these features were not usually provided. According to a newspaper account, this was the only real estate operation Baldwin managed outside of San Francisco.[19] Slow sales due to the 1890s financial panic prompted Newlands to reconfigure the enterprise as a county club with golf, polo, fox hunts, and other pastimes. One of the cottages was used as a clubhouse. After Newlands ended his involvement with Burlingame Park, he enjoyed greater recognition with his project in Chevy Chase, Maryland.[20] The country club idea eventually gave way to large formal estates, forming the exclusive town of Hillsborough in 1910.[21]

San Francisco, the Dense City

As South Park failed to maintain its cachet and other garden suburbs failed to attract residents, San Francisco continued its rapid growth and became a densely built city. The discovery of gold in 1848 quickly changed San Francisco from a tiny hamlet of perhaps 400 people to a city of 35,000 by 1850. Ships anchored at the first suitable place, the northeast corner of the city, and maritime, commercial, and business activities began to concentrate there. Industrial, manufacturing, and warehousing activities spread south of Market Street along the bay.[22]

By the turn of the twentieth century, San Francisco had a population of 350,000 made up of a wealthy business elite, a growing professional middle class, and a large working class. It was the preeminent city on the West Coast: the financial, mercantile, and transportation capital of the West and the entrepôt to Asia. San Francisco businesses controlled Alaska fisheries, Oregon lumber, Nevada mining, and much of the agricultural bounty of California's Central Valley. San Francisco thought of itself as the "New York of the West," even using the moniker "the City" as New York City did. The parallel-to-New-York concept extended to a town across San Francisco Bay called Brooklyn (1856–72), now part of Oakland, named for the ship *Brooklyn* that brought Mormon settlers from New York to California in 1846.

This was a time of the walkable city, where most people lived and worked within a thirty-minute walk or a short horsecar ride (or later a cable car) away. Buildings were close to one another, and development was clustered on the eastern part of the city near San Francisco Bay. The wealthy lived on Nob Hill, along Van Ness Avenue, or in Pacific Heights. Housing for the rapidly growing middle and working classes was met by small-scale builders in the Mission District and South of Market, where land was available, the weather was pleasant, and horse and cable car lines could be easily extended. Twenty thousand similar-looking Victorian houses were erected between 1880 and 1900 by working-class and middle-class owner/builders or contractors. The Real Estate Associates, an atypically large and leading speculative building company of the era, constructed more than one thousand Italianate designs in the Mission and Western Addition. Both speculative and builder-owner development usually occurred on or near street railway lines, on the standard street grid.

The urban form was characterized by high building density, even in wealthy neighborhoods. Although there were some large lots, San Francisco is geographically small, without room to spread out. Most lots were 25 feet wide by 100 or 125 feet long. Early on, the city was platted on a grid; later surveys extended and added new ones. The grid made for fast and unambiguous surveying and recording of real estate. Of course, the grid made no accommodation for hilly topography, views, ground conditions, or many other practical or aesthetic considerations. Streets sometimes ended abruptly when the slopes proved too steep for horses. (Although horses could pull wagons up fairly steep hills, the primitive brakes made it too dangerous to descend.)

As the affluent moved to the Western Addition, they built large houses "with characteristic high Victorian suburban house plans," but they didn't convey a suburban feeling.[23] Building was different than in the midwest or eastern part of the United States; lots and yards were smaller, and houses were built closer together and closer to the street. Builders did not plant trees because shade was not welcome with the persistent summer fog. Front yards, if they existed at all, were shallow. No municipal parks were created during the nineteenth century, except for Golden Gate Park, which was remote from the built-up sections of town. As a result, San Francisco had a denser and more urban feeling than other cities.

To some observers the architecture of San Francisco stagnated during the two decades after the Civil War.[24] Instead of the handsome brick and stone buildings designed during the 1850s, wood became the choice building material, and contractors vied to outdo one another with fanciful gingerbread facades. Wood construction was considered safer after the severe 1868 earthquake and it was cheaper than brick or stone. Old-growth wood was readily available from nearby redwood and pine forests and was the overwhelming choice for the rich and humble alike.

The architects working after the Civil War had learned their trade as apprentices to undistinguished firms and were cut off from architectural developments in the East. As a result, Victorian architecture became the dominant architectural style for San Francisco with increasing ornamental excess. Some critics at the time derided the trend, including architect and furniture maker Charles Eastlake, who said, "I now find to my amazement that there exists on the other side of the Atlantic an 'Eastlake style' of architecture, which, judging from the [California] specimens I have seen illustrated, may be said to burlesque such doctrines of art as I have ventured to maintain … and which by all accounts seems to be extravagant and bizarre."[25]

One acerbic critic was architect Willis Polk, head of the San Francisco office of the firm of Daniel Burnham and John Wellborn Root (pioneers of the Chicago School of Architecture), who complained of San Francisco's Victorian "architecture monstrosities." He didn't blame architects if they made honest mistakes; his scorn was reserved for contractors and builders who used excessive ornamentation.[26]

Tastes in architecture began changing in the late 1880s, as San Franciscans began turning to prominent architects from the Midwest and East to construct major buildings. In 1885, Leland Stanford hired the Boston-based Shepley, Rutan and Coolidge (successor to the prominent architect Henry Hobson Richardson, whose style became known as Richardsonian Romanesque) to design a master plan of Stanford's new university which featured landscaping by Frederick Law Olmsted. In the early 1890s, Burnham Root, was hired to design San Francisco's first high rises, including the Mills Building and the Chronicle building, dramatically changing the skyline.

This odd-looking house is the kind of architectural monstrosity that Polk complained about. Former 948 Haight Street circa 1890, no longer standing (OpenSFHistory wnp.27.5769).

The Chronicle building shortly after completion in 1889. It survived the 1906 earthquake and fire; its clock tower was lost to fire a year earlier. In 1962 the building was clad with aluminum, glass, and porcelain panels; in 2007 it was restored as part of a condominium conversion (OpenSFHistory wnp37.00197).

The City Beautiful

San Franciscans were deeply affected by the 1893 World's Columbian Exposition in Chicago as were most Americans. Burnham and Root organized the massive project with stately buildings surrounded by landscaping and natural features designed by the country's leading architects. Frederick Law Olmsted designed a system of lagoons and waterways fed by Lake Michigan. The exposition buildings were the product of the French Beaux-Arts school of design and emphasized logic, harmony, and uniformity. The fair itself was well-managed and had clean streets, well-behaved crowds, and many advanced sanitary and transportation systems. To the visitors who came from cities with widespread corruption, filthy streets, and poor sanitation, the contrast was dazzling.

Covered with "staff" (stucco), the buildings gave a magnificent whiteness to the scene, which became known as the "White City." Twenty-seven million people—nearly one quarter of the country's population—witnessed the exposition's beauty and serenity, which is often credited with introducing City Beautiful ideals to Americans. Many San Franciscans embraced those ideals.

Prominent San Franciscans visited the exposition, including Michael de Young, owner of the *Chronicle* newspaper, and James Phelan, a prominent banker, civic leader, and future mayor. Two developers of San Francisco's residence parks, George Lyon and Joseph Leonard, are known to have visited the "White City."[27] But whether they visited it or not, builders of San Francisco's residence parks knew about the exposition through newspapers, magazines, and brochures. San Francisco elites were so taken with the

The 1893 World's Columbian Exposition in Chicago (Library of Congress).

Chicago exposition that San Francisco put on its own version of the Columbian Exposition called the 1894 Midwinter California Exposition.

The new high rises, awareness of the World's Columbian Exposition, and the arrival of architects from the East Coast with greater professionalism and sophistication began to change the architecture and form of San Francisco. Most of these architects were academically trained and veterans of McKim, Mead and White or other prestigious architecture firms. Some, including the New York-born Bernard Maybeck and Massachusetts-born John Galen Howard (who was hired to establish the architecture program at University of California, Berkeley), were trained at the École des Beaux-Arts. Others influential architects who had come to San Francisco were A. Page Brown, Willis Polk, Ernest Coxhead, and A.C. Schweinfurth, who developed their own architectural styles.[28]

All the newcomers viewed the Victorian gingerbread city as hopelessly out of date. Wood construction, with its turrets, brackets, and colonnettes, could not compare to the longevity and beauty of brick or stone buildings of the East. Geographer Richard Walker wrote what the newly arrived architects thought of San Francisco's architecture:

> The new architects rejected what they regarded as the falsity and incoherence of Victorian architecture in favor of a studied simplicity and integrity of design—a thoroughly Modern outlook. They favored classical revivals of "Mediterranean" styles, a loose assemblage of Italian Renaissance, Spanish-Moorish, and Roman-Beaux Arts. Californians had suddenly rediscovered their links to Mediterranean civilization through the Spanish conquest. The Mythos of the Missions took Southern California by storm at the turn of the century, giving that region its own identity against San Francisco's favored fantasies of the Pioneers and Argonauts. Ironically, Bay Area architects created the Mission style but abandoned it by the early 1900s. All the leading architects also worked in the Arts and Crafts genre, though this would show up less in the great estates than in smaller houses.[29]

The new guard proposed beautifying San Francisco by remodeling Golden Gate Park in the spirit of Versailles, extending the park in a manner resembling the

Champs-Elysees, creating a monumental terminus for the city's principal street (Market), and building a new Civic Center. Newspaper heiress Phoebe Hearst offered to pay for an international competition to replan San Francisco along the lines of what Baron Hauss-mann recently did in Paris. While none of these proposals were implemented, they were praised and debated extensively.[30]

Other international expositions in Buffalo (1901), St. Louis (1904), Portland (1905), and Seattle (1909) reinforced the City Beautiful ideals of the Columbian Exposition. Walter Rockwell Hoag, brother of Edgar Hoag, a future residence parks developer and brother of the engineer William Hoag who laid out residence parks, attended the Port-land exposition.[31] His experience is not recorded but he may have shared what he saw with his brothers. Although the fairs were a mix of commercialism and civic pride, they also popularized the ideas of city planning, orderly designs, the neoclassical style, and Olmsted's landscaping concepts.

Frederick Law Olmsted and later his sons, Frederick Law Olmsted, Jr., and John Charles Olmsted (the Olmsted Brothers), formed the preeminent landscape-architecture firm in the United States from 1857 to 1950. The firm's work had a huge impact on the design of American city parks and suburban neighborhoods. Not only did the Olmsted firm design hundreds of subdivisions, but it also promoted the coordination of trans-portation systems, naturalistic features, tree-lined streets, landscaping, and underground utilities throughout the United States and abroad.

San Francisco's urban form was ripe for beautification. The city's fame long rested with its economic clout, not artistry or civic beauty. It had a paucity of cultural or scien-tific institutions such as museums and art galleries. There were no grand boulevards or plazas or displays of public art. The city had few parks, and most of them were undevel-oped sandlots. Golden Gate Park was popular, but it was remote and difficult to reach for the poor and people of moderate means. Every square inch of the eastern part of the city was laid out using the relentless street grid.

San Francisco's elites viewed with growing anxiety the population growth and indus-trial output of East Bay cities such as Oakland, Berkeley, and Richmond, as well as other cities including Los Angeles, Portland, and Seattle. San Francisco business leaders were worried that the small physical size of San Francisco (forty-seven square miles) would retard its growth. They tried unsuccessfully to create a super metropolis made up of a number of Bay Area cities.[32]

San Francisco's elites hoped to shed the city's reputation as a rustic boomtown and achieve the ambition of being seen as one of the world's great metropolises, to rival Paris in civic beauty and cultural amenities.[33] To that end, in 1904 James Phelan, a proponent of the City Beautiful movement, hired Daniel Burnham and his assistant Edward Bennett (an English architect who studied at the Ecole des Beaux-Arts) to create a plan for San Fran-cisco. Phelan had been the manager of the California exhibit at the 1893 Columbian Expo-sition, where he became familiar with Burnham and the City Beautiful ideals of the fair.[34]

Burnham's plan was ready in 1905 and consisted of far-reaching recommendations that could be implemented over many years.[35] He focused largely on streets and parks. Inspired by and modeled on Pierre Charles L'Enfant's Washington, D.C., and Hauss-mann's Paris, Burnham called for wide streets, monumental round points or traffic circles, great vistas, and diagonal boulevards. He also called for streets topped with clas-sically styled monuments and curvilinear streets (instead of the unyielding grid pattern) to climb the hills.

As cities become denser, Burnham believed that parks were necessary to good citizenship by providing healthy activities to those who could not afford to travel. According to Burnham, parks were woefully rare in San Francisco. Parks were central to the City Beautiful movement and to Burnham's sense of civic harmony. "Fifty years ago," he explained, "before population had become dense in certain parts of the city, people could live without parks, but we of today cannot." Good citizenship, he argued, was "the prime object of good city planning." Burnham believed parks and civic renewal could provide healthy activities to those who could not afford to travel and depended on the city for recreational and cultural enrichment.[36]

Before Burnham was hired, James Phelan as mayor (1897–1902), had started to acquire land for city parks under the new City Charter of 1900, which allowed him to issue debt. In 1903 voters approved bonds that created Dolores Park (then called Mission Park) on a former Jewish cemetery, a parkway linking the Presidio with Golden Gate Park (called Park Presidio Panhandle on early maps; now Park-Presidio Boulevard), and beautifying Dolores Street with palm trees.[37]

Welcome as these additions were, they did not relieve congestion. Of the existing 1,400 areas of park, almost all (72 percent) were in the difficult-to-reach Golden Gate Park. Burnham recommended adding 8,500 acres, a seven-fold increase, to the park acreage for a total of about 9,900 acres, more than fifteen square miles or about one-third of the entire city. Burnham said San Francisco's population of 400,000 had 285.7 people per acre of park. With a projected future population of two million, the additional acres would bring that figure down to 200 people per acre, just below the average for major cities (206.6)[38]

Burnham's gargantuan parkland seems to have excited little interest or controversy at the time. Perhaps the lack of controversy was because about half its total acreage was a vast swath of land running from the center of the city to the ocean. This land consisted of Rancho San Miguel and Lake Merced (owned by Spring Valley Water Company). Burnham felt the city could purchase the Spring Valley property, and, although the future of the rancho was uncertain, Burnham probably assumed it could be made into a park, which he called Laguna De La Merced Park.

The rest of Burnham's Plan—wide streets, monumental round points or traffic circles, great vistas, and diagonal boulevards—garnered a great deal of popular support. It seemed as if San Francisco would adopt the plan as a long-range planning tool. But then catastrophe struck.

2

After the Earthquake

The great earthquake that struck on April 18, 1906, and the following conflagration, devastated most of San Francisco. The fires incinerated 80 percent of the city, including its core: Downtown, North Beach, South of Market, the Financial District, Russian Hill, and Telegraph Hill. Novelist Jack London wrote: "San Francisco is gone. Nothing remains of it but memories and a fringe of dwelling-houses on its outskirts. Its industrial section is wiped out. Its business section is wiped out. Its social and residential section is wiped out. The factories and warehouses, the great stores and newspaper buildings, the hotels and the palaces of the nabobs, are all gone."[1]

At least 3,000 people lost their lives, and more than 225,000 were homeless. Some sought shelter in the unburned outskirts or camped in the streets or parks, but many left the city. San Francisco's post-quake population fell to a low of 175,000 from its 1900 count of 342,782.[2] Although the loss of population proved to be short-lived, no one knew what the future held; the catastrophe had shocked the city's political, business, and cultural elite.

Rebuilding with Greater Density

Rebuilding started as soon as the ashes cooled. Although attempts were made to implement parts of the Burnham plan, such as widening streets and cutting new ones through downtown, nothing was done.[3] That's not surprising, since even part of the plan would have cost millions of dollars at a time when the city was devastated. It would have taken years to purchase or condemn hundreds of lots and the burned-out but repairable shells of high-rise office buildings, many owned by leading citizens. In addition, the exposure of widescale political corruption and the trials of city officials handicapped decision-making after the earthquake. In any case, there was a strong urgency to rebuild as quickly as possible.[4]

Some of Burnham's suggestions—to widen and create new streets, build a transit subway under Market Street (done in 1973), use curvilinear streets, and preserve the tops of hills for vistas—were common sense. But other ideas were impractical. Diagonal boulevards cutting across dense neighborhoods would have caused horrendous traffic jams and confusion. The vast parkland would have precluded the building of thousands of houses and many residence parks (Ashbury Heights, St. Francis Wood, Forest Hill, Forest Hill Extension, Laguna Honda Park, West Portal Park, Merritt Terrace, Claremont Court, Balboa Terrace, Ingleside Terraces, and Mission Terrace).

Much rebuilding was accomplished during the first three years after the earthquake.

By 1914, when the downtown core had essentially been rebuilt, 174 new steel-frame buildings, 194 reinforced concrete buildings, 2,699 brick buildings, and 25,440 wood frame buildings had been constructed.[5] This impressive performance—and one that consumed everyone's energy and money—is estimated to have cost $290 million, as much as the Panama Canal.[6]

While the steel-framed or concrete-reinforced buildings downtown were well designed, many sub-standard commercial buildings were hurriedly built to fill immediate post-quake needs. The building codes were not uniformly enforced, leading to overcrowding. Chinatown survived efforts to relocate it to the outskirts of the city at Hunters Point, but then it was rebuilt to the same crowded, tenement-like conditions that existed before the earthquake. Some builders took shortcuts with wooden flats or houses that had not burned in the Western Addition and Mission districts, subdividing them into small, substandard apartments. Storefronts were crudely grafted onto the fronts of buildings, wiping out gardens (visible today on Divisadero and Fillmore streets[7]). Looking back, the San Francisco Planning Department concluded:

> In order to accommodate the urgent citywide housing needs, multi-unit flats were increasingly constructed in rebuilt residential neighborhoods.... Reconstruction led to the marked densification of San Francisco, with larger multi-unit structures replacing many single-family houses and commercial spaces.... As development pressure and the value of land in San Francisco increased, it became

Storefronts were added to the fronts of residential buildings spared during the 1906 earthquake and fire. Left to right, Tanaka Bros, Hero Baths, Shirai & Co, and a Buddhist monastery on the corner of Gough and Pine streets in 1907. Baldwin & Howell used this photograph to denigrate the Japanese who had moved into the Western Addition (OpenSFHistory wnp102.0051).

increasingly profitable and common for residential property owners to add commercial space to existing buildings. Entire houses were raised to insert a ground level store. Small commercial buildings were also erected in front yards.[8]

In 1911, the San Francisco Housing Association was appalled by the lack of light and air in the "Latin Quarter" (North Beach). It found: "The people wanted shelter, the workman needed wages, the contractors in many cases had to rebuild shattered financial standing, and lot owners were anxious (for the same reason) to get the greatest possible income from their property. It was a time of turmoil and uncertainty.... The authorities, glad enough to encourage anyone to build, hardly enforced the mild provisions of the exiting building laws. Merely that a building would not fall was all they asked. Thus tenements, not homes, were built."[9]

This wasn't hyperbole. Today, the blocks from Vallejo to Greenwich streets between Columbus and Montgomery are still almost completely covered with buildings: i.e., they have no yards. As a remedy, the San Francisco Housing Association asked whether the outlying districts of San Francisco could be developed along the lines of the "Garden Cities of England."[10]

At the time, some thought that the earthquake was an impetus to build residence parks because San Franciscans were moving to them in the East Bay. But R.C. Newell, a developer who launched several residence parks in the East Bay and San Francisco's Forest Hill, said it was not the 1906 disaster that caused people to leave, but the lack of anything resembling residence parks in San Francisco. The anticipation of an expanded streetcar system in Berkeley and Oakland had caused a flurry of San Francisco residents to buy in the East Bay. Business was so good that Newell opened a branch office in San Francisco; 80 percent of his East Bay sales were to San Franciscans *before* the earthquake.[11] This is confirmed in the Easy Bay city of Alameda, where 67 percent of houses built during the 1890s were sold to people who worked in San Francisco.[12] In 1916 landscape engineer Mark Daniels chided local attitudes for the delay in embracing residence parks:

> The rapidly growing Western cities are just the locations where one might expect to see the art and science of developing residence parks. In spite of the fact that San Francisco is built on hills, hardly a curved or winding street was to be found.... It has only been in the last ten years, however, that any serious attention has been paid to this work ... this tardiness is difficult to understand when it is realized that such subdivisions as Roland Park in Baltimore, Rock Hill, Kensington and Great Neck in New York and the Nichols Tract in Kansas City were meeting or had met with unprecedented success. Chevy Chase, out of Washington, D.C., was developed by a San Franciscan (Newlands in Burlingame) whose heirs and associates never dreamed of applying the same process in their hometown.... The not uncommon statement [was] that if the purchaser of a small lot in an unsightly subdivision didn't like his home-site, let him go out further into the foothills and buy ten acres or so.[13]

While San Francisco was preoccupied with rebuilding, other cities raced to embrace residence parks. Los Angeles started in 1904 with Wilshire Boulevard Heights, whose land use restrictions included a $4,000–$5,000 minimum cost of houses.[14] By 1907, Los Angeles boasted many residence parks, including Chester Place, St James Park, Bernard Park, Alvarado Terrace, Westmorland Place, and Palm Place.[15] Beverly Hills (1906) was Los Angeles' first planned suburb connected to the city center by electric interurban railroads. It was landscaped by architect Wilbur Cook, who had earlier worked with the Olmsteds. Even low-density Sacramento, the state capital ninety miles northeast of San Francisco, was building residence parks.[16]

The cities across the bay, such as Oakland, Berkeley, and Alameda, had warmer weather and lots of space, but it was the system of electric streetcars and fast and economical ferry service to downtown San Francisco that made it possible to live in the East Bay and work in San Francisco. The superior transit system was the result of competition between private transit companies who were eager to sell vacant land they had acquired cheaply by extending rails to undeveloped areas and subdividing them for sale at higher prices.[17] In 1893, Francis "Borax" Smith and Frank Havens formed Oakland Transit Consolidated, which built new lines and integrated them into a unified rail network—the "Key System"—that covered the East Bay. The company's competitor, Southern Pacific, ran its own ferry service, electrified its branch line in 1911, and developed its own network of streetcar feeder lines. As a result, it took only thirty-six minutes to reach downtown Berkeley from the San Francisco Ferry Building.

These transit improvements were a boon to East Bay development. The population of Berkeley tripled in ten years to 40,000 by 1910, making it the fourth fastest-growing city in the United States and the fifth largest city in California. Oakland more than doubled its population to 150,000 by 1910 and reached 216,000 in 1920.[18]

East Bay developers who acted on the opportunities presented by the transit system included Duncan McDuffie, who would later launch St. Francis Wood in San Francisco; Newell Murdoch Company, which would launch Forest Hill in San Francisco; and John Spring, an investor in various San Francisco residence parks. Beginning in 1905, McDuffie and other investors built several residence parks in the East Bay, including the 125-acre Claremont Court, which was located near the historic Claremont Hotel—and on a recently extended streetcar line. McDuffie hired the prestigious John Galen Howard, head of the University of California architecture program, to design formal brick gates at the entrance.[19]

McDuffie followed with the 1,000-acre Northbrae tract in north Berkeley, developed in five phases between 1907 and 1910. The streets were laid out respecting the steep terrain. John Galen Howard was again hired to design a fountain in the center of the tract, where seven streets intersected above an interurban streetcar tunnel (now used by automobiles). McDuffie offered financing (lots typically cost $1,750) and required front setbacks and a minimum house cost ($2,500). Buyers were free to choose their own designs, but McDuffie retained architect Walter Radcliff to assist with house plans.[20]

As McDuffie was planning and launching residence parks in Berkeley, Forest Hills Gardens (1909), a garden suburb located fifteen miles from Manhattan on the Long Island Railroad, achieved nationwide acclaim for its use of English garden suburb concepts. The 142-acre project was a collaboration among the philanthropic Russell Sage Foundation, Frederick Law Olmsted, Jr., and architect Grosvenor Atterbury. The Russell Sage Foundation envisioned Forest Hills Gardens to be for working-class families, but costs rose to such an extent that it proved too expensive for them.[21] McDuffie sought advice from the principals behind Forest Hills Gardens when developing his St. Francis Wood residence park (see Chapter 6). Henry Gutterson, later to become the supervising architect for St. Francis Wood, had worked for Atterbury as a young man during the development of Forest Hills Gardens and must have had a first-hand familiarity with it.

McDuffie's experience and knowledge of other residence parks helped crystalize the residence park ideal: public sculptures to define a sense of place, custom-built houses using locally prominent architects, proximity to streetcar lines, and the exclusion of commercial services. Houses were sited on curving roads with generous gardens creating a park-like setting, and McDuffie advertised that this was an excellent place to raise families in peace and safety. Plus, residents could walk to nearby streetcar lines that would quickly and inexpensively take them to jobs and the newly opened department stores downtown. McDuffie would use many of the same features when developing his residence park in San Francisco, and others followed his example.

The People's Railway

San Franciscans badly wanted to recoup the population lost after the 1906 earthquake and fire. City leaders realized they needed transit to open up the vacant districts for housing development. But, unlike the East Bay, San Francisco did not have transit owners with the vision, financial incentive, or clout to expand service. The monopolistic United Railroads streetcar company had no incentive to improve service—which was criticized as slow and infrequent—or expand service to vacant areas, as East Bay transit companies had. City regulations made it virtually impossible for United Railroads to expand or raise fares.[22] Furthermore, city residents detested the company after a 1907 strike that was characterized by strikebreakers, riots, deaths, and numerous injuries. The company's widespread bribery of officials was exposed in the graft scandals that convulsed city government after the 1906 earthquake, forfeiting whatever public support United Railroads might have retained.

As part of the nationwide Progressive Era and its focus on municipal reform, in 1900 San Francisco implemented a new city charter that called for the eventual ownership by the city of public utilities, including transit. Seeing no alternative, San Francisco took the far-reaching step to build a city-owned streetcar system, the first government-run streetcar system in the nation. A bond issue passed in December 1909 providing the funds to take over the privately owned Geary cable line and turn it into a publicly owned *electric streetcar* line. The new municipal Geary line opened on December 30, 1912, with a new mayor, James Rolph, riding in the first car. He said:

> It is in reality the people's road, built by the people and with the people's money. The first cable road in the country was built in San Francisco, and now the first municipal railway of the country is built in San Francisco. Our operation of this road will be closely watched by the whole country. It must prove a success! We must run it by proper methods. When we have built from the ferry to the ocean, it will be the best single route in the city, and we must extend it wherever possible, until it becomes a great Municipal system. I want everyone to feel that it is but the nucleus of a mighty system of streetcar lines which will one day encompass the entire city.[23]

Mayor James "Sunny Jim" Rolph, was a "good government" progressive who reigned for twenty years (1911–1931). Although the Municipal Railway (Muni) was established before Rolph came to office, he was instrumental in its expansion and growth. According to Roger Lotchin, Rolph, a son of the Mission District and self-made millionaire, was able and effective. He was, "a unique political personality who bridged class and ethnic lines and who could operate well in the old machine political world and in the new pluralist culture replacing it. His ability to manipulate the media was unmatched. He wrapped the mantle of San Francisco so tightly around himself that he became almost indistinguishable from the city itself."[24]

In 1912, in order to build the kind of transit system the city needed, San Francisco hired Bion J. Arnold, a prominent transportation planner from Chicago, to study all

Mayor James Rolph at the dedication of City Hall, 1915 (OpenSFHistory wnp36.01117).

aspects of transit and transportation. His 400-page report called for a series of improvements (such as streetcar tunnels to overcome the city's many hills) that became the basis for subsequent transportation projects. To implement transit improvements and meet other municipal infrastructure needs, Rolph enticed Michael O'Shaughnessy, a respected civil engineer with vast experience in building water systems, to take on the job of city engineer at a salary far less than what he earned in private practice.

O'Shaughnessy spoke as if he were making a sacrifice for his wife, who wanted to return to San Francisco, but what engineer would not relish the chance to reshape a major city? The mayor granted him nearly absolute authority, and O'Shaughnessy quickly became the city's de

Michael O'Shaughnessy, 1915 (OpenSFHistory wnp36. 00691).

facto planner. Known as the "Chief," he presided over the city's engineering staff and cajoled the board of supervisors (equal to a town council; San Francisco is a city and county) to support many public works. His influence is seen today in the design and construction of streets, sewers, boulevards, tunnels, bridges, emergency pumping stations, the fire alarm central station, the municipally owned Muni, and the vast Hetch Hetchy water supply and hydroelectric power system.

O' Shaughnessy fearlessly built new railway lines into previously inaccessible districts west of Twin Peaks, as well as the Marina, North Beach, and Mission districts. Although official city policy was to take over all private transit companies (the city finally did so in 1944), Muni's objective was not to compete with United Railroads, but to open up areas of the city to further development so it could serve a growing population of residents. Muni was willing to operate at a loss for several years in order to do so, although increased property taxes more than offset the losses.

Opening Up the West Side

Of the three tunnels eventually built for Muni, two penetrated the west of Twin Peaks area and were used exclusively by streetcars. (The other was the Stockton Street tunnel built in 1914 that accommodated streetcars, automobiles, and pedestrians.) Conventionally, San Francisco is not known as having an "east side" or "west side" of town; however, a row of hills (Mt Sutro, Twin Peaks, and Mount Davidson) effectively divides the city in half. While the east side of the city was fully built up by 1900, the west side remained vacant. The weather on the west side was cold and windy, with blowing sand and fog (especially in the summer), and there was no transportation or utilities, just a few dirt roads.

Another reason the west side remained vacant was the legacy of a thorny jurisdictional dispute during the 1860s between the federal government and the city of San Francisco. The federal government claimed jurisdiction of the so-called the Outside Lands, given that name because it was literally outside the city's jurisdiction (about at Divisadero Street). Squatters occupied some of the area hoping to win land titles once the ownership claims were resolved. After protracted litigation, Congressional action, and political chicanery typical of the nineteenth century, the City of San Francisco finally acquired ownership, platted the land using a rectilinear grid, and awarded much of the land to squatters.

In return, the city retained a 3-mile long parcel for Golden Gate Park, which runs from about the center of town to the ocean. It cut western San Francisco into two parts: the north became the Richmond District; the south became the Sunset District.

The Richmond District was largely made up of scattered farms and dairies and some houses. By the 1890s, the Richmond was undergoing limited development by small builders, as cable car companies had laid tracks along Clay, California, and Geary streets as far west as Central Avenue (now Presidio Avenue) largely to take visitors to the cemeteries established around Lone Mountain. With so few parks, many people used cemeteries as recreational retreats.

The Sunset, south of Golden Gate Park, was without roads or transit. A grid of paper streets with standard-sized lots covered the district, and some streets were not graded or paved until the 1940s.[25] The land was privately owned by many individuals and that, plus the lack of transportation, made development difficult. Just how difficult can be seen by the experience of William H. Crocker, president of the Crocker National Bank and heir to the fabulously wealthy Charles Crocker (one of the "Big Four" of the Southern Pacific Railway).

By 1905, William Crocker had bought one hundred contiguous blocks in the southern Sunset from dozens of individuals. He named the area "Parkside" and claimed (falsely) that "the climate was 10 degrees warmer than Golden Gate Park."[26] He formed the Parkside Realty Company and tried to launch a conventional development, but he quickly ran into trouble. In addition to the considerable expenses to grade streets and install sewers, gas, electric, and water lines, the company had to overcome public perception (and reality) that the area was a distant wilderness.[27] The most pressing problem was lack of transportation.

In attempting to secure permission to run a streetcar line to the tract, Crocker and the Parkside Realty Company were implicated in the bribery graft trials after the 1906 earthquake and fire.[28] Crocker claimed he personally was unaware if his underlings had resorted to bribery, but bribery was widespread in city government.[29] In 1908 Crocker got a single feeder line laid on 20th Avenue from Lincoln Way to Taraval Street. Although the housing shortage caused by the 1906 earthquake and fire initially stimulated purchases, the streetcar route took too long and was too inconvenient for commuting downtown. Sales fell off.[30]

A few years later, after residence parks became popular, Crocker rebranded part of Parkside as a residence park, awkwardly naming it the *Woodside Addition to the Parkside*. He quickly renamed it *Edgehill Park* to sound more like a residence park, although it is not near a hill. The 142 lots were each supposed be 30-to-60-feet wide and have 12-foot front setbacks.[31] However, this project was built on the existing street grid, the project had no landscaping or amenities, and there does not appear to have been any 30-foot-wide lots.

Crocker did not get far with his early Parkside project, but a huge vacant parcel in the geographic center of San Francisco, on the western slopes of Twin Peaks, might have had better potential for development. Called *Rancho San Miguel*, this was the land Daniel Burnham had suggested should become a huge park. It was closer to the built-up parts of town and was under sole ownership, making it easier to subdivide. The original rancho covered more than 4,000 acres. During the 1860s and 1870s, the eastern part was sold and became the Noe Valley, Eureka Valley, Fairmont Heights, Glen Park, and Sunnyside districts.

In 1880, Adolph Sutro, flush with the fortune he made from the Nevada Comstock mines, bought the remaining 1,200 acres of Rancho San Miguel. It straddled the tallest hills in San Francisco: Mount Parnassus (so named by Sutro but later renamed Mt. Sutro in his honor), Twin Peaks, and Mount Davidson. Sharing a widespread distaste for the treeless hills and captivated by the naturalist Joaquin Miller, Sutro planted thousands of trees and created what became known as Sutro Forest, a private nature reserve running from Ocean Avenue over the hills to the Inner Sunset District. Sutro sold pieces of the rancho and about 800 acres remained when he died in 1898. It was largely covered by a dense forest, except some flat land leased to farmers.[32]

Rancho San Miguel was ideal for the creation of residence parks because the parcel was a blank slate. It could be freely designed without constraints to accommodate relatively low-density development with detached houses, landscaping, and picturesque streets. Sutro's will stipulated that the land should be retained in its current state for an indefinite period; the heirs waged a decades-long battle to overturn the will and sell the land.

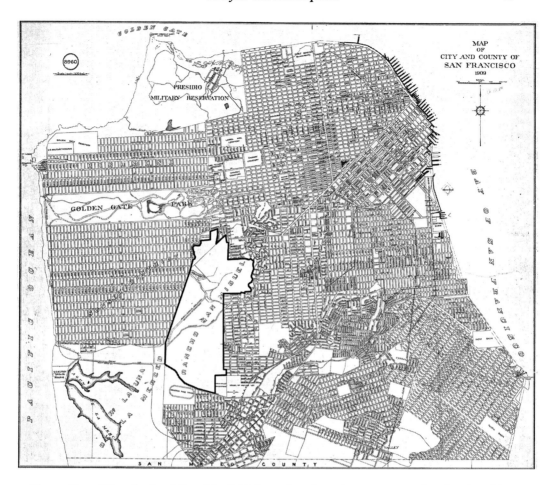

The outline of Rancho San Miguel in 1909 shows how large it was compared to the city of San Francisco. It was roughly in the center of a city surrounded by water on three sides, the Pacific Ocean (left), Golden Gate (north), and San Francisco Bay (right). The large open space at the top (north) is the Presidio military reservation; Golden Gate Park is the rectangular open space south of the Presidio. The street grid south of Golden Gate Park were paper streets and later became the Sunset District. Downtown is located in the upper right-hand side with piers jutting into the bay (University of California Earth Science and Map Collection. Image quality enhanced by Kushal Lachhwani, 2019).

By 1909 the probate of the Sutro estate reached a point where much of the land could be sold. Eyeing the possibilities, in 1910 civic leaders, improvement clubs, and real estate boosters began campaigning for a streetcar tunnel under Twin Peaks to open up the area for development.[33] A streetcar tunnel could connect the west of Twin Peaks area to Market Street with a vastly reduced commute time comparable to the East Bay ferry-streetcar system. Such a tunnel, the longest streetcar tunnel ever attempted, was included in transportation consultant Bion Arnold's 1912 report. Arnold called for starting at Valencia and Market and terminating at a western portal near Sloat Boulevard.

The tunnel idea was so popular that on March 18, 1912, the board of supervisors passed an ordinance declaring the city's intention to build the Twin Peaks tunnel before Arnold's report was finished. O'Shaughnessy shortened the length of the tunnel to start at Castro Street instead of Valencia Street in order to reduce the cost

View of Rancho San Miguel looking northeast at the Alms House (Laguna Honda Hospital) in 1906. Mt. Sutro is to the left, the treeless Twin Peaks are in the right background. The tree line marks the boundary of Sutro's property (OpenSFHistory wnp33.00963).

from $7 million to $4 million. O'Shaughnessy believed that property owners, who were paying the cost of construction through a special assessment, would object to a longer and costlier tunnel. The tunnel was formally authorized in 1913 and events proceeded quickly. Excavation began on November 12, 1914, at the eastern end (Market and Castro streets) and at the western end (site of the future Claremont Court, Merritt Terrace, and West Portal Park residence parks). Construction of the 2¼ mile tunnel proceeded quickly and was finished on July 14, 1917, a little more than three years later. But uncertainty and debate over which streetcar company would use the tunnel—United Railroads, the Municipal Railway (Muni), or both—continued until the last minute. Finally, the city-owned Muni streetcars began exclusively using the Twin Peaks Tunnel on February 3, 1918.[34]

Mayor Rolph was unabashed about claiming a mandate to make infrastructure improvements:

> The people of San Francisco elected me to office with the object of improving conditions in San Francisco and on a platform of "Progress." The City has been suffering from a lack of transportation and an adequate water service more than from any other causes. I have dedicated my energies and my time to endeavor to alleviate those two conditions in particular. The completion of the Geary Street Railway and additional municipal railways, which will be competed January 1, 1915, are some of the results to the success of which I am proud to state I have contributed in a small way. I believe the completion of the Twin Peaks Tunnel, as outlined on the broad plans of Mr. Arnold and the city engineer Mr. O'Shaughnessy, in whose judgement [sic] both myself and the supervisors have the greatest confidence, will prove a blessing to San Francisco as any one project that can be completed for the City's advancement.[35]

Rolph made it clear that the tunnel's purpose was to foster development: "With the coming of the rail and the operation of streetcars through the Twin Peaks Tunnel, it will no longer be necessary to move down on the peninsula or across the Bay to Marin or Alameda Counties [sic] to find suitable home sites. Enough will be provided west of Twin Peaks."[36]

The decision to build the Twin Peaks tunnel was the product of a consensus among

The west portal of the Twin Peaks tunnel in November 1915. The sign says: "Claremont Station," reflecting the proximity to the Claremont Court residence park. Forest Hill is in the upper right. The station was soon renamed *West Portal,* **and the Beaux Arts entrance was a signature for the neighborhood until it was demolished during the 1970s (OpenSFHistory wnp36.01080).**

the political leadership and real estate businessmen to open up the western part of San Francisco to development. Prominent owners and land developers (who later built residence parks on Sutro Forest land) had a major role in getting the Twin Peaks tunnel built. They formed an association, the Twin Peaks Property Owners Association, to lobby for the tunnel. The association consisted of owners/developers of residence parks west of Twin Peaks,[37] including A.S. Baldwin (Baldwin & Howell) as president; R.C. Newell (Forest Hill) as vice president; and directors Joseph A. Leonard (Ingleside Terraces), C.C. Young and Duncan McDuffie (St. Francis Wood), J.E. Green and Charles A. Hawkins (El Por-tal Park, Laguna Honda Park), Fernando Nelson (West Portal Park), and George N. Merritt (Merritt Terrace). They also paid most of the $4 million construction cost of the tunnel and donated land for its stations.

The developers even helped draft the ordinance to build the tunnel. "Four owners of large real estate tracts beyond the Twin Peaks hill took a very earnest part in aiding this project—they were A.S. Baldwin, Joseph Leonard and J.E. Greene, since deceased, and Duncan McDuffie, the planner of St. Francis Wood. A tunnel ordinance was especially drafted for the purpose of carrying through this work, and a special counselor, Theodore J. Savage, was retained by the interested property owners to assist the City officers in its legal consummation."[38]

A.S. Baldwin of the prominent real estate firm Baldwin & Howell supported bonds for Muni, even though he opposed municipal ownership. He wrote the following letter to San Francisco's chief engineer, Michael O'Shaughnessy:

Dear Chief:

Your editorial in the *Journal of Commerce* is the best article in favor of the bond election to-morrow that I have read. I confess I have been weakening considerably of late on the subject, and considering the fact that I have stood for everything proposed by the Rolph administration up to date, I feel (notwithstanding the strong convictions I have always felt against the municipal ownership of street railroads) that it would be inconsistent on my part to vote against the bonds tomorrow, and I have come to the conclusion that I had better make peace with my conscience either by voting for them or not voting at all.

Yours for success,
A. S. Baldwin[39]

O'Shaughnessy responded: "My dear A.S. I think a solution of this question at the present time means a great deal for the immediate prosperity of the City of San Francisco. We need those railways and this office will see that they are built promptly on time, without graft, and a credit to the new San Francisco."[40] It is no secret that O'Shaughnessy admired Baldwin. He later wrote to the mayor that he held A.S. Baldwin's "judgement [*sic*] in the highest regard and believe he is one of the most unselfish and patriotic citizens we have."[41]

And developers thought highly of O'Shaughnessy. Duncan McDuffie, developer of the St. Francis Wood residence park, thanked O'Shaughnessy. He wrote:

After returning to the office this morning I found I had neglected the main purpose of my call upon you, which was to personally thank you for the generous and unremitting support you have given to those of us who are endeavoring to develop a real residential section for San Francisco on the further side of Twin Peaks. But for your tenacity, patience and unfailing good nature, the Twin Peaks Tunnel never would have been constructed nor would the track be laid which for the vital connection between the lovely section on the west slope of the San Francisco Peninsula and the business heart of the city. I therefore feel we all of us owe you an obligation which it will be quite impossible for us ever to repay.[42]

Today it might appear wrong for city officials to consult for wealthy and powerful developers or endorse their projects, but it was a common practice at the time. There is no suggestion anything improper was going on. There was no graft or corruption like what had been routinely practiced in San Francisco before the 1906 earthquake and fire. Everyone agreed that the city needed housing; the time had come to lay out more attractive residential tracts. The developers were willing and eager to lay out these tracts, and the city was willing to provide the engineering, political support, and infrastructure to support the developments.

The combination of the Twin Peaks tunnel and a new transit agency (Muni) fulfilled the dreams of city leaders to open up the vacant western part of San Francisco for residential development of all kinds, not just residence parks. Thousands of houses in conventional subdivisions platted on the grid sprang up in the Richmond and Sunset districts during the following decades.[43] But the first to rush in were the developers of residence parks.

3

Building Residence Parks

A flood of residence parks opened between 1910 and 1917. Of the thirty-six residence parks in this book, twenty-one were launched or announced between 1910 and the beginning of World War I in 1914. Another nine were launched between 1915 and 1917.

It is not surprising that developers rushed to get in on the act. The East Bay was leading the way in constructing residence parks. Garden suburbs and residence parks were being constructed all over the country. The economy was expanding and money was available. After years of rebuilding the downtown area, pent-up demand for housing was strong. New streetcar lines were reaching vacant areas. The Sutro estate, the largest piece of land in private ownership, was finally available for development.

The idea of residence parks was popular. Many remembered Burnham's 1905 plan for curvilinear streets, scenic roads, and parks. The English Garden Cities movement was at its peak. Garden Cities were widely promulgated by Ebenezer Howard as a utopian model (or fantasy) of a self-contained town of 30,000 with residences, businesses, and agriculture surrounded by green spaces and located a substantial distance from other urban areas.

Support for the idea of residence parks benefited from the new field of city planning. Although the aesthetics of the City Beautiful movement were a strong component, city planning also searched for the functional and humane city. The efficacy of formal plans was confirmed by the 1902 McMillian Plan for Washington, D.C., by Frederick Law Olmsted, Jr., Daniel Burnham, and Charles McKim. This comprehensive plan featured classical architecture, statuary, and parks that would transform the city suffering from haphazard development and lack of grandeur.

Locally, Charles Mulford Robinson's plan in 1905, for the beautification of Oakland, and Werner Hegemann plans for Oakland and Berkeley in 1915 reflected popular support. At the First National Conference on City Planning in 1909, Frederick Law Olmsted, Jr., introduced a detailed account of orderly German city planning, and many American cities began seeking advice from German city planners. Frederic C. Howe, managing director of the People's Institute in New York, invited Werner Hegemann from Germany to organize a lecture tour across the nation. Daniel Burnham's plan for Chicago in 1909 became a blueprint for transforming the downtown over the following decades.

Several influential books and journals were published about city planning, such as Raymond Unwin's *Town Planning in Practice: An Instruction to the Art and Design of Cities and Suburbs* and Benjamin Marsh's *Introduction to City Planning: Democracy's Challenges to the American City*. The journal *American City* was launched with articles covering municipal improvement projects in the United States. By the early 1910s, city planning was seen as a legitimate, even necessary, tool far superior to the ad hoc speculative development that had characterized San Francisco's early growth.

San Francisco's residence parks are a particular type of garden suburb. Robert A.M. Stern, in his encyclopedic *Paradise Planned,* identified the existence of 954 garden suburbs in thirty-five countries. Stern identified several distinct types of garden communities: garden villages, garden suburbs, and garden enclaves. Garden villages were located outside a city, along a railroad line, and were self-contained with their own shops and neighborhood-serving businesses, such as schools, shops, and churches. Residents were dependent on a major city for their livelihoods. Garden suburbs were also located outside a city but had few or no services. Residents relied on commuting to the main city for employment and nearby hamlets or small towns for services and supplies.

San Francisco's residence parks fall under Stern's definition of a garden enclaves: the neighborhood versions of a garden suburb, sharing many of the same ideals and traits, but situated within the city limits. The residence park is almost exclusively residential, with coordinated land-use planning, such as setbacks and landscaping, and with no services within their boundaries. They are close enough to existing services or are able to attract services to locate nearby.[1]

By the early twentieth century, residence parks were widely known in San Francisco. As mentioned earlier, in 1911 the San Francisco Housing Association was concerned about excessive density and asked whether the outlying districts of San Francisco could be developed along the lines of the "Garden Cities of England."[2] San Franciscans were well aware that many areas of San Francisco were worse than before the fire as a result of post-earthquake shoddy construction and overcrowded conditions. That situation made the idea of residence parks even more appealing.

In 1912, when Duncan McDuffie launched his residence park in San Francisco, he compared it to "the famous residence parks of Cleveland and St. Louis."[3] He may have been referring to Cleveland's Euclid Heights (1892) and the many *privates places* in St Louis. He likely assumed that prospective buyers were familiar with these places because he didn't name them in the ad.

Attitudes in San Francisco about the planning and developing of cities held by the press, developers, and public officials changed, as reflected in a 1911 editorial in the *San Francisco Call*:

> The time has come when the residential growth of San Francisco must proceed along new lines. Realty dealers are daily confronted with the competition of the cities across the bay, which offer large lots in sightly [i.e., good looking] locations and "houses with four sides to them." The Richmond and Sunset Districts are adapting themselves to the new trend of enlarging lots to a slight extent in some favored localities. But the 25-foot lot is such a fixture in those sections and the land has attained such a value that it is slow and expensive to change over to a larger unit…. The solution … lies in the country beyond Twin Peaks and extending to the ocean. Today this sweep of hill and valley is almost uninhabited….
> In such a setting, the 25-foot lot would be an absurdity. An acre if possible or half or quarter acre lot at least, sufficient for a stretch of greensward and to take in a number of the lordly pine and eucalyptus trees, would make this an ideal suburb.[4]

City engineer O'Shaughnessy knew firsthand the advantages of naturalistic planning principles and was experienced with the problems of large residential subdivisions. As a young man, he had laid out Mill Valley in 1889 and Belvedere in 1890–91 in Marin County, where the streets were platted with the terrain.[5] O'Shaughnessy also worked on Burlingame Park, south of San Francisco, in the 1890s.[6] In 1907 he identified sources of water for the Crocker Family Estate in San Francisco for its Glen Park tract and an Amazon Street/ West End project, which, in 1912, became the Crocker-Amazon residence tract (see Chapter 13). In 1908 he evaluated pumping equipment and water systems for the Lyon & Hoag project in Burlingame.[7] And, in 1909 he provided recommendations to the Catholic Archdiocese for developing the former St. Mary's College site, which in 1924 became a residence park.

O'Shaughnessy applauded the construction of residence parks. He publicly endorsed Ingleside Terraces residence park saying, "I have seen the residence parks in most of the Eastern cities and as well as on the West Coast and [Ingleside Terraces] is superior to any of them. There is nothing anywhere that equals Ingleside Terraces."[8]

It was natural for O'Shaughnessy to support residence parks because he detested what the street grid had done to the hills. He wrote:

> By contour streets on easy grades some of the picturesque hillsides of San Francisco, which have been ruined by the rectangular street system, could have been made the most attractive home sites imaginable. In the districts southwest of Twin Peaks broad, winding, contour streets, with artistic parked [planted] borders with appropriate ornamentation have been adopted and add to the attractiveness of the adjoining property. Many fine homes are being created in residential parks which are several miles distant from the congested districts but will be easily accessible by reason of the tunnel and boulevard system now under construction.[9]

Another powerful figure supporting residence parks was John McLaren, superintendent of Golden Gate Park from 1890 to 1943. He was an exalted figure whose opinion carried great weight. In 1910, McLaren designed the Hanchett residence park in San Jose using slightly curving streets complete with cement sidewalks, gas, underground electricity, water, sewers, and small parks. McLaren also laid out the adjacent Hester Park.[10] He publicly endorsed the stock offering of the Baldwin & Howell's Residential Development Company syndicate (see Chapter 5). In 1917, he was hired to landscape the Visitacion Valley Garden Cities project, although the project died before he did much.

While Daniel Burnham famously urged the making of "Big Plans," developers of residence parks made little plans. The developers of San Francisco's residence parks were what historian Marc Weiss calls "community builders." In contrast to the typical nineteenth-century subdividers who often did little more than place a few stakes in the ground to mark lots and ungraded roads (and sometimes sold land with invalid legal titles to the property), community builders improved large tracts of land with utilities, extensive landscaping, and paved streets, with deed restrictions controlling land uses, building lines, setbacks, building size, minimum construction costs, and racial exclusions. They often set aside areas for retail, apartments, parks, churches, and schools.[11] San Francisco residence park developers by and large were consistent with Weiss' concept of community builders, except that they did not provide spaces for commercial or institutional uses.

Deed Restrictions

Residence parks were planned by developers who wanted to create model communities of quality houses with gardens and quiet, tree-lined streets. And, before the adoption of city and state planning ordinances and environmental review, property owners enjoyed considerable freedom to use their land as they saw fit. But developers felt they could not give buyers discretion over how to use their land; otherwise buyers could sub-divide lots or operate businesses that might destroy the living-in-a-park ambiance. People would not purchase a lot if they feared that their neighbors could do whatever they liked with their property.

To avoid these problems, many conditions governing land use were written into the deeds covering lot sales. These restrictions limited what was built, how the land was used, and who could buy. The deeds also sometimes taxed buyers, through a homeowner's association, for the upkeep of the grounds.[12] Restrictions were intended to create a consistent neighborhood character so that the tracts would remain desirable places to live. These restrictions almost universally required:

- Buildings be single-family residences,
- Fence heights be limited,
- Houses have only two stories,
- Houses have setbacks,
- House designs be reviewed for conformity with the restrictions,
- Minimum construction costs to prevent cheap houses, and
- Prohibition non-whites from owning or renting (see Chapter 4).

To prevent the nuisances of city life—traffic, congestion, noise, vices, and pollution—the deed restrictions prohibited multiple family buildings, stables, saloons, and businesses of any kind. Activities associated with country life, such as animal husbandry, chicken coops, and agriculture, were also banned. Indeed, the term "restricted park" was often used in advertisements interchangeably with "residence park." A residence park was not an escape into a rural, small-town, or country setting, but a "park in the city." Duncan McDuffie, developer of St. Francis Wood, explained:

> An exclusive residence park in a metropolis is not a suburb. It is not a village removed from the city and consisting of a variegated collection of houses, cottages, bungalows, stores and saloons. In the great Eastern cities, residence parks are laid aside in the most desirable section of the metropolitan area. Within their boundaries no shops are permitted. The houses measure up to a certain standard. The streets and boulevards are wide, usually lined with trees and flowers. Although part of the city, they are removed from the bustle and noise. They have the air of seclusion, an atmosphere of refinement and substantial comfort. Because of their restrictive area, the property in such parks is extremely valuable, and continually increases in value.[13]

Deed restrictions have a long history. In 1869, the Riverside Improvement Company in Illinois required a mandatory 30-foot setback and a minimum cost of construction. Roland Park in Baltimore, Maryland (1891) was a successful residential development in large part because of its extensive set of deed restrictions on lot sizes, building lines, setbacks, minimum dwelling values, and requirements for owner residency. By the 1920s, deed restrictions had become widespread across the nation.[14]

Usually the developer or homeowner association enforced the restrictions, but transgressors could be sued, if necessary. Public mention of such enforcement is rare, but one case involved Edward C. Mussel, Jr., who built a house that was 70-feet long in Windsor Terrace. Residents Evelyn Andres and Carolyn Blum, calling themselves the "home guards" of Windsor Terrace, went to court to enforce the deed restrictions that no home could be more than 40-feet long.[15] The result of the lawsuit is not known.

Private deed restrictions were so effective that mayor James Rolph and city engineer Michael O'Shaughnessy opposed the creation of the city planning commissions when the State of California authorized their formation in 1915. Although the San Francisco Board of Supervisors passed an ordinance authorizing a planning commission, Rolph refused to appoint its members. The mayor and city engineer were satisfied with the way civic improvements were being planned and implemented by informal relationships among city agencies, private contractors, and private lenders.[16] Presumably Rolph and O'Shaughnessy felt a planning commission was unnecessary or would delay or politicize subdivision development.

A few residence park developers bought land on the existing street grid (Jordan Park, Windsor Terrace, Clover Terrace, 4th Avenue and Fulton), but most developers preferred unplatted land so that they could lay out curvilinear designs better suited to hilly topography or on level terrain could create winding, picturesque streets. They took advantage of natural features, such as views of the ocean, forests, or the bay. Some graded the sites to create better viewsheds. And they all sought to create lush park-like ambiences no matter how closely the houses were built together (although they were invariably detached).

The typical residence park business plan offered improved lots with curbs, sidewalks, and all utilities (electricity, sewer, water, telephones and gas) installed; however, it did not provide the actual houses. Before the 1920s, lot buyers were responsible for selecting their own architects and builders. While some buyers did so, it became apparent that relatively few people had the wherewithal to select and pay for the services of an architect, locate and contract with a builder, and finance the construction.

In the 1920s, most developers broadened their offerings by hiring architects either to design custom houses for customers or to provide stock plans, sometimes free with the purchase of a lot. Smaller-sized houses appeared, in addition to larger custom designs. Developers also built houses on speculation using in-house or independent builders, financed the purchase of lots, and offered construction financing or even created their own construction companies. In some parks, the developers hired an architect and a builder to design and construct the entire tract. It was common to sell lots to builders or contractors who built either on speculation or for a client.

The Automobile

While the electric streetcar made many residence parks commercially viable, residence parks coincided with the rapid commercialization of the car. Henry Ford had relentlessly reduced the price of his Model T, introduced in 1908, so that everyone who wanted one could afford one. He famously promised, "When I'm through about everybody will have one," and his boast was accurate.[17] In 1913 he unveiled the moving-chassis assembly line that dramatically increased output and produced cars in many cities, including San Francisco (at 2905 21st Street).[18] In three years, the number of automobiles tripled in San Francisco, from 12,000 in 1914, to 32,000 in 1917. It tripled again by 1924.

San Francisco's Victorian-era streets were no match for the car. Streets were widened or extended, sidewalks narrowed, and new streets cut through. Cars were parked in any available place. There was little room to build detached garages in San Francisco's high-density neighborhoods, so front yards were sacrificed to allow a garage to be inserted on the ground floor, sometimes dug below grade. Some houses were raised to

824 Page Street in 1886. The front yard, shallow to begin with, was later sacrificed for a driveway and garage (OpenSFHistory wnp70.0527).

provide adequate clearance. These changes reduced the already meager landscaping or greenery.

Residence parks, on the other hand, were better able to accommodate the car. With wider lots, detached houses, and lower densities, cars could be parked on the street or to

824 Page Street with driveway and garage (photograph by author, 2019).

the side or rear of houses. Soon garages were incorporated into new house designs. Some residence parks were equipped with rear alleys, so cars could be driven into garages out of sight. West Clay Park, Merritt Terrace, Lincoln Manor, Sutro Heights, and parts of Seacliff, Ingleside Terraces and Mission Terrace all feature rear alleys.

Sales of residence parks also benefited from the construction of new "scenic" boulevards in San Francisco. Built by O'Shaughnessy between 1915 and 1920,[19] these boulevards were constructed to give views of the ocean or along hills, giving panoramic views of the city or bay. The scenic boulevards included the Great Highway, Sloat Boulevard, Twin Peaks Boulevard, Junipero Serra Boulevard, Monterey Boulevard, and El Camino Del Mar. Although the boulevards were intended to provide a means for pleasure driving, they also provided easy access to many residence parks.

One of the new boulevards was made possible by the removal of houses and the realignment of streets for the excavation of the Twin Peaks tunnel at the eastern portal at 17th and Castro streets. This provided an opportunity to make Market Street a cross-town drive by extending it along the slopes of Twin Peaks. O'Shaughnessy was ecstatic about the new road: "We're going to extend Market Street to a connection with Portola Drive and make it the greatest and grandest scenic boulevard in the world…. Why drive an automobile through a tunnel 2½ miles long when you will be able to enjoy this wonderful Portola boulevard for a third less [than] the cost of a vehicle tunnel."[20]

O'Shaughnessy must have felt vindicated that the route was being built at last. Twenty-five years earlier he surveyed a similar route that wasn't built and for which he wasn't paid.[21] He wrote, "I was authorized by the Democratic Board of Supervisors in

1883 to make surveys for the extension of Market Street over Twin Peaks Mountain to the Pacific Ocean, at an expense of $5,000, and through political juggling got cheated out of the fee for all my work."[22]

Residence Park Architecture

One important characteristic of residence parks is the widespread use of architects, instead of builders or contractors, to design houses. Most of the housing stock of several thousand houses was designed by architects. Buyers were free to choose their own architect and designs, subject to review by the developer or tract architect, but no architectural styles were imposed. As result, there is a great deal of individuality.

The architecture of residence parks broke the hold the Victorian style had on San Francisco. In other parts of the city, Victorian style houses continued to be built, and even the subsequent Edwardian-style retained the form, wood cladding, and some of the spindle work and detailing of Victorians. In contrast, the houses in residence parks were often stucco clad and reflected the more modern styles and forms—those influenced by various Mediterranean, English, and northern European historical styles, as well as the Arts and Crafts movement and Craftsman styles.

Developments in domestic architecture in Berkeley influenced the way houses were sited on the streets of San Francisco residence parks. Instead of endless rows of elaborate Victorians, poet and naturalist Charles Keeler engaged architect Bernard Maybeck in 1894 to design a hillside home that would blend into its natural surroundings. Maybeck responded with an unpainted redwood house with shingle siding, exposed beams and rafters, steep rooflines, and a stone fireplace. Its woodsy, natural character is credited with originating a Bay Regional style. The Hillside Club was founded to promote Keeler's ideas for a new kind of urban development, one that would retain the natural topography and produce "artistic homes that appear to have grown out of the hillside and to be a part of it." They opposed houses laid out in a strict street grid and instead wanted winding lanes that followed the contours of the land and a network of pedestrian paths. In 1904, the club published Keeler's *The Simple Home*, an extended essay outlining his views on architecture and how it could influence the way people lived.[23] Many residence parks feature houses influenced by this so-called Bay Region style.

Architectural style classifications are renowned for a lack of consensus and the limitations of classification. There is a debate whether a Bay Area style should be called a style at all.[24] In any case, few pure examples of any style exist, and it was common, if not universal, for houses to fuse elements associated with several styles. The supervising architect for the St. Francis Wood residence park, Henry Gutterson, did not favor uniformity when he said, "California is a melting pot socially and the architecture should express that fact … the use of many styles and variations of styles, we shall have with us for years to come, and properly so since to be truthful, architecture should express the people."[25]

The description of how architect Earle Bertz designed houses in Sea Cliff can be applied to other residence parks and other architects: "In designing homes no hard and fast rules apply, but rather Mr. Bertz studied each precise location with an artist's perception, drawing upon any school or vogue that would produce the most satisfying result, sometimes the English Gothic gave a charming effect to the general vistas, in others the Spanish or Italian example was applied with delightful impressiveness; or the architect's own conception, was used broadly and in a way to create diversity in the ensemble without disturbing the harmony."[26]

Dozens of architects designed houses in residence parks, but in some cases one or two were responsible for many or most of the designs: Joseph Leonard in Jordan Park and Ingleside Terraces; Henry Gutterson and Masten & Hurd in St. Francis Wood; Carl Bertz in Sea Cliff; Harold Stoner in Balboa Terrace; Ida McCain in Lincoln Manor and Westwood Park; and Charles A. Strothoff in Westwood Park, Westwood Highland, and St. Mary's Park. As tract architects, they approved other architects' designs for conformity with a residence park's guidelines, and they designed custom houses.

In some residence parks, such as Westwood Park, Westwood Highlands, St Mary's Park, Mission Terrace, and the later phase of Sea Cliff, the developer hired an architect to design houses for the entire tract, or a large portion of it, to be constructed by one or several builders. In this case, the tracts usually had a primary style with minor variations to avoid monotony. In the more homogenous tracts, styles reflected the time period when the style was in favor. For example, Harold Stoner designed many Storybook houses in Balboa Terrace. (The Storybook style, also referred to as Fairy Tale, Disneyesque, and Hansel & Gretel, originated in Los Angeles in the early 1920s.)

Although they differed in design and style, the diverse designs looked harmonious together because they practiced traditional architecture. Whether they were Beaux-Arts–trained, embraced the ideals of the Arts and Crafts movement, or favored their own idiosyncratic approach, architects shared an appreciation for classic concepts of order, composition, proportion, hierarchy, balance, and scale. They strove to balance these concepts with the client's program, budget, and site. Architects also were conscious of producing designs compatible with neighboring houses in terms of scale, massing, and context.

Certainly, many owners were consciously trying to show their wealth or taste, but no matter how grand or expensive, the houses invariably fit in with the neighborhood. A further refinement in some residence parks is that all facades were to be treated equally, recognizing that freestanding houses in close proximity would be seen from all sides. If the house was clad in stucco on the primary façade, stucco would be used on all the facades, instead of cheaper wood siding. This was not always the case in practice, but when it was used it did reinforce the overall concept of houses set in a garden. Similar to New York's Forest Hills Gardens, architectural style did not guide the design of the tract, but each house and its landscaping was designed to contribute to a garden feeling.[27]

As a result of these design principles, residence parks look nothing like the repetitive, densely packed Victorian houses of the nineteenth century or the stucco row houses of the twentieth. Builders used the latest construction methods and materials, but they also used natural materials, such as slate and clay tiles, metalwork, and wood carvings, all coupled with high standards of detailing and craftsmanship.

Boom, Bust and Boom

San Francisco residence parks were launched during a decade punctuated by recession, war, and inflation. A long economic boom that began in 1896 ended around 1913 when a national recession hit the country. World War I broke out in August 1914, disrupting financial markets, increasing inflation, and creating material shortages. Between 1914 and 1920, prices increased 107 percent for clothing, 95 percent for food, 60 percent for fuel and lighting, and 35 percent for rent.[28] These shocks resulted in steep declines in sales and building activity.

In San Francisco, overall construction activity in 1915 fell 30 percent to $14 million from $23 million in 1912. The decrease was worse for residential real estate.[29] An uptick in the national economy in 1916 had minor effects in San Francisco, with the result that "1917 and 1918 were depression years for real estate in San Francisco."[30] In 1917, city engineer Michael O'Shaughnessy wrote, "Commercially things are very quiet in San Francisco with a great many business houses and practically suspension of building operations, and I believe this will continue for at least two years or until the end of the war."[31] Duncan McDuffie reflected on the difficulties in St. Francis Wood's early years:

> From the summer of 1914 to the spring of 1919, almost no lots were sold. I remember that in 1915 our total sales aggregated $5,000. In the meantime, interest, taxes, and upkeep charges went on as usual.... They exhausted our every resource and if it had not been for the wise and generous attitude of the banks, and particularly George Kennedy's bank [George Kennedy was an early resident of St. Francis Wood and an officer at First National Bank of San Francisco, later Crocker Bank], we would not have

Advertisement for San Carlos Park at Market and Geary circa 1908. Reads in part, "Beautiful San Carlos Park, No Fog, No Winds, No Ferries" (Source: OpenSFHistory wnp26.853).

kept St. Francis Wood afloat. This difficult situation created the temptation to turn from our original idea. Among the temptations was pressure to cheapen street improvements, to reduce the size of lots, to encourage "jerry builders" and to let down on restrictions and architectural supervision. There were also opportunities to dispose of the property, but a sense of responsibility for our purchasers and an overwhelming desire to carry on … induced us to hang on no matter what the cost.[32]

Furthermore, San Francisco residence parks were facing competition from the East Bay and San Mateo County, south of the city. Real estate developers and speculators attempted to entice the wealthy and the professional middle class to San Mateo County by emphasizing the lower costs and better weather compared to San Francisco. For example, in 1916, promoters advertised that lots in the city of San Mateo were one-fourth to one-fifth the cost of lots in West Clay Park or Presidio Terrace and practically no farther from the center of San Francisco. They claimed the time it took to travel from San Mateo to the Southern Pacific train station at 4th and Townsend streets was comparable to traveling from West Clay Park.[33] An advertisement for San Carlos Park extolled, "No Fogs, No Winds, No Ferries," taking aim at the disadvantages of San Francisco.

The high prices in San Francisco were a sore point. High prices prompted a project to build a "Garden City" project for workers so they could remain in San Francisco. The location of the Garden City project was Visitacion Valley, which straddles the San Francisco/San Mateo County lines near the bay. The plan was envisioned as a semi-philanthropic effort to provide low-cost housing for workers who couldn't afford decent housing in San Francisco. Lack of affordable housing meant that workers would move to the East Bay, industry would follow them, and San Francisco's clout would diminish.

The president of the firm created to build the project, George C. Holberton of Conservative and Building & Investment Company, told the Downtown Association that the Forest Hill, St. Francis Wood, and Ingleside Terraces residence parks were too expensive for workers earning less than $100/week. Holberton said that the Garden City project's first unit would contain one thousand houses priced at $2,000, much lower than the

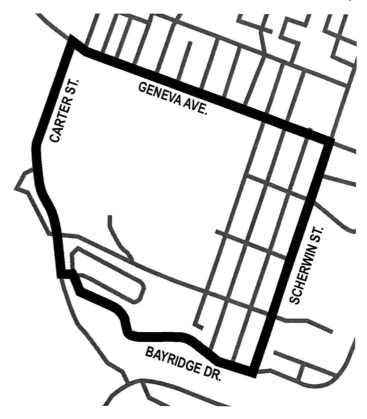

Garden City Visitacion Valley (map by Kushal Lachhwani, 2019).

price of a house in a residence park: Westwood Park, $3,250; Parkside, $3,500; Claremont Court, Merritt Terrace, and Forest Hill Extension, $4,000; Ingleside Terraces, $7,400; Forest Hill, $10,000, and St. Francis Wood, $12,500.[34] (It was also lower than the average national price of $3,400.)

The Garden City project was called semi-philanthropic because its purpose was not so much to bring financial profit as to furnish homes for workers.[35] The financial scheme was taken from English Garden suburb philanthropic projects: a limit of 6 percent profit, installment plans for workers, payments limited to 20–25 percent of workers' salaries, and refunds if workers moved. The company needed one million dollars in financing.

Holberton was also the district manager of Pacific Gas and Electric Company, and John A. McGregor was vice president of the Conservative and Building & Investment Company and the president of Union Iron Works, a major shipbuilder on the West Coast.

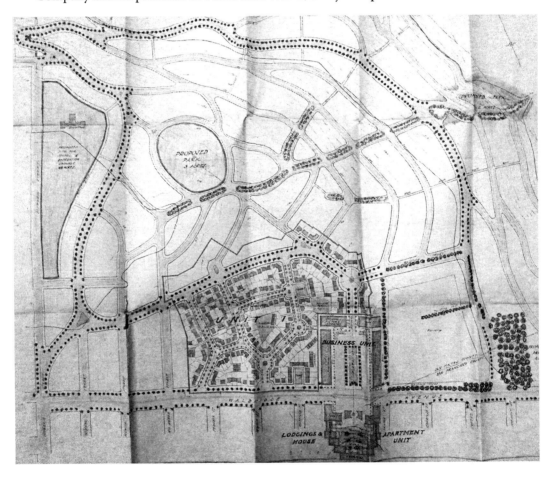

Plan for Visitacion Valley Garden City by Charles Cheney. Walbridge (now Geneva Avenue) runs east and west along the base of the plan. North is at the bottom; south is at the top where San Bruno Mountain rises to 1,300 feet. Cheney's plan features a plaza lined with shops, apartments, and a theater. Single family houses, duplexes, and parks were planned on curvilinear streets. In 1941, a livestock pavilion called the Cow Palace was built on the site and is used for concerts and expositions. It was not possible to lay flat the archival map or remove the folds prior to photographing it (California State Library Sacramento. Image quality enhanced by Kushal Lachhwani, 2019).

Many other prominent businessmen bought shares or helped in the effort, including R.C. Newell, developer of the Forest Hill residence park.[36] John McLaren would create the landscaping, which included waterfalls.[37]

The company bought 170 acres for $1,850/acre in the Schwerin Tract (the site of the present Cow Palace) in Visitacion Valley. The entrance was off Walbridge Avenue (now called Geneva) and Santos in San Francisco, but nearly all of the tract was in San Mateo County and close to San Francisco Bay.

The Conservative and Building & Investment Company hired architect Charles Cheney, who produced a plan with a physical form, layout, and architecture taken directly from the English garden suburbs he had visited. Charles H. Cheney was a city planning pioneer. He graduated from the University of California in 1905, studied at the Ecole des Beaux-Arts in Paris from 1907 to 1910, and then toured the cities of Italy, France, Spain, and England. In 1912, he joined the San Francisco architectural firm of Lewis P. Hobart and became an advocate for city planning and zoning. He organized the first California Conference on City Planning in 1914 and was influential in city planning efforts the rest of his life.[38]

Cheney's plan for Garden City featured an entrance with a plaza lined with shops, a theater, and apartments for a village of 10,000 people. Landscaped curvilinear streets would climb the slopes with children's playgrounds and small parks. A variety of housing stock would be built: single family, duplexes, and apartments.

As the project got underway, the United States entered World War I, and the country struggled to meet arms and munitions goals as well as gear up a massive ship-building program to replace millions of tons lost to due German U-boats. The promoters recast the Garden City project as a means to house thousands of war workers who were expected to pour into the shipyards in San Francisco and South San Francisco. Garden City was located near the shipyards, so commuting time and expenses would be minimal. The proponents hoped to receive federal funds similar to those of the federally financed Emergency Fleet Corporation.[39] The local real estate board and Chamber of Commerce supported the project out of patriotic fever and the recognition that private industry could not produce low-cost housing (or any housing) during the war.

Some land was purchased, but the project never began. George C. Holberton resigned from PG&E in early 1918 as part of a companywide layoff due to the lack of building activity.[40] The end of the war in November 1918 negated the justification for government funding, and the traditional hostility of the real estate industry to government-sponsored housing re-emerged. With the housing downturn, there was no sentiment for semi-philanthropic projects. The Visitacion Valley Garden City project is unknown today, but it shows how widespread the idea of garden cities was at the time.

About the same time the Garden City project was being planned, Charles Cheney drew up a sophisticated plan for the Crocker Estate Company's Bayshore Tract, also located in Visitacion Valley along San Francisco Bay.[41] The Crocker Company may have contemplated developing a residence park on part of the site. The plan featured a plaza and curvilinear streets that climbed the base of the hill. Cheney laid out spaces for residences but also for industrial and commercial uses, which are incompatible with a residence park. The incompatibility reflected the proximity to the Southern Pacific Railroad's large marshaling yard and machines shops that were adjacent to the tract.

This was obviously not an ideal location for a residence park, and the timing was bad. The tract was conventionally developed during the 1920s on a grid with detached

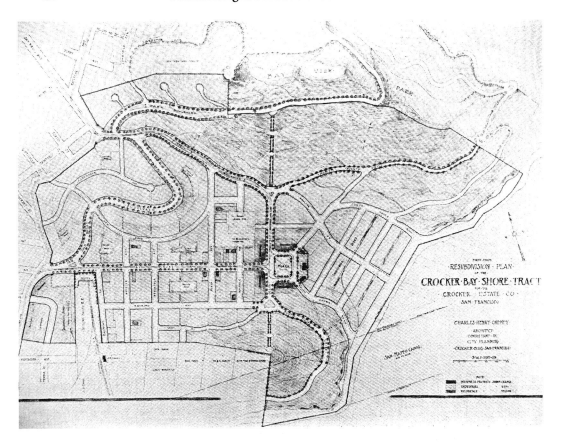

Charles Cheney's plan for the Crocker Estate Company's Bayshore Tract. Located on San Francisco Bay (right) the tract was bounded by San Mateo County line (bottom), Bayshore Boulevard (left) and a hill, Bayview Park (top). The plan features a plaza and curvilinear streets but also industrial and commercial uses, incompatible with a residence park but understandable because of the nearby Southern Pacific railroad marshaling yard ("Work of Charles Henry Cheney Architect and City Planner," *Architect and Engineer*, LIII; 3, June 1918. Image quality enhanced by Kushal Lachhwani, 2019).

craftsman houses, all built to the same design. During the 1920s and 30s, some stucco-clad houses were constructed with architectural elements reminiscent of houses in Los Angeles, and the area became known as Little Hollywood.

The effects of the war on construction lasted for some time after peace was restored. An article in *The Building Review* magazine in May 1919 said, "For the past two years, building construction in the United States, except for the War Department, has been practically at a standstill.... Labor is available, money is at hand, material is abundant and the need for construction is pressing, but construction does not resume. Many people of the United States seem to feel that we shall revert to pre-war prices and they are apparently postponing construction until the reductions in prices are realized."[42]

The 1910–1920 time period was a tough time for residence parks. Yearly data on residential construction activities is available for Parkway Terrace, and it shows how abrupt the downturn was.[43]

All the developers of residence parks faced similar problems during this time, but they reacted in different ways. Some left the business; others constructed cheaper

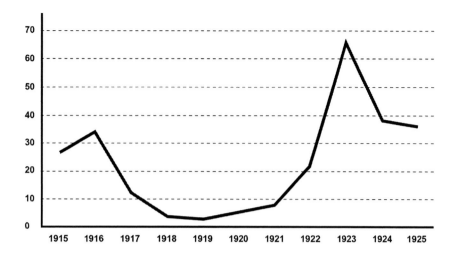

Construction in Parkway Terrace declined from 1916 through the early 1920s (data taken from Inge Horton, *A Jewel Restored: Fernando Nelson's House in Parkway Terrace*, www.outside-lands.org/parkway_terrace_jewel.php. Graph by Kushal Lachhwani, 2019).

developments. Some maintained their standards but deemphasized custom houses. Other developers scaled back amenities like clubhouses or recreation facilities.

Boom Times

After a brief recession in 1921, the economy took off and house building rebounded with a vengeance across the country. The majority of residence park houses were

Construction activity in West Portal Park peaked in 1925 mirroring the national trend (author's analysis of 332 houses on Forest Side, Madrone, Wawona, Ulloa, 14th Avenue, 15th Avenue, Vicente, and Taraval lying within West Portal Park, dates from San Francisco Planning Department. Graph by Kushal Lachhwani, 2019).

constructed during the national housing boom of the 1920s. The West Portal Park residence park mirrored national trends.

The Great Depression retarded building during the 1930s, but by the onset of World War II, nearly all of San Francisco's residence parks had been built out. A few scattered lots remained, and limited house construction occurred during the 1940s and 1950s, especially as some larger lots were subdivided. As a result, San Francisco's residence parks make up a time capsule of the styles and fashions of domestic architecture that were popular during the first third of the twentieth century. They also reflect the prejudices, cultural mores, and racial discrimination of their day toward Blacks and Asians.

4

The Residents, the Excluded
and the Displaced

Residence parks were designed as model communities with gardens and quiet, tree-lined streets for white, middle- and upper-income buyers. Before the adoption of city planning ordinances, civil rights laws, and environmental review, developers could and did exclude nonwhites, ignore the lives of tenant farmers who worked the land, and disregard the environment. In this regard, they operated the same way many subdivision developments did nationwide.

The Residents

Developers marketed residence parks to be socially exclusive. Except for a few tracts designed for the very wealthy or the working class, most were built for the professional classes with families. For example, in 1920, Ingleside Terraces published a list of thirty-six recent buyers; ten were managers or in sales, six were physicians or dentists, six were in real estate or were builders, and four were attorneys.[1] The 1930 U.S. Census for St. Francis Wood shows about one-third of the heads of households were business executives or in sales. Doctors, lawyers, and architects made up 20 percent. The average number of people was 3.4 per household, and 38 percent of the households had at least one servant. Typical occupations were accountant, agent, architect, artist, attorney, broker, cashier, clerk, contractor, dentist, engineer, executive, lawyer, manager, manufacturer, merchant, physician, president, professor, proprietor, sales manager, salesman, superintendent, and vice president.[2] The more exclusive Presidio Terrace attracted an even wealthier crowd, including builder Fernando Nelson, A.S. Baldwin, and other millionaires.

Some residents were leaders in civic affairs and politics.[3] Perhaps the most consequential in forming the modern state of California was Edmund G. (Pat) Brown of Forest Hill, the two-term governor of California between 1958 and 1966 who shaped much of the state through the huge expansion of higher education; 1,000 miles of freeways; a state commission to guarantee equal employment opportunities; and the State Water Project, a massive system of canals, pipelines, and dams.[4]

Other leaders included George H. Casey of Lincoln Manor, Leland W. Cutler of Sea Cliff, Edward G. Cahill of West Clay Park, John Francis Neylan of Balboa Terrace, and Chester MacPhee of Ingleside Terraces. George H. Cassey was a member of the executive board of the 1934 successful campaign to elect Republican Frank F. Merriam as governor and was general manager of the Pacific Fruit Exchange. Leland W. Cutler persuaded the Reconstruction

Corporation to invest in bonds for the construction of the San Francisco-Oakland Bay Bridge and was instrumental in the financing of the Six Companies consortium that constructed Hoover Dam. Edward G. Cahill cofounded with his brother John the Cahill Brothers Construction Company in 1923 and was the manager of the city's Public Utilities Commission in the 1930s. John Francis Neylan was an attorney and publisher of the *San Francisco Examiner*. Chester MacPhee started as a real estate broker in the working-class Mission District and then became a member of the board of supervisors in the 1940s.

But most residents were not movers and shakers. More typical are Morris and Minnie Riskin, early residents of West Portal Park. On December 21, 1921, Riskin, a diamond merchant, bought a house for $10,000 at 180 Madrone from the previous owners, Perry Small and his wife Petrica C. Small. Built in 1919, the house had not been lived in before Riskin bought it. His daughter said that her father was:

> just absolutely enthralled with the Sunset District. And there was nothing in the Sunset District and that's why he liked it. But this Nelson guy [Fernando Nelson & Sons] was building homes then … my God, you could go for miles and there would be nothing, and my dad just loved it. That was the farthest corner of the world at that time in San Francisco…. My dad came from a very large family, 13 children. He said he wanted to get as far away from the family as possible…. His brother Sal asked him, "Why do you want to live in the sand dunes?" My dad said (good naturedly), "You know I'd rather live in the sand dunes than live with you."[5]

The remoteness that appealed to Riskin was touted by developers as being ideal environments for raising families, enjoying the health benefits of marine air, and enjoying scenic views of forests or the ocean. Developers advertised residence parks as being ideal for families that desired a garden, safe places for kids to play, and the feeling of living in the country with like-minded people.

An ad for Forest Hill said, "Under the trees, there is sand, just as good as the beach. Every home will have a garden and a sleeping porch, and the youngsters can skip rope on the lawn or the streets that are like driveways in a big country estate. There will be a community of probably 3,000 people like yourselves with the same tastes and the same ideals. And you, Mr. Renter and Mr. Parents, can get home in 15 minutes through the new Twin Peaks Tunnel."[6]

The ad illustrates several themes common to most residence parks. The buyers had been renters, they were not independently wealthy, and the father needed to commute downtown. But the family could have the feeling of living on a country estate, like the rich. The promise of living surrounded by people with "the same tastes and same ideals" was meant to ensure there would be no unpleasant lifestyles and no different people to associate with—particularly non-whites.

Buyers were typically becoming first-time homeowners. The former addresses were located for some of the newcomers to residence parks, and all were renters.[7] For example, in Ashbury Terrace, Dr. William G. Hopper of St. Mary's Hospital had lived at 1456 Page Street an eight-unit apartment building, and Louis Ferrari was an attorney who had lived in a flat at 627 Castro. In Windsor Terrace, Dr. H.H. Stirewalt had lived in a five-unit building at 702 Oak Street, Dr. Adolph J. Kahn had lived with his wife Edith at 86 Post Street in a three-unit building, and Henry M. Ambrose (a clerk at Wells Fargo Bank) had lived with his wife Mabel in a flat at 1033 Page Street. Frank E. Brown, a draftsman for the Board of Public Works, lived in a seven-unit Victorian building at 2915 California Street before moving to Ingleside Terraces. Realtor Reardon T. Lyons lived in a flat at 135 10th Avenue before moving to Jordan Park.

Residence parks succeeded in creating something new in San Francisco: intentional communities of strangers who were attracted by the promise of suburban amenities and social exclusivity for a class of buyers that could not afford more expensive options. The privately planned tracts were very different from most communities found in San Francisco. Developers created distinct identities and provided residents with opportunities to socialize and work together for common goals. These were self-governing neighborhoods; the residents participated in the decisions affecting them. At the same time, residents got to know one another and developed social networks, especially during the early years when services were scarce. These social networks excluded Asians and Blacks.

Racial Exclusion

Non-whites were prohibited from owning or leasing property in residence parks. In San Francisco, the discrimination specifically listed people of African, Chinese, and Japanese descent. Language differed slightly; some deeds banned anyone other than "Caucasians," and others specifically listed Chinese, Japanese, Mongolian, and even Ethiopian. Across the United States, housing covenants commonly banned Asians, Mexicans, Blacks, and Jews, each specific ethnicity named or unnamed depending on the racial attitudes of the area.[8] Contrary to other parts of the country, San Francisco residence parks did not exclude Jews or Latinos.

Racial discrimination toward Asians and Blacks was widespread in major subdivisions across the country and throughout California. The rationale for discrimination in residence parks was the same as the one used in other subdivisions: if racial minorities were allowed, white residents would flee or not buy in the first place, and property values would drop. According to Richard Walker:

> Every integrated development came with racial covenants and other deed restrictions from the 1890s onward, and the first exclusionary zoning laws in the country were adopted in the 1880s by Modesto and San Francisco to rid Anglo zones of Chinese. Subdivision maps were first required in California in 1893 and the regulations upgraded again in 1907, 1915 and in the 1920s. Berkeley's McDuffie came up at the same time with the idea of single-use and large-lot zoning to confine commercial activities to designated areas and restrain further subdivision of exclusive domains. These ideas became the norm throughout the United States between the World Wars.[9]

Developers used racial restrictions in San Francisco even though at the time Asian-American immigrants

Restrictions in Sea Cliff Bar Alien Owners

NO Oriental or Ethiopian can own property in Sea Cliff.

All buildings must set back from front property line sufficiently to carry out the general plan of parking.

The restrictions in "Sea Cliff" protect your home, family and investment.

"Sea Cliff" prices are not prohibitively high.

The man of moderate means can build or the owners will build for him on terms.

The man or woman seeking a home or homesite should see "Sea Cliff" before deciding on a location.

The owners of "Sea Cliff" have an exceptionally liberal offer for homeseekers.

Sea Cliff advertisement proudly states "No Oriental or Ethiopian can own property in Sea Cliff" along with other restrictions (*San Francisco Chronicle* December 4, 1920).

were not allowed to buy property. The long period of discrimination, exclusion, and violence directed against Chinese in California during the nineteenth century and against the Japanese after their victory in the Russo-Japanese war of 1905 culminated in 1913 with the Heney-Webb Alien Land Act, which forbade property ownership by "aliens ineligible for citizenship."[10]

Language against Asians often included a racist and apocryphal warning: "It is not an uncommon sight to see a mansion located between a Chinese laundry and a delicatessen store simply because the mansion was constructed in an unrestricted district."[11] Chinese laundries were a favorite example of the "nuisances" that deed restrictions were meant to prevent. (There were indeed many Chinese-run laundries dating from the Gold Rush, when Chinese men were barred from the gold fields and found work doing laundry. By 1880, of the 320 laundries in San Francisco, 240 were owned by Chinese.)

The Chinese population was significant and Japanese immigration was increasing but although Blacks were few in number at the time, they also were banned. As Robert Fogleson wrote:

> The belief, more than anything else, drove many subdividers to impose racial covenants even in cities with very few African- and Asian-Americans (and hardly any could afford to buy a lot, much less build a house, in suburbia) … the Mason-McDuffie Company, subdividers of St Francis Wood, banned any persons of African descent even though only 1,600 of San Francisco's 417,000 residents (or less than four-tenths of one percent) were African American.[12]

In San Francisco, St. Francis Wood developer Duncan McDuffie said that that nearly all residential subdivisions (not just residence parks) built in the Bay Area since 1905 had used building restrictions, including the exclusion of "various aliens" from ownership.[13] By "aliens," McDuffie meant ethnic minorities.

McDuffie was based in Berkeley, where zoning was often accompanied by restrictive covenants, not just in residence parks. These covenants prohibited buyers from selling or renting their property to Asians and Blacks. Real estate agents also tried to prevent racial groups from buying or renting in other "white" areas of Berkeley. Most Asians and Blacks lived south of Dwight Way and west of Grove Street (now Martin Luther King Way). When Dwight Uchida rented a home on Ward Street, a few yards east of Grove, the neighbors asked him to move. He had crossed the racial dividing line.[14]

Residence parks developers and sales agents didn't prominently advertise the racial exclusions. Usually these restrictions were buried in a list of "amenities." However, an advertisement by Fernando Nelson & Sons candidly listed "No African or Asiatics," along with other restrictions in selling his houses.

Baldwin & Howell played the race card in promoting Presidio Terrace. An ad in *The Argonaut* magazine in 1906, a time of particularly virulent anti–Japanese sentiment, led with the headline "The Japs [sic] Have Invaded the Western Addition," and

350 HOMES 350
Eight Blocks of Homes
NOTHING BUT HOMES

No Flats, Stores, Apartments or Saloons.
No Africans or Asiatics.
No Home Without a Front Lawn.
No Unsightly Poles in Front of Your Home.
No Two Houses Alike—Distinctive Architecture.
A WHOLE BLOCK OF

Fernando Nelson & Sons refused to sell to "Africans" and "Asiatics" in all of their housing development, not just residence parks (*San Francisco Chronicle* January 22, 1916).

trumpeted that Presidio Terrace was the "only one spot in San Francisco where only Caucasians are permitted to buy or lease real estate or where they may reside."

In 1917, the U.S. Supreme Court outlawed local government segregation ordinances, but racial discrimination could continue legally under private contract. In 1927, Harry Allen, the developer of Sea Cliff and president of the California Real Estate Board, sent a questionnaire to local realty boards throughout the state asking about what he called "the factor of color" in selling real estate. The questionnaire asked if segregation existed in realtors' jurisdictions and what races were affected. All the realtors who responded took it for granted that segregating the races was the proper thing to do, arguing that property values would fall if the races comingled. Respondents to the survey said that towns with racial minorities were segregated but realty boards took no action as long as the races stayed in "their own neighborhoods." Otherwise, realty boards used deed restrictions, covenant restrictions, or "gentlemen's agreements" to keep white areas white. Cities did not rely on municipal ordinances to enforce segregation, saying, "The question is apparently too delicate a nature to be handled by city ordinance."[15]

Allen found that "practically all subdivisions are provided with restrictions to protect them from future deprecation [*sic*] as far as possible through encroachment of a foreign race." The term "foreign race" usually encompassed Chinese, Japanese, Mexicans, and Blacks, while a few towns added the Latin races, Russians, Greeks, Armenians, "Madres Italians" [*sic*] or people from the Turkish Empire. In 1927, W.H. Fitchmiller, secretary of the Santa Monica Realty Board, explained his animosity toward the Latin races in a letter to Harry Allen in 1927:

> Personally, I place the Latin races, in exactly the same category as the color line. The Spanish, French, Italian, and the Grecians [*sic*] are to my way of thinking of most objectionable type. As a rule, the families are large, their cultures marked by its absence, there is no such thing as the finer qualities demanded by American citizenship apparent in them, dignity and charter is lacking. I am speaking of course of the general run. There are exceptions to the rule, but for one I do not believe it proves the rule … crime is in the greater number of cases traceable to these particular races. I am real hard boiled when it comes to a sale of these people, I would prefer not to sell, than to place them where they do not fit in.[16]

In 1948, the U.S. Supreme Court outlawed private racial covenants, such as those used in residence parks. The residence park deed restrictions concerning race became null and void. But racial prejudice was deep-seated and hard to eradicate. After racial covenants were illegal, informal exclusion of non-whites continued in many San Francisco residence parks. Minority buyers were discouraged and steered away from these communities by real estate professionals, who were in turn lobbied and warned by residents not to show open houses to non-whites.

At that time and for many years afterward, racial discrimination by the government was illegal, but private discrimination wasn't. In 1963, the California State Legislature passed the Rumford Fair Housing Act, which prohibited discrimination based on race, religion, color, national origin, and ancestry in private housing. In response, the real-estate industry funded an initiative campaign to overturn it, using the slogan "A man's home is his castle." The initiative would repeal the act and amend the state constitution, providing "the right of any person, … to decline to sell, lease or rent such property to such person or persons as he, in his absolute discretion, chooses." The proposition passed in a landslide of more than 2 million votes. But in a 5–2 ruling, the California Supreme Court overturned the initiative, holding that it violated the U.S. Constitution's Equal Protection Clause. The U.S. Supreme Court affirmed the California Supreme Court by a vote of 5–4.[17] As attitudes began to slowly change, the residence parks became more diverse.

Contemporary demographic data about several residence parks reveals a range of results. Compared with the population mix of San Francisco and taking no account of income or any other factor, whites are overrepresented in Sea Cliff and Forest Hill while underrepresented in Mission Terrace. Asians are overrepresented in St. Francis Wood, Balboa Terrace, Ingleside Terraces, and Mission Terrace and are underrepresented in Sea Cliff and Forest Hill (slightly). Hispanics are overrepresented in Mission Terrace and underrepresented in Sea Cliff, Forest Hill, St. Francis Wood, Balboa Terrace, Ingleside Terraces. Blacks are underrepresented in all the parks.

	San Francisco	Sea Cliff	Forest Hill	Forest Hill Extension	St. Francis Wood	Ingleside Terraces	Bal Terrace	Mission Terrace
White	40%	71%	57%	48%	45%	45%	45%	15%
Asian	34	15%	28	33	45	41	45	48
Hispanic	15	8	7	14	5	5	4	34
Black	5	0	3	1	0	0	0	1
Mixed	4	5	5	3	1	3	6	2
Other	1	0	1	1	3	1	0	0

Rounded to nearest percent. Source: https://statisticalatlas.com/place/California/San-Francisco/Race-and-Ethnicity, 2019.

The Displaced

While residence parks excluded Asians and Blacks, another group of people were displaced by residence parks. These were the farmers and field hands who labored in fields that became the site of residence parks such as Ashbury Terrace, Presidio Terrace, St. Francis Wood, West Portal Park, Merritt Terrace, Mission Terrace, St Mary's Park, Presidio Gardens, and Ingleside Terraces. As far as we know, these people were not compensated unless they owned the land, and few did.

Truck farms, or growing vegetables on relatively small plots and offering them for sale, was once a big business in San Francisco. As early as the 1860s, produce farming was a profitable business, as fruits and vegetables were scarce and expensive. Many immigrants from France and Italy realized that they were not going to strike it rich in the gold fields, but they saw an opportunity in providing fresh produce. Some bought the land they farmed, but more commonly they rented in the outlying areas and sold their produce in the Colombo Market at Davis and Front streets.

Colombo Market was established in 1876 and moved after the 1906 earthquake and fire to Washington and Front streets between Davis and Drumm.[18] By the 1950s, the produce market and related businesses covered 50 acres of prime real estate. City leaders for decades thought the land was too valuable to be used for a produce market (they tried to move it as early as 1916; see Chapter 13). In the early 1960s, after several attempts to relocate the market, the San Francisco Redevelopment Agency purchased the land under eminent domain. Colombo Market was razed for the Golden Gateway/Embarcadero Center project. The farmer/vendors moved to markets in South San Francisco or San Francisco Bayview/Hunters Point District.[19] Both markets are still in business. The 23-acre San Francisco Market in Bayview/Hunters Point has 1,000 workers and is a city-designated historic legacy business.[20]

Little information is available about the people who farmed In San Francisco. The *San Francisco Call* summarized the history of farming in what became the Mission Terrace residence park:

A windmill to pump water for farming on Cayuga Avenue near the Mission Terrace residence park in 1912. The view looks south toward San Bruno Mountain in the distance (OpenSFHistory wnp36.00213).

In 1851, French immigrant M. Crochet bought 40 acres and he built a country home with flower gardens, vineyards and an orchard. It became known as Crochet Gardens and was an attraction until Crochet returned to France. Around 1870, his daughter Alexandrine leased the land to French and Italian truck gardeners where they grew vegetables on 5 to 10-acre plots on the naturally fertile soil that had an abundance of groundwater [due to nearby Islais Creek]. The land was dotted with windmills, shack houses, and barnyards and goats…. The Italian truck farmers left the city to continue farming. When the land was being graded, there was a scramble to pick up cabbages, artichokes and other vegetables.[21]

On what would later become Forest Hill, the Burfiend family grew potatoes and ran a dairy near the Alms House (now Laguna Honda Hospital).[22] In 1860, Herman H.W. Burfiend (also spelled Burfeind), age 25, opened a ranch on land then owned by the Alms House. In 1888, he added a dairy and sold milk to the Alms House. His sons, George, Henry, and Dietrich, worked on the farm, and his daughter Annie was a cook at the Alms House. The Alms House furnished the dairy with water at $15 a month and, in turn, received payment in milk. Burfiend died in 1897, leaving an estate of $1,100 to his wife Mary. The sons then worked as teamsters for the Alms House.[23]

Adolph Sutro rented part of Rancho San Miguel to farmers who had to leave when the land was sold to residence park developers.[24] Some moved south to San Mateo

Portrait of an Italian truck farm in Visitacion Valley circa 1901. First row left to right: Rose Sechini, her son Paul Sechini, Frank Piasoni, Rico Piasoni, Mrs. Piasoni, unidentified baby, Albert (Bill) Armanino, John Armanino, Joseph Sechini, unidentified, Mr. Cossalla-Coulterni, Henricata no last name, unidentified. Second row: unidentified, unidentified, unidentified, Joseph DeMartini, unidentified, unidentified, Richard Sechini, unidentified. Third row: unidentified, unidentified, Anthony Sechini, unidentified, unidentified. The unidentified are believed to be hired hands or neighbors (author's collection).

County, which was still relatively undeveloped, and continued farming. One tenant, Alberto Afonso, moved to Colma and continued farming.[25] Santino Bottini (1884–1971) and his wife Carolina Paccioretti Bottini (1897–1986) leased 34 acres from Sutro. They moved to South San Francisco, where they owned and operated the Liberty Market from 1928 until 1982.[26]

Giuseppe Merlo made the transition from farmer to hired hand. Merlo owned a stall in Colombo Market and for decades during the 1800s farmed south of Sutro's property, along a ravine about where St. Francis Circle is today. He and his family worked the farm until 1915, when the ravine was filled in with tailings from the Twin Peaks tunnel and became West Portal Avenue. He found work felling trees for the building of the Forest Hill residence park.[27]

The impact of having to relocate has not been chronicled, but by the turn of the twentieth century farming in San Francisco was becoming less attractive. Water was a perennial problem, and the newer generation preferred to work for wages and live in houses with indoor plumbing, electricity, and other modern conveniences. Farmers who owned the land could sell it to developers, while their offspring and laborers had to move or seek other jobs. For example, the five-year-old Paul Sechini in the illustration of the Sechini ranch later became a boiler maker for the Southern Pacific Railroad.[28]

Residence parks were not the only reason for the reduction of farming in San Francisco. As San Francisco's population grew, so did the demand for home sites, and the number of farms took a precipitous decline. In 1900 San Francisco had 304 farms on 8,219 acres. By 1920 the number of farms had shrunk to 74 on 1,295 acres and then to only 17 on 138 acres in 1925.[29]

Residence parks were a notable achievement, as will be shown in later chapters, but they were built at a time of racial discrimination and displacement, and when the loss of the native environment was not valued or respected. This does not excuse the developers but puts their actions in historical context.

5

Baldwin & Howell

Baldwin & Howell (B&H) was one of the most important residential development companies in the Bay Area during the late nineteenth and early twentieth centuries. The firm acted in many capacities: selling lots, developing subdivisions, appraising and marketing real estate, selling houses, leasing, and more. Headed by Archibald S. Baldwin (1858–1924) and Josiah R. Howell (1868–1916), the company had a prominent clientele, including the Adolph Sutro and Charles Crocker estates. One gauge of the firm's status is that it was listed as one of the largest taxpayers in San Francisco in 1901, along with Southern Pacific Railroad Company, Hibernia Bank, and the Spring Valley Water.[1] Baldwin was a member of the Pacific Union Club and listed in the society Blue Book. Howell was one of the Committee of 50 formed after the 1906 earthquake and fire.

Baldwin & Howell was instrumental in the development of residence parks in San Francisco. B&H promoted the residence park concept among landowners, investors, real estate firms, newspapers, politicians, and the public. The company built and marketed San Francisco's first residence park, Presidio Terrace, which became a model for others. Baldwin & Howell oversaw the development of the largest vacant land holding in San Francisco, the Sutro estate with more than 700 acres. In less than three years B&H had appraised it, convinced the contentious heirs to sell it to them, created a stock company, raised $1.5 million, purchased the land and subdivided it, and selected the developers who would create six residence parks. B&H created three kinds of residence parks for the wealthy (Presidio Terrace), the middle class (Westwood Highlands), and the working class (Mission Terrace). They also agitated for, promoted, and paid part of the $4 million cost of building the Twin Peaks tunnel and other transportation improvements.

Archibald S. Baldwin was born in Winchester, Virginia, and arrived in California in 1879 at age 21. In 1886 he joined a well-known real estate firm, McAfee Brothers Land Agents and three years later became a partner of the firm, along with R.P. Hammond, Jr., a civil engineer and park commissioner. The firm was known as McAfee, Baldwin and Hammond, Real Estate Agents and Auctioneers. Richard P. Hammond, Jr., was born in San Francisco in 1857, the son of a prominent early settler, Richard P. Hammond senior.[2] Hammond Jr. became the surveyor-general of the United States and also supervised construction of the Del Monte Hotel in Monterey.[3]

In 1892 Archibald Baldwin and Richard Hammond, Jr., bought out McAfee, and the firm became Baldwin and Hammond. In 1894, Hammond retired and sold his interest to Baldwin. In 1897 the firm became Baldwin & Howell (B&H) when Josiah Howell became a partner with one-third interest in the firm. The *San Francisco Call* said of the move: "Some of the largest properties in the City are under the control and management of Mr.

Baldwin, and in admitting Mr. Howell to the firm is a recognition of the valuable services rendered by him over the long period of his employment. The result must necessarily serve to further strengthen one of the oldest and most reliable real estate houses in the City."[4]

Glen Park Terrace

During the late 1890s Baldwin attempted to develop a residential subdivision in Glen Park, in the Outer Mission District, then at the outskirts of the city. Although Baldwin did not conceive of the subdivision as a residence park, this project illustrates his grappling with the problem of providing amenities in residential subdivisions, an unusual step in nineteenth-century California.

Baldwin was the agent for the owners of land now located along Diamond Street at Surrey and Sussex streets and Poppy Lane. These holdings, and indeed much of the Outer Mission, were mostly composed of dairy farms and vegetable gardens.[5] Glen Park Terrace had a strong selling point, an electric streetcar line—the city's first—the San Francisco to San Mateo Electric Railway, which ran nearby on its way to and from downtown and the cemeteries in Colma in San Mateo County. A wealthy businessman, Behrend Joost, built the streetcar line in order to access his Sunnyside subdivision, just south of Glen Park, which had opened in 1892. Joost's subdivision was a typical nineteenth-century speculative venture, with hundreds of lots platted on a grid without regard to the topography and without amenities of any kind. Many streets were too steep to build on.

Streetcar access was an advantage, but Baldwin needed something else to entice buyers to the outskirts of the city at a time when property values were weak due to the depression of 1893–97. Baldwin hit upon a novel idea to attract lot buyers. He would build a zoo and amusement grounds. The idea was not as ludicrous as it might sound. San Francisco did not have a zoo until 1929. As mentioned earlier, parks were scarce in San Francisco. Golden Gate Park was located across town and necessitated a long roundabout trip from the Outer Mission. Residents were unhappy about how difficult it was for them to reach Golden Gate Park, and they agitated for a park in their own district. Baldwin believed that a park or resort might be just the thing to entice lot buyers.

Baldwin's plan was influenced by the closure of Woodward's Gardens, a popular San Francisco destination. In 1866 Robert B. Woodward, a wealthy hotel proprietor and former South Park resident, filled his four-acre estate with stuffed animals, a large collection of fine art, a conservatory with rare and exotic trees and tropical plants, and the first public aquarium on the West Coast. Ostriches, flamingos, and deer roamed freely, while wolves, bears, lions, camels, and monkeys were kept in cages. As many as ten thousand people a day visited Woodward's Gardens during its heyday.[6]

Woodward's Gardens had closed in 1891 after the death of its founder. In January 1897, Baldwin organized the Glen Park Company for the purpose of constructing "museums, parks, zoological gardens and other places of public resort and entertainment" called the Mission Park and Zoological Gardens. Baldwin hired a prominent architect, Frank S. Van Trees, to design classically inspired buildings to house the animals; hired landscape architect George Hansen to map out boulevards and circular paths that followed the topography; and contracted with Anson C. Robison, an importer of exotic birds and animals.

Plan for animal house, 300x250 feet, for the proposed Mission Park and Zoo, drawn for the "Daily Report" by
Frank S. Van Trees, architect, Crocker Building ; estimated cost - - - - - - - - - - - $12,000
Estimated cost of zoological collection, as per offer of A. C. Robison - - - - - - - - 1,910
Cost of grading and preparing the court and construction of artificial lake for sea lions - - - 3,000
              Total cost - - - - - - - - - $16,910

The Beaux Arts style is reflected in architect Van Trees' design for Baldwin's Glen Park zoo in 1897 (General Sub File-Mission and Park Zoo [SF] Society of California Pioneers).

Van Trees' "Italian renaissance" design was published in the *Daily Report* newspaper on August 7, 1897. In Van Trees' own words:

> The building as designed … will be built about a court, 300 feet by 250 feet. In general style the structure, which will be permanent in character and constructed in a substantial manner, will be what is known as the Italian renaissance. There will be a colonnade on three sides, with three grand entrances, and in the arcade in front of the animals' cages will be a walk. The part of the roof to be seen from the court will be of tiling…. There will be thirty-eight large cages from 13 feet by 15 feet to 15 feet by 18 feet with some very large ones of 40 feet, and in addition to these the designs provide for two large, open cages to connect with the closed ones say for monkeys, lions or exercising the animals. The depth of the building, giving an idea of its generous proportions, will be 33 feet, and the general height will be 16 feet to the eaves and 32 feet to the extreme top. The cost of this building will be $12,000.[7]

This was a costly and ambitious scheme for what was a highly speculative venture. Perhaps for that reason, Baldwin changed his mind and instead offered to sell the raw land to the City of San Francisco in 1897. At the time, the City was entertaining bids from landowners to establish a zoo. But Baldwin demanded $400,000—ten times the City's appraised value—and after an acrimonious dispute, the parties could not come to terms. Baldwin resumed plans for a zoo, although a drastically downscaled one. The grandiose plans by Van Trees were tossed, and Baldwin turned to a rustic (and cheaper) style for the buildings.

In 1898 the zoo opened as the Glen Park and the Mission Zoo. It was equipped with seal ponds, a bear pit, a herd of elk, and the Morro Castle, which housed an aviary, a tea house, and a children's playground. By this time, the San Francisco economy had rebounded due to the effects of the Yukon Gold Rush and the Spanish-American War. The zoo was popular, with 8,000 to 15,000 weekly visitors. Baldwin thought its popularity would drive lot sales, and he was not alone.

The *San Francisco Call* wrote, "Every lot in Glen Park Terrace has a fine sunny exposure and commands a good view of this new and popular resort, Glen Park … all property adjacent to public or private parks enhances rapidly in value. It is also conceded that no park has ever attained such popularity within the same time as Glen Park. What Woodward's Gardens was to the city years ago so is Glen Park to-day. Wherever such crowds go real estate values must increase. Glen Park Terrace commands the key to the whole situation."[8] In 1900, with the zoo a success, Baldwin & Howell filed a development map of Glen Park Terrace with forty-eight lots located between Surrey and Chenery. Baldwin graded the lots, provided sewers, and paved the streets, features that were often left up to the lot buyers to deal with after the developer got his money.

However, the zoo did not drive lots sales as expected. Thousands of noisy pleasure seekers inundated the area, some of them drunk (alcohol was served at the zoo, contrary to Woodward Gardens). Mismanagement and accidents caused the zoo to close after several years of operation. Around 1901 Baldwin ended his involvement.[9] After the 1906 earthquake, the G.H. Umbsen & Company and the River Brothers took over and began selling cottages on the installment plan.[10] Historian Evelyn Rose said, "I came to realize that Glen Park Terrace was an early concept of a residential park. In this case, he was 'bringing the people to the park.' In his later developments, he seemed to have realized that 'bringing the park to the people' was a better approach. Building homes in a park-like setting would be more practical."[11]

Partnership with Antoine Borel

After Glen Park Terrace, Baldwin & Howell teamed up with wealthy businessman Antoine Borel, and their collaboration would lead to San Francisco's first residence park, Presidio Terrace. Borel brought experience in real estate, a prominent reputation, and strong financial assets to the firm.

Antoine Borel (1840–1915) was a banker with vast holdings and interests in many businesses across the state. After arriving in San Francisco from Switzerland in 1855, he worked as a commission banker and became involved in a plethora of businesses, including Death Valley borax mines and the Spring Valley Water Company. When the Bank of California failed in 1875 and had to be reorganized, Borel became its director.[12] In 1884, Borel organized a syndicate to purchase the California Street Cable Car Line from Leland Stanford, and he orchestrated the construction of the Hyde Street Line.[13] He and his associates operated the line for more than thirty years.[14] According to a newspaper account describing Borel's firm:

> They are always ready to buy large pieces of real estate which they think can be resold by them in subdivisions at an advantage. Although they thus purchase to sell, they are not speculators in the accepted meaning of the word, as their transactions are based on good, sound business principles. They have also invested heavily in local securities such as bank, water and street railroad stock, and in local and county bonds. No better illustration of their implicit faith in San Francisco and California is needed than this fact. The firm has always endeavored in any way it could to encourage local enterprises and to that end it has used its money freely.[15]

Borel and B&H formed another syndicate, the San Mateo Improvement Company, to develop a large tract in San Mateo.[16] In these projects, Borel bought the land and B&H organized the development activities.

Presidio Terrace

Antoine Borel had acquired land next to the Presidio and First Avenue called the Tibbitt's Track as early as 1898.[17] This became the site for Presidio Terrace, a 9-acre tract built beside a golf clubhouse on the southern border of the Presidio. The tract was laid out as an oval street that formed an island on the interior of the parcel. The entrance was from Presidio Avenue, which was at the end of Pacific Heights, a well-to-do neighborhood. Iron entrance gates designed by noted architect Albert Pissis conveyed exclusivity and privacy. Sites for forty houses were laid out around the oval street with irregularly shaped lots that were two or three times wider than the normal 25-foot lot. The developers also installed formal landscaping, underground utilities, paved streets and sidewalks, and trees.[18]

Presidio Terrace is different from all the other residence parks in San Francisco in that the streets are private property, owned by the homeowner's association. Although many residence parks in San Francisco maintain common grounds, they do not include the

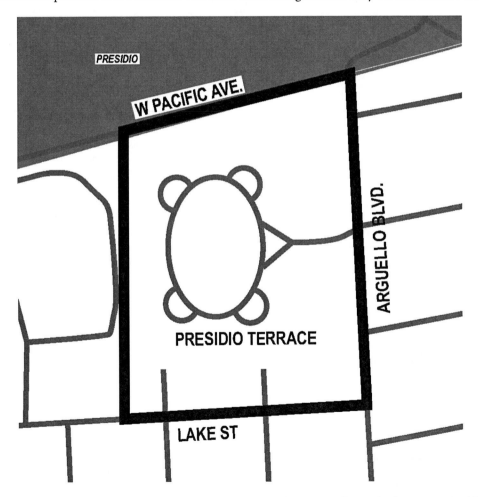

Presidio Terrace is located on the southern border of the Presidio and adjacent to Pacific Heights, a well-to-do neighborhood. The entrance is off Arguello (formerly First Avenue) (map by Kushal Lachhwani, 2019).

streets, which were dedicated to the city to avoid the financial burden of maintaining them. However, Presidio Terrace is similar to the private places of St. Louis, where the streets are privately owned, and no-trespassing signs are posted. And the no-trespassing edict is enforced in St Louis. In 2015, the author was driving through Portland Place, one of the private developments in St Louis, with a St. Louis resident and native, when a private security guard pulled us over and told us to leave immediately. In San Francisco's Presidio Terrace, the entrance gates were rarely closed until recently.

Presidio Terrace's deed restrictions included a number of items that became standard in later residence parks: a minimum cost of constructing a house ($7,000, in this case); and no flats, hotels, laundries, saloons, or stables allowed.[19] A homeowner's association was created, and the members were assessed to pay for the upkeep of streets, landscaping, and privately maintained streetlights. With ownership comes the responsibility to pay property taxes, but the Presidio Terrace Home Association apparently lost track of its tax liability for the streets and owed $995 in back taxes. In 2015, the streets were sold at auction for $90,100 to individuals with no connection to Presidio Terrace. In 2017, the association filed a lawsuit to rescind the sale, and the San Francisco Board of Supervisors did so in December 2017. At this writing, the result of a lawsuit to overturn the board's action is not known.[20]

The 1906 earthquake and fire provided Baldwin & Howell with the justification for the land use restrictions. After the fire, a frenzy of construction in the unburned Western Addition District resulted in shoddy alterations to the otherwise well-constructed

Presidio Terrace entrance gates. For many years the gates were not closed (photograph by author 2019).

buildings. Also, the genteel nature of the district changed, as saloons, gambling houses, and brothels, displaced by the fire, moved in.

The *San Francisco Call* ran a number of articles about the vices that had descended on the neighborhood. One article read: "Women of the Western Addition have taken up the fight against vice. The advance of the vicious element from the ruins of the old tenderloin to the homes of the decent has been winked at by a lethargic Police Department until it is unsafe to women or children to leave their homes without fear of pollution."[21] An article on September 14, 1906, ran with the headline, "Vicious Resorts Must Close" and explained that Jimmy Lawler, was openly running a "notorious resort" (i.e., brothel) at 1822 O'Farrell Street. The "notorious" Lazarene also ran another disorderly house at Steiner and Turk streets. He had operated a number of disreputable houses on Commercial Street before the fire.

"Fallen Women Flaunt Calling in Menace to Innocent" introduced an article that lamented the passing of the old neighborhood and the birth of a "new Tenderloin" in the Western Addition. Many brothels emerged, including one at 848 McAllister Street run by Helen Sherwood, a "middle class woman schooled from infancy in all the craftiness of her craft." Other brothels operated at 3032 Fulton, 1822 O'Farrell, 2928 Fulton, and 2912 Fulton.[22] The *Call* identified an opium den on the once reputable Garden Avenue (now Garden Street between Divisadero and Broderick streets). Children playing in the street called it the "hop joint," and the *Call* said, "it is a constant menace to every home in the neighborhood."[23]

Baldwin assured buyers such things would never happen in Presidio Terrace: "Grocery stores, saloons and disreputable resorts have made their appearances in many portions of the Western Addition which no one ever dreamed of before the fires. There is only one place in San Francisco where one can find absolute protection from such nuisances and that is Presidio Terrace."[24] As discussed in Chapter 4, B&H also used the influx of Japanese moving to the Western Addition from the burned-out South of Market area to justify and promote racial exclusions in the residence park.

B&H advertised Presidio Terrace as San Francisco's first and only residence park with panoramic views of Golden Gate Park and the Pacific Ocean.[25] The hope was that buyers would not speculate but would commission architects to build custom houses. Presidio Terrace clients were well-do-to San Franciscans who could afford to engage the services of an architect to build a custom house. In November 1905, Baldwin moved into the first house in Presidio Terrace, designed by architect Frank Van Trees (whom Baldwin had hired for the Mission Zoo). In 1909 Fernando Nelson, a wealthy builder responsible for later residence parks, hired architects MacDonald and Applegarth to design a three-story monumental Elizabethan "cottage" at 30 Presidio Terrace.

Only three buildings had been built by the time of the 1906 earthquake and fire, but sales quickened afterward, and twenty-six houses were completed by 1911. But many lot buyers did not relish the task of building a house from scratch. Sensing this, Moses Fisher, owner of a large building company, bought seven lots and constructed houses (at 10, 11, 19, 24, 25, 28, and 32 Presidio Terrace) to designs by architect Charles F. Whittlesey of Los Angeles. Fisher also built three more houses (20, 27, and 34) making up one-quarter of Presidio Terrace. Presidio Terrace was considered a success and became a model for the residence parks that followed.

Mission Terrace

In 1910, Borel and Baldwin & Howell announced a new residence park—for the working-class called Mission Terrace, on a truck farm in the outer Mission District. A project-specific company, the Mission Terrace Company was formed with Josiah Howell (a partner in Baldwin & Howell), Edward Coleman, and J.H. Meyer to develop the land Antoine Borel had acquired. Coleman and Meyer would lay out the streets, install utilities, and sell lots.[26]

The location may explain why Baldwin & Howell chose to develop a residence park for the working class. The area consisted of scattered farms and a few working-class houses. The site was even farther away from downtown than Glen Park Terrace and was located next to the Southern Pacific steam railroad line with its noise and smoke. Nonetheless, Mission Terrace would have many features of residence parks. B&H explained its approach:

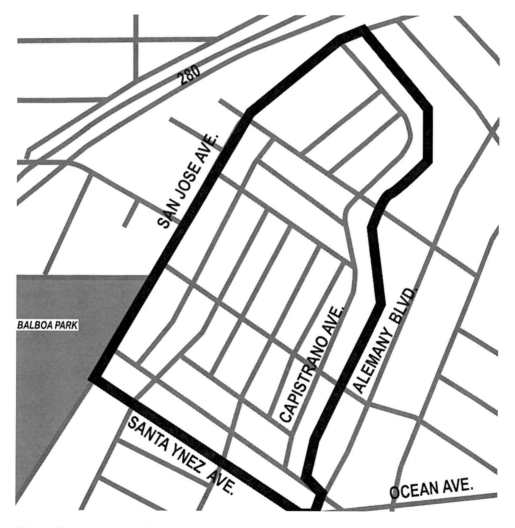

Mission Terrace is located between San Jose Avenue and Alemany Boulevard in the Outer Mission (map by Kushal Lachhwani, 2019).

Mr. Borel has given us instructions to be liberal in the subdivision of these tracts and to see that broad avenues are opened through the property.... We do not intend to follow absolutely the conventional methods usually employed in the subdivision of tracts in San Francisco. The policy of getting the most lots without regard to appearance, which now prevails, will be departed from.... Reasonable building restrictions will probably be adopted, and it is more than likely that saloons, laundries and manufacturing establishments will be prohibited within the boundaries of the property, which we intend shall serve for modest but attractive homes exclusively.[27]

This was to be their last collaboration. Borel died in 1915 leaving a $3 million estate, and each of his employees was bequeathed a year's salary.[28]

Rather than a small, exclusive community, Mission Terrace would have 400–500 lots, ten times as many as Presidio Terrace. Baldwin & Howell optimistically promised a 20- to 30-minute trip to downtown on streetcars that ran along the western and eastern borders of the tract along San Jose Avenue and Mission Street. The main through street, Capistrano, roughly followed the course of Islais creek. To reinforce the Mission theme, streets were given Spanish-sounding names and houses would to be designed in the "Spanish style."

In contrast to Presidio Terrace, there was no expectation that lot buyers in Mission Terrace would commission architects to design houses. In a generous gesture, Baldwin & Howell hired MacDonald & Applegarth, high status architects, to drawn up stock plans for lot buyers. Applegarth had studied at the University of California under Bernard Maybeck and then attended the École des Beaux-Arts, as did his partner Kenneth MacDonald, Jr. The two collaborated on more than thirty commercial buildings and many residences before their partnership ended in 1912.

Sales were delayed several times during 1911 in order to put in sewers, but lots were for sale by September 1911 with ads that targeted contractors, not home buyers.[29] Lots were priced at $900–1,250 with 10 percent cash down and the rest in monthly payments. Plans for houses that could be built for $1,500–2,500 were given free to contractors. Deed restrictions prohibited saloons and laundries and required a minimum cost of $1,500 for bungalows and cottages. Houses were to be set back 15 feet from the sidewalk, and alleys would be used to avoid cutting driveways through front lawns. Businesses were allowed only on San Jose Avenue, a major traffic artery.

Lot sales and house building started well. In 1912, Mission-District builder Nils F. Nilsson bought fourteen lots on Delano between Santa Ysabel and San Juan to build bungalows, and seven more lots on San Gabriel. Twenty-seven lots were sold during last few months of 1911, with several builders buying lots and constructing houses. It appears Baldwin & Howell built a few spec houses to seed the tract and encourage others. An undated brochure for Mission Terrace features drawings of houses on wide lots in the Craftsmen style that resemble the house at 35 Delano. These drawings may have been created by MacDonald & Applegarth, but it's not clear whether any houses were built to their design. Wide lots are not found in Mission Terrace, and the Craftsman style was not the only style of houses erected.

Contractors also built stucco row houses of the type seen in many San Francisco neighborhoods.

Baldwin & Howell reported that tennis and croquet courts were being added for the residents, but did not mention where these facilities would be located (none are extant).[30] Sales and building slowed during World War I. In August 1914 there were "unsettled conditions in the money market," and sales slackened.[31] Builder Nilsson, who had by then

35 Delano, built 1912 (photograph by author, 2019).

Stucco row houses were built across the street from 35 Delano in 1912 (photograph by author, 2019).

bought at least forty-two lots, declared bankruptcy in 1917. There is no further mention of Mission Terrace in the newspapers until 1920, when Baldwin & Howell announced that nineteen houses had been built or were under construction after a pause of "several years."

When Baldwin & Howell returned to Mission Terrace after the war, the company changed its selling approach. Complete houses were now being sold "at cost." B&H discovered that the business model of selling improved lots and asking buyers to design and build their own homes wasn't working. "People are not looking for lots. They want homes."[32] Houses were attached and set on the narrow 25-foot lots typical for San Francisco.

In 1921, the residents of the Mission Terrace Improvement Club paid $500 to the Mission Terrace Company for a lot at 467 Capistrano Avenue and then built a clubhouse there. In March 1922, Frank J. Pullen, president of the Mission Terrace Improvement Club, was quoted as saying "we are very proud" of the residents' new clubhouse on Capistrano Avenue, and "we expect to make good use of it, both for club meetings and social purposes." The residents used the clubhouse for a few years and then sold it.[33]

Appraisal of the Sutro Estate

About the time that Baldwin & Howell was launching Mission Terrace, Mrs. Emma L. Merritt, daughter and executrix of the estate of silver millionaire and ex-mayor Adolph Sutro, asked Baldwin to appraise the land holdings of her late father. Sutro was a major landowner in San Francisco and at one time owned about 1/12 of the city.[34] About his land holdings, Sutro was quoted as saying, "I took my money and invested in real estate … when everyone was scared and thought the city was going to the dogs. I bought every acre I could lay my hands on until I had 2,200 acres in this city."[35]

The bulk of Sutro's undeveloped land consisted of Sutro Heights; some additional ocean front property near the Cliff House; and the former Rancho San Miguel, a hilly and heavily forested parcel along the western slopes of Twin Peaks. Sutro left little cash ($473) when he died, and his heirs were eager to dispose of the land as quickly as possible. The properties cost money to maintain and the tenants on Rancho San Miguel paid little rent. As Mrs. Emma L. Merritt said, "The note of tenant Lynch for $126 for 18 months' rent at $7/month has never been collected. We have always considered it worthless, as Mr. Lynch is old and feeble. We reduced his rent for the first of March 1901 to $2.50. Lynch was unable to pay and we thought it better to have him occupy the place as if it were vacant, some tramp might set fire to it and the adjoining forest."[36]

The terms of Sutro's will specified that Rancho San Miguel could not be sold until ten years after the death of the last heir, at which point the proceeds would be used to fund a trust for charitable purposes. Seeing that they would get nothing, the heirs sued to break this provision, and Mrs. Merritt was opposed to breaking her father's wishes. The battle took twenty years to fully resolve.

Baldwin saw the Sutro land holdings as a once-in-a-lifetime chance to create residence parks on a vast scale. His report reads more like an attempt to persuade the heirs to take advantage of the natural setting and create residence parks than a real estate appraisal. He wrote, "It offers an opportunity to establish in San Francisco one of the most picturesque residential districts in the United States and one which can hardly be surpassed anywhere in the universe."[37] He also warned that using a street grid, as had been done for most of San Francisco, would be a mistake:

> The mistakes of the past should not be repeated and when this tract is opened up wide and graceful avenues should be constructed through it on easy grades, conforming as near as possible to the topography of the tract, instead of following the plan of the Richmond and Sunset districts, as well as most of the other suburban additions, where rectangular blocks have been carved out of property and in many instances streets have been projected on paper over grades which are inaccessible and in many cases prohibitive ... lots would be as wide and cost no more than tracts in Piedmont and Berkeley.[38]

Baldwin proposed laying out streets that respected the topography, subdividing the land into large lots, preserving the trees, and providing scenic views. He also suggested how streetcar service could be provided to Sutro Heights while avoiding the political quagmire involved in securing street railway franchises. His appraisal made no mention of other potential uses nor did he refer to the concept of the "highest and best use." He admitted his scheme might not generate the most money for Sutro heirs but would provide for beautiful residential uses.

Baldwin's Proposal for Sutro Heights

To illustrate what could be done to the Sutro Heights property, Baldwin turned to engineer John Punnett to lay out a prototypical residence park consisting of a combination of the existing platted grid of the Richmond District and curved streets with large lots. Baldwin suggested placing a private park (on what had been Sutro's house and grounds) for the exclusive use of the owners of the tract. Although he acknowledged that the park site would fetch a premium if sold for lots, he argued that using it as a park would drive sales for rest of the tract. He said its upkeep should be provided by a corporation similar to that in Presidio Terrace.

With the nearby Cliff House and Sutro Baths being major tourist attractions, Baldwin sought to protect the ambiance of the residence park by limiting commercial uses to Merrie Way and the Cliff House for "saloons, restaurants, art and curio stores, galleries, and such other places of business as now exist or are likely to spring up in the future."[39] He also addressed the need to reroute an existing streetcar line away from the entrance to the private park and instead recommended granting a right of way through the residence park to the streetcar company. It would forgo some lot sales, but it was worth it to avoid the intransigence of the streetcar company in rerouting the line. He was confident that if the property were improved the way he suggested, it would bring twice as much as a grid plan. He recognized that the heirs would not want to pay for grading, streets, sewers, and a park, but such improvements would help them dispose of the property as a whole, as they desired.

However, one serious drawback remained. The U.S. Army conducted artillery target practice from Ft. Miley and "the concussion from the guns ... made the use of that portion of the Sutro Property lying west of Fort Miley for residential purposes prohibitive."[40] The fort was constructed in 1899 and named in honor of Lieutenant Colonel John D. Miley who had died during the Spanish American War. Sutro never lived to hear the cannonade from the sixteen 12-inch mortars or three 12-inch cannon.[41] However, the

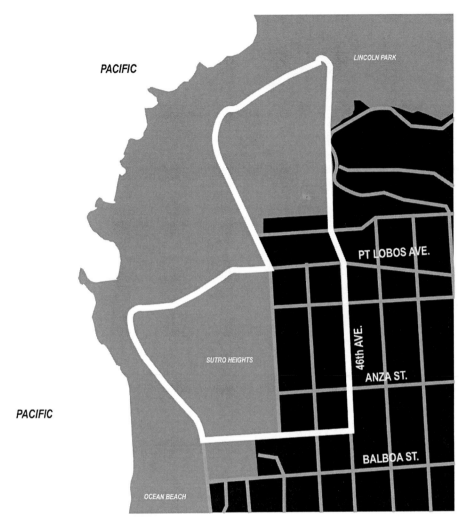

The proposed Sutro Heights residence park faced the Pacific Ocean and the Cliff House (map by Kushal Lachhwani 2019).

commanding officer, Major Lamoreux, assured Baldwin that target practice would be discontinued if houses were going to be built nearby.

Instead of developing the land into a residence park, the Sutro heirs offered to sell most of their ocean-front property to the city for $688,000 and donate Sutro's house and grounds for use as a public park. The heirs were cantankerous and wanted cash, so perhaps they thought it was simpler to sell the whole parcel instead of creating a residence park. A bond measure was placed on the 1912 ballot to purchase the property. It was supported by the tourism industry, which opposed the creation of a residence park. In what might have been the first objection to development based on environmental concerns, James Wood, manager of the Hotel St. Francis, said: "If this city should ignore this opportunity to acquire the Sutro lands and permits this wonderful public scenic playground to be converted into residence parks, posterity would execrate us for the irreparable blunder. The loss of such a distinctive public feature would be like leveling Telegraph Hill."[42]

SCHEME FOR RESIDENCE PARK SUTRO HEIGHTS AND ADJACENT PROPERTY

SUGGESTED RESIDENCE PARK
No. 33. THIS IS A PHOTOGRAPH OF A SKETCH MADE BY MR. W. H. BULL, WHICH DOES NOT DO JUSTICE TO THE PROPOSED SCHEME, BUT WHICH WILL GIVE SOME IDEA OF THE COMPREHENSIVENESS OF IT.

Baldwin's suggested residence park for Sutro Heights. The streets are largely a continuation of the Richmond District grid. A private park is shown with trees and scrubs. The Cliff House is on the coast. Fort Miley is to the right. The Sutro heirs did not proceed with the idea (image courtesy of the California State Library. Image quality enhanced by Kushal Lachhwani, 2019).

However, the bond issued was defeated. In 1915, Lyon & Hoag launched what they claimed was a residence park with marine lots called *Sutro Heights Park* on a portion of the land (see Chapter 10). In 1920, the Sutro heirs sold some of the land to the city and donated Sutro's house and grounds under the condition that it be "forever held and maintained as a free public resort or park under the name *Sutro Heights*."[43] It is now part of the Golden Gate National Recreation Area.

Rancho San Miguel

The Rancho San Miguel property comprised about 800 acres, the largest piece of privately-owned land in San Francisco under one ownership. It surrounded the city-owned Alms House for the Poor (now Laguna Honda Hospital), established in 1862, and the nearby Laguna Honda reservoir. It was a blank slate—it had not been platted, it contained almost no residents or buildings, and only two dirt roads traversed it—making it ripe for the building of "homes in a park." Yet there were problems.

This steep and hilly area was covered with a dense eucalyptus forest that Sutro had planted. It was nearly impassible due to the steepness and underbrush. Ocean Avenue formed the southern border of the property, which had streetcar service but was unpaved. The dirt roads through the tract, Corbett Road and Dewey Boulevard, washed out regularly during the rains. The rancho land had almost no commercial value, the trees were not commercially valuable, and the few relatively flat portions were leased to farmers for a pittance. Baldwin called on engineer John Punnett to survey the land, plan roads, and

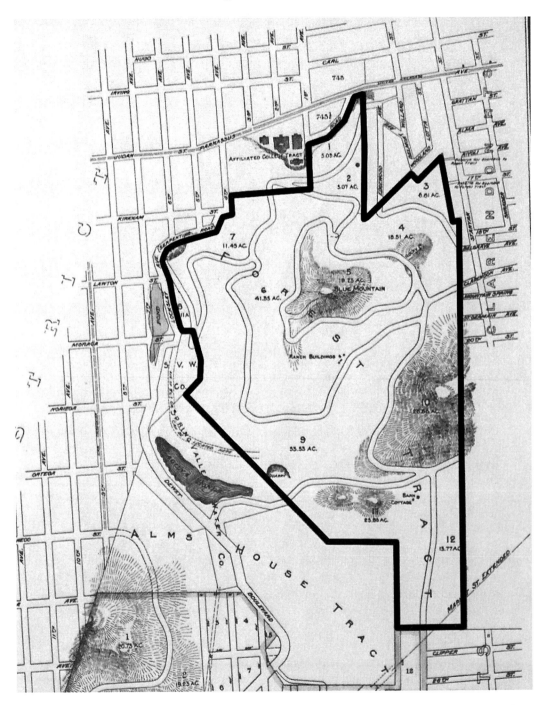

Due to the steepness of the site, only a few roads with large lots were suggested for the northern section of Rancho San Miguel. Parnassus Avenue runs east and west on the top (north), Mount Sutro (elevation 908 feet) is in the middle of the tract, 7th Avenue/Laguna Honda Boulevard will later run along left side (west) of the tract (from "Map of Forest Tract and San Miguel Ranch showing lands owned by estate of Adolph Sutro, deceased with projected avenues throughout the same and referred to in the Report of A.S. Baldwin, 1910." Map Collection, Map 971; California Historical Society. Image quality enhanced by Kushal Lachhwani, 2019).

sketch lot sites. Punnett divided the land into northern, central, and southern portions and proposed different treatments to account for the topography.

The northern part, which included the Affiliated Colleges (now University of California, San Francisco), Mt Sutro, and Seventh Avenue, was so steep that Baldwin suggested it should have large lots (so-called "villa" lots of ½ to 2 acres) that would be reached by a new road that would hug the contours of the hills. The entrance to this area was problematic because the easiest place along Parnassus Avenue was blocked by the Affiliated Colleges. Another possibility was at the Laguna Honda reservoir site, if it were filled in. The third option was to extend Clarendon Avenue over the hill to the Alms House property.

The central section lying between the Alms House and Corbett Road was relatively flat and more easily accessible than the other portions. John Punnett laid out a continuation of the Sunset District grid with standard-sized blocks measuring 240 × 600 feet. This would produce nearly 1,900 lots with 25 × 100-foot lot dimensions. It contained two hills

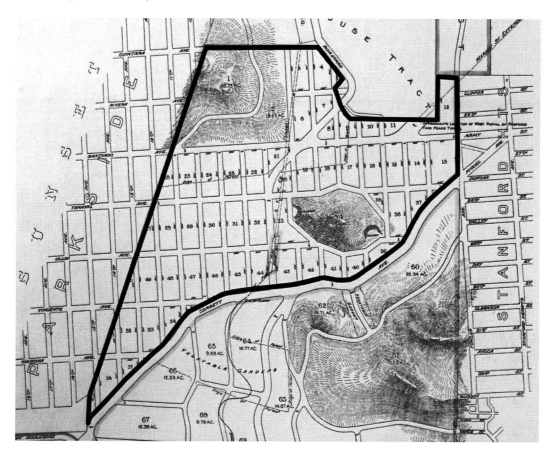

The center section of Rancho San Miguel was flat enough so that the streets were originally proposed to be laid out as a continuation of the Sunset grid. The circular looking hill is Edgehill. Corbett/Portola Drive forms the southern border (bottom). None of the streets were laid out as shown on the map (from "Map of Forest Tract and San Miguel Ranch showing lands owned by estate of Adolph Sutro, deceased with projected avenues throughout the same and referred to in the Report of A.S. Baldwin, 1910." Map Collection, Map 971; California Historical Society. Image quality enhanced by Kushal Lachhwani, 2019).

(Edgehill and part of what is now Forest Hill) that were considered too steep for development. Baldwin thought they should be used as city parks, but both hills were later covered with houses.

Baldwin opposed using the grid, what he called the "square block method," even though it might lead to a quicker sale. He explained his reasoning, saying, "I do not wish to be construed as recommending the square block method of subdivision. On the contrary I am opposed to it, and if I owned the property, I would adopt some other plan. It is possible, however, that a quicker sale could be effected by adopting [it]."[44]

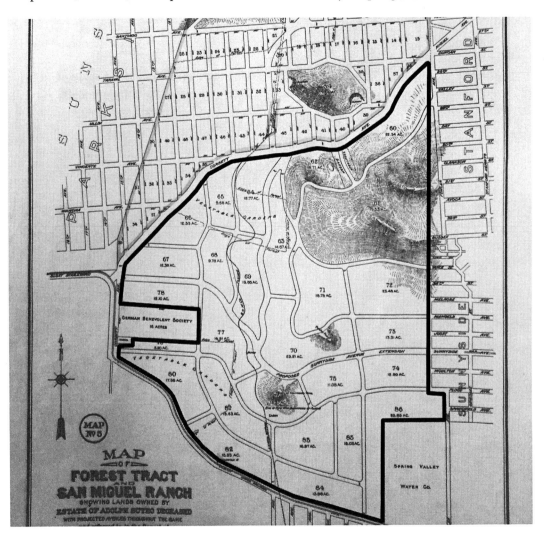

The southern section of Rancho San Miguel, on the slopes of Mt Davidson (elevation 927 feet), was proposed with curvilinear streets except for the hill; Baldwin thought it was too steep for development. Corbett/Portola Drive is the northern border (top) and Ocean Avenue is the southern border (bottom). Streets were eventually laid out somewhat similar to this map (from "Map of Forest Tract and San Miguel Ranch showing lands owned by estate of Adolph Sutro, deceased with projected avenues throughout the same and referred to in the Report of A.S. Baldwin, 1910." Map Collection, Map 971; California Historical Society. Image quality enhanced by Kushal Lachhwani, 2019).

The southern section between Corbett Road and Ocean Avenue contained Mt. Davidson, which was also considered too steep for anything except a public park or reservoir. It eventually became a public park. For the remainder of the land, Baldwin recommended curvilinear streets and villa-size lots. Baldwin admitted that curvilinear streets and villa-size lots would not maximize the potential revenue, and he took a swipe at the heirs: "...the projection of avenues throughout this portion of the San Miguel Ranch is one which will probably not be acceptable to those who are trying to get 'all there is in it' out of the property. It serves the purpose, however, for an appraisement..."

Throughout the appraisal report, Baldwin tried to persuade the heirs that the land should be developed based on the topography, trees should be preserved, and lots sited to take advantage of the views. He clearly had a vision of turning the land into his version of the City Beautiful, using many of the same planning concepts of Presidio Terrace but on a far larger scale. And he soon was able to do just that.

Residential Development Company (RDC)

Knowing that the heirs wanted to sell the entire Rancho San Miguel as quickly as possible, Baldwin offered to buy the central and southern sections himself. He did not include the northern section presumably because it was the most difficult to develop. By purchasing the land, he would be in the position to subdivide it into tracts for residence parks and hopefully do so at a profit. A sales price of $1,417,877 or about $1,719 per acre was agreed upon. This seems to have been a fair price, as the entire rancho land was appraised in 1898 for $783,750.[45]

Rather than borrow the money and assume all the risk, Baldwin formed a syndicate with other prominent real estate firms, including A.J. Rich & Co.; Shainwald, Buckbee & Co.; and Lyon & Hoag to create a special purpose company, the Residential Development Company (RDC). RDC would sell stock to the public and use the proceeds to purchase the rancho. RDC was capitalized with 20,000 shares at $100 each, with 12,000 shares offered to the public. The $1.2 million generated through stock sales would provide for the down payment of $862,337 and leave roughly $338,000 to pay for surveying and building roads through the tract. The Sutro heirs agreed to carry back a mortgage of $555,000 for five years at 6 percent.

On January 5, 1911, the public was solicited to buy stock. Baldwin expressed his intention to create a "city beautiful," by retaining Golden Gate Park superintendent John McLaren to landscape and preserve as many trees as possible.[46] The land would be developed with villa sites and artistic homes, surrounded by evergreen trees, serpentine roads, and views of the forest or the ocean. The area would include a golf and country club, and Baldwin also promised to build a scenic road up Mt. Davidson and possibly an electric incline railroad or funicular road to the summit. (None of these features were built.)[47] Prospective investors were promised they would make $5 for every $1 invested. Baldwin ran an ad with endorsements from leading merchants and capitalists, who appealed to investors not only for profit, but also for the beautification and advancement of San Francisco. The list included:

- John McLaren: "This property could be made into the most beautiful residence park in the United States."

- Marshall Hale, Hales Brothers department store magnate: "We will be able to keep many people here who would otherwise go out of the city to live."
- Howard H. Allen, president of the Downtown Association: "I hope the enterprise will succeed … it would be too bad to see such a district cut up into little inferior 25-foot lots … and streets which begin and end nowhere."
- William J. Dutton, president of Fireman's Fund Insurance Company: "I know of no enterprise recently planned which means so much for the advancement and betterment of this city.… So many mistakes have been made in the past in relation to the subdivision of properties in the outlying districts that it will be a source of satisfaction to prevent a recurrence of them so far as the magnificent Sutro tract is concerned."[48]

Baldwin professed to want many small investors to take advantage of the opportunity. However, most people were unfamiliar with the area, and those that were familiar with it knew that transportation was a problem. Curiously, Baldwin did not mention in the ad the proposed Twin Peaks tunnel, which was widely discussed at the time. Although Baldwin promoted the sales to locals, his group was forced to turn to eastern capitalists to raise the money. The deal closed on May 4, 1912, but it took until October for last of the heirs living in Europe to sign the agreement.

Only eight days after the sale was consummated, Baldwin announced that he had accepted offers from two East Bay developers, Newell-Murdoch and Mason-McDuffie. There was no public auction or sale. Baldwin had approached men that he knew shared his vision, brought relevant experience, and had good reputations. In fact, an advertisement for St. Francis Wood by Baldwin & Howell (who acted as sales agents) said that they solicited Mason-McDuffie based on the company's record in the East Bay.[49]

Newell-Murdoch and Mason-McDuffie each paid $3,000 per acre, 70 percent more than what RDC paid the Sutro heirs.[50] In all, RDC received $1,665,000 from developers and realized a profit of $248,000. RDC also retained 269 acres that Baldwin & Howell would later develop as Westwood Park and Westwood Highlands residence parks.

Baldwin consummated the largest land development deal in San Francisco with little public notice or scrutiny. If the deal lacked transparency, it had the virtue of speed. Within three years, Baldwin and his colleagues had reached a deal with the Suto heirs, raised funds and purchased the land, subdivided it into large sections, selected developers, and negotiated sales to developers who launched the residence parks Forest Hill, Forest Hill Extension, St. Francis Wood, West Portal Park, Claremont Court, Merritt Terrace, El Por-tal Park (later Laguna Honda Park), and Balboa Terrace.

Westwood Park

In 1916, Baldwin & Howell began developing a residence park on land they had retained from the purchase of Rancho San Miguel. At the time, the company was also developing or selling outside San Francisco: San Mateo Park and Hayward Park in San Mateo, Stockton Acres with lots suitable for farming, and Pullman Park in Richmond with housing for an industrial town.

At 667 houses, Westwood Park would be the largest development project undertaken by B&H. It was located on Ocean Avenue, nestled by Monterey Boulevard to the north. The land was nearly flat with a gentle rise to the north, making it cheaper to develop than the hilly residence parks nearer the Twin Peaks tunnel.

Engineer John Punnett laid out a symmetrical street design with a double oval intersecting a grid in the Beaux Arts tradition. The oval is inwardly focused with limited access. Streets running east and west in Westwood Park end abruptly at the edge of the tract. This suggests that Punnett might have anticipated possible extensions, should the land have become available. (The land on both sides was vacant,

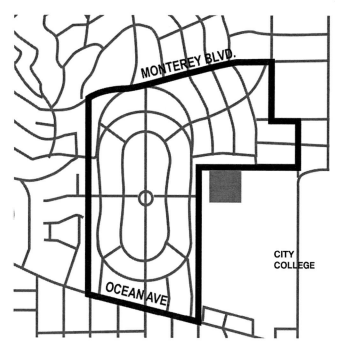

Westwood Park is located between Monterey Boulevard and Ocean Avenue (map by Kushal Lachhwani, 2019).

North entrance to Westwood Park at Miramar and Monterey looking south. The gates were designed by architect Louis Christian Mullgardt (photograph by author, 2019).

although in 1921 Homewood Terrace, a Jewish orphanage, was built to the west.) Louis Christian Mullgardt, a respected architect known for his work on the Panama-Pacific International Exposition and the de Young Museum, designed Westwood Park's gateways and pillars at the north and south entrances.

B&H targeted the middle class. Baldwin said, "We propose to put Westwood Park on the market at conservative prices, placing it within the reach of those who desire moderate priced homes in highly artistic surroundings. This will be one of the first subdivisions of this character to be offered in San Francisco."[51] Westwood Park would still have most of the amenities of other residence parks: wide lots, yard space, front setbacks, buried electric lines, landscaped medians, and ornamental concrete lamp posts. Lots in Westwood Park were wider than the typical 25 feet, and the detached bungalows with front yards gave a suburban feeling to the tract.

Presumably, Baldwin & Howell had learned from their experience with Mission Terrace that moderate-income buyers could not be expected to hire an architect or finance the construction of a house. Given the financial squeeze gripping the nation during World War I, Baldwin & Howell might have concluded that mass production using proven contractors could overcome both problems. Buyers could still buy a lot, but B&H brought in the large construction firm Barrett & Hilp to construct houses in any of thirty-four plans for an advertised fixed price ranging from $1,400 to $5,000. Furthermore, B&H would finance the construction. If buyers could not afford the payments, B&H would try to arrange monthly payments that they could afford. It appears, however, that the only people buying lots were contractors who built speculative houses.

By October 1916, Barrett & Hilp had bought thirty lots, but it was only one of several companies active in Westwood Park. Author Kathleen O. Beitiks has identified twenty individual builders of Westwood Park houses, but the great majority were built by Hans Nelson (not to be confused with Fernando Nelson & Sons). Beitiks says that although about a dozen architects were active in Westwood Park, Charles F. Strothoff designed 70 percent of the homes for Hans Nelson.[52] Strothoff specialized in designing single-family dwellings for merchant builders in San Francisco's West of Twin Peaks area and Crocker-Amazon.[53] He boasted, "It's So Easy for Me, Bungalows—different, artistic, home-like—are my specialty. Small or large, inexpensive or quite costly, I will design a bungalow that will meet your fancy in every particular."[54]

Charles F. Strothoff was born in San Francisco on May 9, 1892. He majored in architectural drafting at the Wilmerding School of Industrial Arts, a technical high school for working-class youth (now the college-preparatory Lick-Wilmerding High School). He continued his architectural studies at night schools and architectural clubs. Strothoff worked as a draftsman in the offices of Albert Farr, a prominent society architect who worked for Allen & Co. and other residence park developers. In 1915, Strothoff began practicing on his own and developed a relationship with several builders/developers, including Walter E. Hansen, Bauer & Quinn, Emil Nelson, the Stoneson Brothers, G.J. Elkington & Sons, Parkside Realty Company, and St. George Holden. He designed houses in West Portal, Westwood Park, Westwood Highlands, Crocker-Amazon, Monterey Heights, Parkside, Pine Lake Park, and St. Mary's Park. By the late 1920s, Strothoff began working in Burlingame, San Mateo, and Millbrae. During World War II, he was the director of the Housing Authority in the city of Richmond, where he oversaw the construction of thousands of permanent and temporary housing units for shipyard workers. He died in 1963.

Typical streetscape on Miramar Avenue. Architect Charles F. Strothoff designed approximately 70 percent of the houses in Westwood Park for the builder Hans Nelson (photograph by author, 2019).

Baldwin & Howell also figured prominently in the career of female architect Ida McCain, who designed upwards of one hundred houses in Westwood Park. B&H described McCain as an expert in designing bungalows.[55]

Despite a pause due to restrictions during World War I, Westwood Park was sold out by 1925.

Woodcrest/Westwood Highlands

In 1922, flushed with the success of Westwood Park, B&H launched Woodcrest, a residence park north of Westwood Park on steep terrain. A portion of the land had been purchased by Duncan McDuffie for St. Francis Wood, but he sold it back (see Chapter 6). Attempting to lure higher-income buyers, Baldwin again engaged engineer Punnett to lay out a formal Beaux-Arts tract with a fan-shaped street design on the lower slopes of the tract and a curving road winding up to the summit of Mt. Davison. Large lots, called "villa sites," were laid out on the steeper section, as fewer houses could be constructed on the hilly terrain.

The high-status nature of the tract is suggested by the large classical gates designed by prominent architect John Reid. Reid, a native San Franciscan, earned an architecture degree from University of California, Berkeley; attended the Ecole des

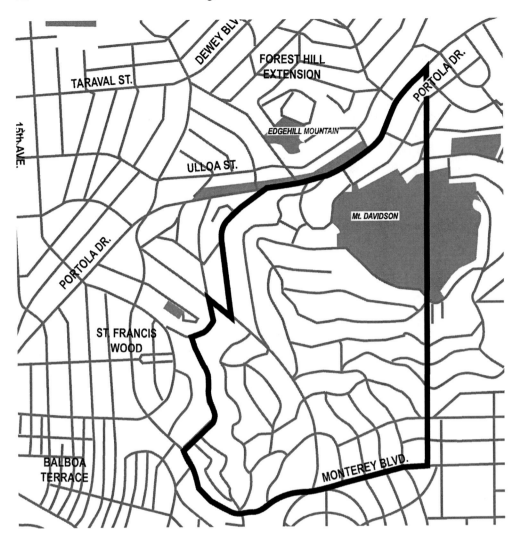

Woodcrest would have been located between Portola and Monterey Boulevard (map by Kushal Lachhwani, 2019).

Beaux-Arts in Paris; and worked for Willis Polk and Daniel H. Burnham before opening his own practice in 1911. He was well connected professionally and politically; he was Mayor James Rolph's brother-in-law and was the San Francisco city architect from 1917 to 1927.

However, B&H soon had second thoughts. The company scaled back its plans and adopted a more conservative and less expensive design for Woodcrest. The streets follow the terrain but less formally than those contemplated by Punnett. B&H dropped the monumental gates and statuary, limited the area of development to the lower slopes adjacent to Westwood Park, and eliminated the villa-sized sites. The only markers of the tract would be small metal signs attached to lamp posts. B&H renamed the tract Westwood Highlands, probably to associate it with Westwood Park.

In Westwood Highlands, B&H adopted a business plan different from prior projects. With a new understanding that most buyers did not want to be responsible for

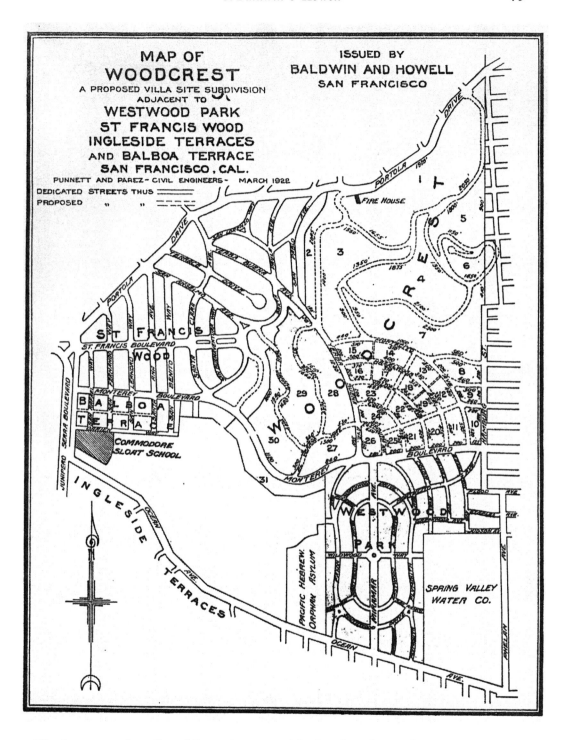

Woodcrest started as a formal Beaux Arts tract with a fan-shaped street design on lower slopes of the tract and a curving road winding up to the summit of Mt. Davison. Portola Drive forms northern border (top), Ocean Avenue forms southern border (bottom), and Monterey Boulevard runs through the middle, left to right (courtesy of Carolyn S. Loeb, *Entrepreneurial Vernacular: Developers' Subdivisions in the 1920s*, Johns Hopkins University Press, pp. 96, 98).

Plan of architect John Reid's for classically inspired statuary at the entrance gates to Wood-crest (courtesy of Carolyn S. Loeb, *Entrepreneurial Vernacular: Developers' Subdivisions in the 1920s*, Johns Hopkins University Press, pp. 96, 98).

building their own houses and to control costs that had risen greatly with the infla-tion caused by World War I, the entire tract would be the responsibility of builder Hans Nelson and architect Charles Strothoff, Westwood Park veterans. Together they would design and build all the houses. Buyers would pick one of Strothoff's Mediterranean revival designs in a variety of sizes but could not buy lots and hire their own architects. The tract targeted the professional class with houses that cost about twice the national average.[56]

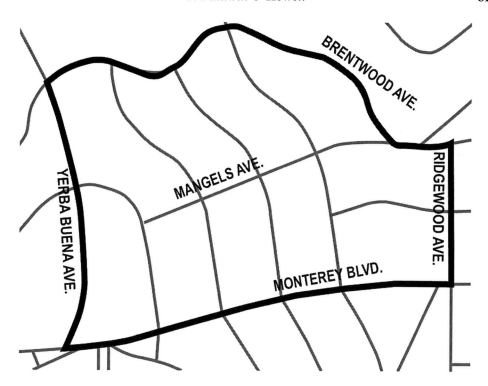

Westwood Highlands is smaller than the proposed Woodcrest tract and looks like a continuation of Westwood Park (map by Kushal Lachhwani, 2019).

Small signs on lamp posts are the only physical markers of Westwood Highlands (photograph by author, 2019).

Westwood Highlands along Monterey Boulevard (photograph by author, 2019).

St. Mary's Park

About the same time that Westwood Highlands was being built, the Roman Catholic Archdiocese of San
Francisco undertook the
development of a residence
park, St. Mary's Park, using
architect Charles Strothoff.
This was not a Baldwin &
Howell project but, in a
curious twist of fate, Baldwin had bid for the land
some twenty years earlier.

The site was south of
Bernal Heights then on
the outskirts of town. It
had been the location of
St. Mary's college, founded
in the 1860s by Joseph Alemany, the first archbishop
of San Francisco. He paid
$1,600 to Jesus Bernal for
land on the Rancho Rin-
con de la Salinas y Potrero
Viejo, four miles south of
City Hall. Alemany picked
the location to escape the

St Mary's Park is located on the site of the former St Mary's
College off Mission Street and south of Bernal Heights (map
by Kushal Lachhwani, 2019).

St Mary's is a California Registered Historical Landmark #772. The plaque reads: "In August 1863, Archbishop Joseph Sadoc Alemany, O.P. opened St. Mary's College at this location with a faculty of two diocesan priests, four laymen, and two student teachers. In August 1868, at the invitation of the archbishop, Brother Justin McMahon and seven Christian Brothers took charge of St. Mary's. The Christian brothers have manifested the principle characterized by the best educational institutions, excellence" (photograph by author, 2019).

congestion of the Gold Rush boomtown, but it was cold and foggy, as well as remote.[57] This was not a seminary, where seclusion and quiet were desired, but a college for lay students. The college existed at this location from 1862 until 1889, when it moved to Oakland. In 1928 it moved to Moraga, California, where it operates today.

After the college left, the land was rented to truck farmers. The archdiocese periodically entertained offers to sell the property but never did so.[58]

A.S. Baldwin took out a four-month option to purchase the land for $250,000 on June 21, 1897. Other bidders included United Railroads, which bid $200,000 on August 6, 1907; Dudley Kinsell offered $150,000 on January 4, 1909; Morrison Cope & Brobeck offered $175,000 on February 19, 1909; Stanford & Co. Investments offered $140,000 on March 15, 1909; and Armond Levy offered $280,000 (and paid a $1,000 deposit) on December 22, 1911. In addition, L.A. Kelly & Co Real Estate bid $225,000 on August 5, 1911. Kelly said the site could be divided into 550 lots and estimated it would cost $106,636 to grade the site and put in sidewalks, curbs, sewers, and street paving.

Michael O'Shaughnessy, before he became San Francisco's city engineer, reviewed the site and concluded that the archdiocese could sell the lots over a four-year period for $289,930, with expenses of $64,855 for improvements and $12,500 in sales expenses, leaving a net profit of $212,575. But he recommended that the archdiocese sell the entire property as a whole, not be "bothered by the annoyances from petty sales."

The archdiocese decided to keep the land and develop it. In 1914, with the success of residence parks in other parts of the city, the archdiocese announced the creation of

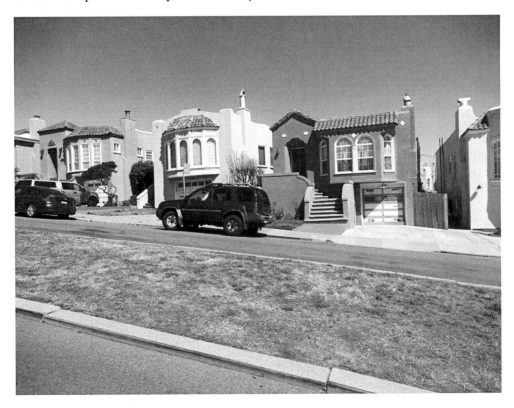

Houses by Charles A. Strothoff on College Avenue. It appears that the houses have similar floor plans with some variation in facades (photograph by author, 2019).

St Mary's Park, a residence park with four hundred lots, each 35- to 60-feet wide, featuring bungalows for people of moderate means. To handle sales and development they retained R.D. Blake,[59] a member of the archdiocese's building committee for the Young Men's Institute on Fell Street and a veteran of Balfour Gutherie & Co., a venerable British company where he had worked in the land and loan department.[60] Nothing happened for the next ten years. Presumably, the archdiocese confronted the World War I financial disruptions that inhibited so many other residence parks at the time.

In 1924, with the real estate market booming, the archdiocese hired engineer John Punnett (not Mark Daniels, as some sources say) to draw up a subdivision plan. Punnett created a roughly circular street in the center of the tract bisected by a primary street (College Avenue) with a lawn median. To some, the shape resembles a bell, perhaps a subtle reference to the church. Blake was again engaged, and he offered to build houses to suit buyers.[61] However, it is not clear how many took him up on that offer, as architect Charles A. Strothoff, "San Francisco's Famous Home Architect," was featured as the designer in advertisements. He apparently designed most of the houses that were constructed by a number of builders, including F.W. Varney, Gordon W. Morris, F.A. Soracco, and the Stoneson Brothers & Thorinson. The houses cost $8,750 with a low down payment and monthly payments of $60.[62]

The archdiocese held the mortgages and offered low down payments and easy terms but showed no Christian charity as they banned non-whites from buying or residing in St. Mary's Park.[63]

Baldwin & Howell

The firm of Baldwin & Howell was held in high esteem and was well connected with the city's business and political elites. The firm acted as de facto city planners at a time when no municipal city planning existed. Baldwin & Howell used its influence to introduce a new way for San Francisco to grow. The company agitated for "wide and graceful avenues … on easy grades, conforming as near as possible to the topography of the tract," instead of merely extending the street grid. This was not a new idea, but it was something of a revolution for San Francisco, which had been wedded to the rectangular street grid for generations.

Baldwin & Howell selected the developers who would build residence parks on the Sutro estate. One of the first developers B&H chose was an East Bay developer who would produce St. Francis Wood, perhaps the fullest realization of the residence park concept in San Francisco.

6

Duncan McDuffie

Baldwin & Howell's Residential Development Company sold one of the first parcels of Sutro's Rancho San Miguel to the Berkeley real estate firm Mason-McDuffie, which created the St. Francis Wood residence park. In many ways St. Francis Wood typifies what all the developers of residence parks were trying to achieve.

Early on, it was lauded by experts. In 1922, the internationally known German city planner, architectural critic, and author Werner Hegemann wrote that the plan for St. Francis Wood was a "beautifully framed area with effective perspectives." The main street, St. Francis Boulevard, with gates at the entrance and a fountain at the end, reminded Hegemann of the great Italian Renaissance architect Andrea Palladio, who called for the principal streets to be straight and lead from the gates in a direct line to the greatest and principal plaza.[1]

Writing in 1959, historian Mel Scott lauded St. Francis Wood for its "brilliant suburban development."[2] More recently, St. Francis Wood was called a "regional trend setter."[3] It is an "outstanding achievement, … [whose] … lushness and continuity of the landscaping … is integrated with the general plan."[4] It is also credited for having "retained its cachet for nearly a hundred years."[5]

More information is known about St. Francis Wood than about any other residence park for a number of reasons: the developer's business records are available at the Bancroft Library; the records of the tract landscapers, the Olmsted Brothers, are available at the Olmsted Archives at Fairsted, the Frederick Law Olmsted National Historic Site in Brookline, Massachusetts; many of the house plans are available in the University of California Environmental Design Archives; and much has been written about the tract. This chapter is based on a book by the author.[6]

St. Francis Wood is located in the center of San Francisco on the western face of the city's highest peak, Mount Davidson (938 feet). George Davidson, who surveyed the area in the 1850s, named the hill Blue Mountain after the colorful native plants that thrived on its slopes: blue-blossom ceanothus, blue-eyed grass, and Douglas and long-pedaled iris. The peak was later renamed in Davidson's honor.[7] Mt. Davidson is part of a range of hills (Diamond Heights, Twin Peaks, and Mt. Sutro) that divide San Francisco. Adolph Sutro had planted blue-gum eucalyptus, and the trees blanketed the land from Ocean Avenue to the Inner Sunset District, broken only by a few open plots leased to vegetable growers.[8] A wood flume carrying water from sources in San Mateo County to the Laguna Honda reservoir wound its way through the land approximately along what is now Santa Clara Avenue.[9]

St. Francis Wood is located between Portola Drive, Monterey Boulevard and a series of small streets to the east. The dotted line shows the original extent of the tract, but McDuffie sold back that section to the Residential Development Company (map by Kushal Lachhwani, 2019).

Duncan McDuffie, Community Developer

The man primarily responsible for conceiving and building St. Francis Wood is Duncan McDuffie (1878–1951).[10] McDuffie, along with business associates Louis Titus, C.C. Young, Perry T. Tompkins, and Elmer I. Rowell, scouted the property in March 1912 and came up with the concept for St. Francis Wood. McDuffie wrote that the group "climbed over the wooden fence that marked the western boundary of the Sutro property on Junipero [Serra] Boulevard. The day was sunny and brilliant; the trees rustled in the light breeze, the ground was carpeted with California poppies, cowslips, buttercups, wild pansies, baby blue eyes and iris. From open spots among the trees we could see the narrow ribbon of Sloat Boulevard unrolling to the beach, the shining shield of the Pacific and on the horizon the jagged rocks of the Farallons."[11]

The Mason-McDuffie Company became one of the region's largest real estate and development firms. During the East Bay building boom following the 1906 earthquake and fire, the firm prospered. The company developed traditional subdivisions, conducted general real estate activities, and formed a number of special purpose real-estate companies with Louis Titus as president and McDuffie as secretary. In 1906 C.C. Young (California governor, 1927–31) and Perry T. Tompkins joined the firm.[12] In 1914 McDuffie was founding vice president of the California Conference on City Planning, initiated and headed the first planning commission in Berkeley in 1914 and also served on the National Association of Real Estate Boards City Planning Committee with Edward Boulton and J.C. Nicholas, among others.

Before zoning laws were widely used, land and lots were divided and sold for whatever purpose the new owners desired. McDuffie was among the first of the "community builders" who subdivided and sold land for a specific use. Community builders were developers who adopted a longer timeframe for sale, exerted a great deal of land use control, and insisted on higher design quality than what was used by other developers, even if such requirements delayed profits. Through deed restrictions, a private contract between the original seller and buyer of the lot, many conditions were imposed that restricted what an owner could do with his land. A purchaser was assured that his investment was safe from other buyers who might degrade the qualities that made the subdivision valuable.[13]

Deed restrictions existed in other California communities, but McDuffie went further in breadth and mechanisms for enforcement. St. Francis Wood allowed only single-family residences that were no more than two stories tall and were set back on the lots at least 20 feet from the street and 10 feet from the rear lot line. Free space on both sides of a house had to be at least 25 percent of the width of the lot, and the minimum on any side was 10 percent. Detached, one-story garages were allowed for automobiles but not as living quarters. Houses had to cost a minimum of $3,500, and plans had to be submitted to a supervising architect to ensure the design met restrictions. In addition to a supervising architect, McDuffie established a homeowner's association vested with the legal power to enforce covenants, maintain common areas, and make needed repairs to the tract infrastructure.

As mentioned earlier, McDuffie used deed restrictions in two residence parks in Berkeley—Claremont and Northbrae—before creating St. Francis Wood and would also employ features from the East Bay in St. Francis Wood: public sculptures to define a sense of place, custom-built houses using locally prominent architects, proximity to streetcars lines, and the exclusion of commercial services.[14]

McDuffie created a special company, West Gate Park Company, and in 1912 he bought a sloped, heavily forested, 175-acre tract just east of the future Twin Peaks tunnel entrance.[15] This tract was one of the most desirable portions of RDC's land holdings. It was located on a gentle slope that made building easier and cheaper compared to the steep hillsides of Forest Hill. And bordered the existing crossroads, Sloat Boulevard and Corbett Road (now Portola Drive). It was close enough for residents to walk to the entrance of the future Twin Peaks tunnel, while far enough away for them to avoid the noise and crowds that the streetcar would bring. The plan for St. Francis Wood was a bit bold, for the nearest store was miles away, but the streetcar's right of way leading up to the tunnel's entrance (or portal) was expected to be used for business purposes.[16] The right of way became West Portal Avenue, which by the 1920s had become a neighborhood commercial center, offering a Post Office, movie house, butcher dry cleaners, and hardware stores, as well as supermarkets, banks, cafes, coffee shops, beauty salons, professional offices, doctors, and dentists.

McDuffie launched St. Francis Wood on October 12, 1912, initially offering improved lots, not houses. The streets were paved and included curbs and sidewalks. All utilities, including electricity, sewer, water, telephones, and gas, were to be placed underground to eliminate unsightly poles, wires, and visual clutter. Lots were 50-feet wide, twice the width of the standard San Francisco lot. The developer would plant trees to ensure complete landscaping of the site, as well as build community parks throughout the tract, a children's playground, and tennis courts. Houses would be detached with generous setbacks. To avoid monotony, there would be no model homes or standard plans. To ensure the construction of only high-class homes, all building plans would have to meet the planning restrictions of the development. Residents with automobiles would store their cars in a community garage to avoid spoiling the visual ambiance (the community garage was not built). McDuffie would act as the president of the homeowner's association (1912–17 and 1919–22), until there were enough residents to elect a president.

McDuffie turned once again to John Galen Howard, the region's most prominent architect of the time, to design the ornamental entrance, a fountain, entry pillars, and sidewalks.

John Galen Howard (1864–1931) had come to California in 1902 to serve as the architect for the design of the University of California campus in Berkeley and to create and head the university's architecture degree program. Schooled at Massachusetts Institute of Technology, Howard apprenticed with H.H. Richardson and then with McKim, Mead & White, two of the most famous architectural firms in the country. Charles McKim thought so highly of Howard that he paid for him to study at the Ecole des Beaux Arts in Paris, where Howard received the highest marks of any American.[17] In addition to his classical training, Howard was also a fan of California Mission architecture and the Arts and Crafts movement. As a young man, he had traveled to southern California and fallen in love with abandoned adobe houses and missions.[18]

Howard was the supervising architect for the exposition buildings of the 1909 Alaska-Yukon Exposition held in Seattle, Washington. In addition to his university duties, Howard maintained a lucrative private practice and served on civic planning groups for the 1915 Panama-Pacific International Exhibition, the design for the San Francisco Civic Center, and other projects.

Howard brought the Beaux Arts planning aesthetic to St. Francis Wood. He designed a loggia, with a gable roof clad in red clay tiles and a garden and reflecting pool on both sides of St. Francis Boulevard at the main entrance at Sloat Boulevard at a cost of $12,000, the price of a large house at the time. It is believed that this entrance was inspired by the Villa Borghese and the Vatican gardens, and Howard's intention was that it would evoke the ambiance of the Italian Renaissance.[19]

He also designed a fountain at the intersection of St. Francis Boulevard and Santa Ana Avenue (similar to his work in Northbrae), the street posts (topped with gas lights), and the sales office (now the St. Francis Wood tract office).

St. Francis Wood was conceived when the automobile was becoming a practical and affordable mode of transportation, not just a novel and expensive luxury. Although the proximity of the Twin Peaks tunnel streetcar line was an important selling point for St. Francis Wood, residents also wanted the convenience of automobiles. As originally designed, residents would use a common garage instead of individual garages. The

At the main entrance to St. Francis Wood, Howard designed a loggia, with a gable roof clad in red clay tiles, a garden, and a reflecting pool inspired by the Villa Borghese and the Vatican gardens (OpenSFhistorywnp36.01641).

The fountain on St. Francis Boulevard by Howard was similar to his fountain design used in Berkeley's Northbrae. Both fountains were damaged by car collisions but were restored (photograph by author, 2019).

common garage would have been located in a semi-circular building at the end of Terrace Drive. The idea was impractical, as residents would have had to walk several blocks, in some cases uphill; the common garage was not constructed. Instead, detached garages were added at the rear of the lots with driveways sited between the houses.

St. Francis Wood has two prominent private parks and several smaller miniparks. The two-acre park along Terrace Drive includes a recreation area for children and adults, and was the proposed site for a communal garage and clubhouse. Inspired by the Forest Hill clubhouse, plans were drawn up for a clubhouse and community center in 1921. It was to have one and one-half stories, with an auditorium seating 250, a stage, ballroom, lounge, and kitchenette, plus committee rooms, and showers for use by the tennis club.[20] Money was raised, but the total fell short, and the St. Francis Wood board decided to abandon the idea. No drawings or plans are known to have been made.[21]

Although the communal garage and clubhouse were not built, the park has become a place for residents to socialize. The former sales office building was relocated from near the entrance to St. Francis Wood to Terrace Park. Although modestly sized, it functions as the office and meeting place for the homeowner's association board of directors.

The Olmsted Brothers

McDuffie was unique among San Francisco developers in that he hired the Olmsted Brothers, the nation's most prestigious landscaping firm. The only other developer to hire the Olmsteds in the Bay Area was Wickham Havens for his Lakeshore Highlands residence park in Oakland. The Olmsted Brothers firm was known for designing large city parks and private estates. Perhaps other developers thought the firm was too expensive or brought a level of sophistication that wasn't warranted for their projects. McDuffie, however, was personally familiar with Olmsted Brothers' reputation and had previously hired the firm to landscape his residence in Berkeley.

Much of the credit for Olmsted Brothers' work in St. Francis Wood is due to James F. "Fred" Dawson, an associate in the firm. He and John Charles Olmsted worked with John Galen Howard on the 1909 Alaska Yukon Pacific Exhibition in Seattle. (John's uncle was Frederick Law Olmsted, Sr.; he adopted John after his father's death. In other words, John and Frederick Law Olmsted, Jr., were cousins *and* stepbrothers.) Dawson and John Charles Olmsted were involved with the detailed planning for St. Francis Wood. Frederick Law Olmsted, Jr., was involved in city planning activities at the time, and he and McDuffie were good friends.[22]

McDuffie asked the Olmsted Bothers to revise the street plan done by a local engineer, lay out private parks, landscape the entire tract, and consult on designs for statuary and fountains. In the comparatively flat section near the entrance, the Olmsted Brothers retained the local engineer's plan for parallel roads in a horseshoe-shaped design. The firm channeled traffic along a few major streets so that the residential streets would be free of traffic. But in the hilly sections, they used winding street designs with some sharp curves.

Olmsted Brothers made a big change in the eastern end of the main axial road, St. Francis Boulevard. Original plans had the road terminating abruptly, but the Olmsteds extended and widened the road to 150 feet with a landscaped median taking up much of the width. Although eliminating a number of lots, the extended street's 7 percent grade provided a view of the ocean from a belvedere and a future park.[23]

The design of the belvedere provoked a year-long debate among Olmsted Brothers, McDuffie, and his architect, Henry Gutterson. The main disagreement revolved around cost; Olmsted Brothers' plans called for expensive grading at a time when the tract was struggling. Reading the letters, it is clear that McDuffie was anxious to have the Olmsteds' approval. At least seven designs were traded back and forth before the final plan was selected.[24]

McDuffie and the Olmsteds took considerable pains to make St. Francis Boulevard reflect its importance as the main entrance and axis of the development. But the entrance posed a serious problem because it was located at the junction of five roads: St. Francis Boulevard, Corbett Road (now Portola), Sloat Boulevard, Junipero Serra Boulevard, and the future West Portal Avenue. In addition, three streetcars lines—the United Railways #12 and two new Muni streetcar lines, the K and M—were projected to run through the intersection. Olmsted cautioned McDuffie: "Any scheme which brought trolley traffic directly in front of the area in front of your entrance would be a serious objection … assembling so many lines of roads and trolleys at one point would completely break up the periphery of such an area that little would be left for appropriate development."[25]

The Olmsted firm proposed to run the Muni streetcars from the tunnel along both sides of an existing creek (located about where today's West Portal Avenue is today) and then run the tracks through an underpass beneath Sloat Boulevard, 450 feet away from the entrance to St. Francis Wood. The plan would leave a one-block area for shops in front of St. Francis Wood. The Olmsteds felt that so many streetcar lines would inevitably draw commercial activities, but that if the shops were limited to a specific area, they would not threaten the ambiance of the tract. McDuffie liked the idea, but the owners of the adjacent land, L.E. Green and A.S. Baldwin of RDC, did not support him.

The belvedere was the simplest and least expensive design of many by the Olmsted Brothers and Gutterson. Constructed at a time (1916) when McDuffie was under severe financial pressure, it is a grand gesture and one not seen in other residence parks. It is still possible to glimpse the Pacific Ocean two miles away (photograph by author, 2019).

St. Francis Circle looking north shortly after completion in 1919. Houses in St. Francis Wood are visible to the right; the two-story house in the center of the photograph lies in West Portal Park. The two small buildings are sales offices for West Portal Park and Forest Hill Extension. The house on the left predates the residence parks (OpenSFHistory wnp36.02158).

In any case, the cost-conscious City Engineer Michael O'Shaughnessy vetoed the concept. He was adamant that the streetcar tracks run on the street and not in an underpass, due to the greater cost of constructing an underpass. McDuffie argued with O'Shaughnessy about the dangers of streetcars and automobiles crossing the intersections, but O'Shaughnessy assured him that all traffic would stop at the intersection and a traffic officer would be provided.[26] At the time, auto traffic was negligible.

In light of O'Shaughnessy's rejection, McDuffie asked the Olmsted firm to come up with a solution. Perhaps recalling Northbrae, Olmsted Brothers responded with a traffic circle, a first for San Francisco. The intersection is still known as St. Francis Circle, despite the removal of the circle sometime before 1930. The issue of undergrounding the streetcar tracks surfaced again in the early 1970s. During the construction of the Muni Metro the city decided to keep at-grade crossings. Today, this intersection is one of the most complicated and busiest in San Francisco, handling 40,000 cars a day and having one of the longest red lights in the city.

Marketing and Sales

In the first advertisements for St. Francis Wood, McDuffie touted the advantages of the residential park restrictions; high-quality streets; underground utilities; and amenities such as parks, tennis courts, fountains, and extensive landscaping. If these amenities weren't enough, McDuffie also promised buyers good views, a sunny climate, and a central location. The last two were a bit of a stretch. McDuffie assured buyers that St. Francis Wood was no foggier than the average San Francisco neighborhood, but he made this comparison during the fall and winter months instead of the summer fog season.[27] A "central location" in most cities implies a convenient distance from downtown, but McDuffie was referring to the geographic center of San Francisco. On the west side of Twin Peaks and at the far edge of the city's development, St. Francis Wood lacked convenient transportation to the primary business districts. McDuffie stressed in early advertisements that the trip downtown would be fast once the new Twin Peaks tunnel electric streetcar service started. Until it did, McDuffie urged prospective buyers to take advantage of the low prices that would surely rise once the tunnel was built.

McDuffie did not open the entire tract for sale at once. He improved the property and offered lots in phases. The initial offering consisted of 283 lots in the "horseshoe" section where St. Francis Boulevard formed the spine. In 1917, he extended the tract twice. San Anselmo Avenue and Monterey Boulevard were laid out, as was the tract north to San Pablo Avenue. In 1924, the final phase extended to San Andreas Way and part of San Jacinto Way. The sketches drawn by the Olmsteds show the streets laid out as far east as Yerba Buena and Monterey. This eastern portion was sold in 1921 to RDC and was later developed by Baldwin & Howell as Westwood Highlands.

Mason-McDuffie's business plan was to offer lots for sale with curbs and sidewalks, as well as all utilities (electricity, sewer, water, telephone, and gas)—but not the actual houses. Buyers were free to choose their own architects. But soon the firm broadened its offerings by hiring architects either to design custom houses for customers or provide stock plans, sometimes free with the purchase of a lot. Mason-McDuffie also started a construction firm and offered to finance lot purchases and construction costs. Finally, the firm built a number of homes on speculation to sell to customers.

Although St. Francis Wood prices were well above the average, Mason-McDuffie did offer a range of house sizes and prices. These houses were not just for the very rich. In 1915, McDuffie advertised complete houses on 50- to 60-foot-wide lots in a range of prices: $7,900, $8,350, $11,500 and $12,500.[28] A year later, Mason-McDuffie was offering "small" but "not cheap" bungalows. Nonetheless, these efforts brought small rewards. World War I and an economic downturn hurt Mason-McDuffie as it did other developers. By the end of 1915 only fifteen houses were completed. Eleven were added in 1916, five more in 1917, and another six in 1918.[29]

The growth of St. Francis Wood began in earnest after the end of World War I and the commencement of Muni streetcar tunnel service in 1918. In 1919, McDuffie launched the lower-priced St. Francis Gardens, 103 lots located north of Terrace Drive. Instead of the 50-foot-wide lots offered in the original sales, these were 40-foot-wide lots and priced at $1,950. Buyers could live in St. Francis Wood for under $7,000 if they built the minimum-cost house (at that time $5,000). All it took was $50 down and $19.50 a month.[30] McDuffie later had second thoughts about the wisdom of requiring houses to have a minimal cost, which did not guarantee a quality design as intended, and prospective buyers balked at it. He thought that architectural supervision was a more effective way to maintain quality.

While these lower priced lots were for sale, the supervising architect of St. Francis Wood was urging people to buy. Henry Gutterson extolled the virtues of home ownership and urged people not to delay their home construction plans waiting for material prices to fall after the war, since labor was the major cost component. He summed up his argument saying:

Good construction has always proven to be a worthwhile investment. When that investment involves the center of our affections it should allow for progress. Our house should be a substantial, adequate, artistic background for the expression of our development. How could it be better set than in a garden with free space and sunshine on all sides—a garden home. Build now![31]

A year later, the lots were offered at even lower prices: $1,750, with $50 down.[32] By early 1922, prices had stabilized, and Mason-McDuffie was offering "Homes for All Purses." Buyers had a choice of company designed and built houses at $10,250 to $13,500, built-to-order houses as low as $8,750 to $9,250, or view lots for $2,150 to $2,650 with financing and construction provided by the company.[33] In 1923 Mason-McDuffie was offering to construct five principal types of houses, seeking to correct the impression that prices were out of reach. By commissioning architects to design thoughtful plans, buying materials in bulk, and passing along cash discounts to buyers, the company could offer houses that were compatible with those already built in St. Francis Wood "at the lowest possible price."[34]

At the low end was a two-bedroom, one-story house with approximately 980 square feet, priced $9,850 to 10,250. The house had a side entrance and a hall that avoided the need to walk through the dining room to reach the bedrooms, a common problem with other bungalows. The bedrooms were located at the rear and reached by a short staircase. The garage was detached at the sidewalk.

Architects Masten and Hurd's two-bedroom bungalows on the west side of San Pablo Avenue priced from $9,850 to 10,250 ("St. Francis Wood Homes," undated brochure in Bancroft Library, University of California, Berkeley, Mason-McDuffie collection, Banc Mss 89/12, box 22 (photograph by author, 2019).

Larger three-bedroom bungalows designed by Earle B. Bertz were priced from $11,500 to $13,500 ("St. Francis Wood Homes," undated brochure in Bancroft Library, University of California, Berkeley, Mason-McDuffie collection, Banc Mss 89/12, box 22. Photograph by author, 2019).

Larger two-story houses in the Colonial, English, or Italian style with three or four bedrooms and a maid's room were offered at prices up to $25,000 ("St. Francis Wood Homes," undated brochure in Bancroft Library, University of California, Berkeley, Mason-McDuffie collection, Banc Mss 89/12, box 22. Photograph by author, 2019).

Slightly larger three-bedroom, one-story bungalow models with approximately 1,100 square feet were priced from $11,500 to $13,500. Here the garage is part of the house, under the bedroom.

Larger two-story houses in the Colonial, English, or Italian style had four bedrooms and a maid's room. These 2,000-square-foot houses were offered at prices up to $25,000. All these models had only one bathroom, except the maid had a separate bath. Larger, even more expensive houses were sold in St. Francis Wood; Mason-McDuffie offered a house on St. Francis Boulevard for $40,000.[35]

Although the smaller houses may have been reasonably priced for St. Francis Wood, they were substantially higher than nearby Westwood Park, a Baldwin & Howell development off Ocean Avenue. Westwood Park was targeted to the middle class, with bungalows priced from $6,500 to $8,500.[36]

Architecture

St. Francis Wood initially advertised that houses were to be designed in the "Italian Renaissance" style.[37] This term was not defined but refers loosely to a style popular during the 1890s to the 1930s, now known for symmetrical facades and low pitched, hipped roofs covered with red clay tiles, recessed entry porches, and entrances accented by small classical columns or pilasters. The first-story windows were usually full length with arches above, and the walls were clad in stucco or masonry. Roofs typically had broad overhanging boxed eves, often with brackets.[38] Although Howard designed the entrance gates with his interpretation of the Italian renaissance in mind, he did not design of any houses in St. Francis Wood.

The first houses were built by Mason-McDuffie to kick-start sales. They were loosely inspired by various Mediterranean sources with stucco facades and red-clay-tile roofs. In 1913 Mason-McDuffie hired Louis Christian Mullgardt to design 44 San Benito. This house was part of a unique three-house ensemble that shared a common garden called San Benito Court. Henry Gutterson, supervising architect for the tract and designer of many homes in St. Francis Wood, was responsible for the other two houses, 50 and 58 San Benito in 1914.[39]

McDuffie did not encourage the use of any stylistic requirements and the deed restrictions did not require a particular style. Nor did any of the other residence parks in San Francisco. For an example of a development that did so, the Palos Verde Estates in southern California required that designs had to be "reasonably good"; conform to the Mediterranean style; be light in tone; clad in plaster, stucco, or stone; have a roof pitch of less than 30 degrees; and be approved by an Art Jury.[40] Architects and builders in St. Francis Wood (and other residence parks) had no such strictures and freely borrowed and adapted features and forms from various historical styles to meet programmatic needs and clients' tastes. The time was a period of revivals in architecture, and many styles were popular.

During the 1920s, approximately 347 houses were built in St. Francis Wood, more than 60 percent of the total. House construction accelerated in the early 1920s and peaked in the mid–1920s, as it did nationwide. By the early 1930s, much of St. Francis Wood had been built out. Most of these houses were designed in traditional or historical styles.

Nearly all of these houses were designed by architects.[41] Approximately 149 architects are known to have worked in St. Francis Wood, including nationally known figures such as Willis Polk, Louis Mullgardt, Mario Ciampi, William Wurster, Julia Morgan, and Bernard Maybeck. Others who were better known locally include Clarence Tanatu, Walter Ratcliff, John Reid, Ward & Blohme, Miller and Warnecke, H.C. Baumann, Harold Stone, Albert Farr, Charles Strothoff, and Masten and Hurd.

One of the most prolific architects was the tract's supervisory architect, Henry Gutterson. All plans for St. Francis Wood homes had to be submitted to Gutterson for "criticism and advice." With the goal of maintaining the high character of the tract, Gutterson's advice could focus on anything from proposed color schemes and designs of radio aerials to setbacks and fence heights.[42] Homes built without his approval could be removed at the expense of the owner. Gutterson's contract was renewed yearly by the association for four decades, reflecting both approval of his performance and recognition of the need for architectural supervision to maintain the cohesiveness of the tract. Gutterson was the supervising architect of St. Francis Wood for forty years, until his death in 1954. In addition to being responsible for reviewing and approving the plans of other architects, he designed speculative houses on behalf of Mason-McDuffie and designed custom houses for individual buyers.

Henry H. Gutterson (1884–1954) attended University of California, Berkeley, from 1903 to 1905 under John Galen Howard.[43] Gutterson assisted on the Burnham Plan and then studied at the École des Beaux Arts in Paris from 1906 to 1909, working in the same atelier that John Galen Howard had. Due to financial difficulties, Gutterson left before graduation and worked briefly for Grosvenor Atterbury in New York City.[44] Atterbury was designing and building Forest Hills Gardens in Queens, New York; Gutterson undoubtedly became aware of and was influenced by that development.

When he returned to Berkeley, Gutterson taught at U.C. Berkeley and joined John Galen Howard on the design staff for the 1915 Panama-Pacific International Exposition. Gutterson also designed a house in Berkeley for Sophie McDuffie, the sister of Duncan McDuffie.[45] His appointment as supervising architect was a tremendous vote of confidence for the thirty-year-old architect. With his Beaux Arts training, close relationship with Howard, and firsthand experience with Forest Hills Gardens and the Burnham Plan, Gutterson was well qualified to supervise the building of a garden suburb.

Although Gutterson received training in classical architecture at the École des Beaux Arts, he was also influenced by the Arts and Crafts movement and became one of its acknowledged practitioners in the Bay Area, building small-scale homes that were woodsy, sheathed in redwood inside and out, and looked rooted in the landscape. This work placed Gutterson alongside luminaries such as Bernard Maybeck, Julia Morgan, Louis Mullgardt, and John Hudson Thomas.[46]

Henry Gutterson is credited with designing at least eighty-three homes in St. Francis Wood from 1913 to 1948, most between 1913 and 1925. As was characteristic to many upper-middle-class residential developments of the period, house exteriors assumed a wide range of expression, alluding to Italian villas, English medieval manor houses, thatched cottages, Dutch colonial, Spanish Colonial, French Norman, and even a house made of large stones.

Not all the houses credited to Gutterson were designed exclusively by him. As was common practice, draftsmen and architects in his office produced plans under his guidance, although the final designs were credited to Gutterson as the architect of record. He hired women architects at a time when the profession was almost exclusively male. Dorothy Wormser Globlentz remarked that any particular design could be done by one of several draftsmen: Jack Ballentine, Louis Schalk, Elizabeth Austin, John Wagener, or Globlentz herself.[47] Globlentz contrasted Gutterson's work environment with that of Julia Morgan. Under Morgan, Globlentz felt closely supervised and never met the clients, whereas Gutterson was "sweet and nice" and would turn a job over to a draftsman to be responsible for the design. "He assumed that you knew enough to carry through, whereas she [Morgan] assumed nothing."[48]

During 1918–19, when Gutterson was in France performing "canteen work" for the Christian Science Church, he left the office in charge of Gertrude Comfort, who worked for Gutterson from 1916 to 1925. Her 1918 design of a Dutch Colonial at 70 Santa Monica Way was widely copied by other architects in the neighborhood after the war.[49] She married architect Irving Morrow, and formed the architecture practice Morrow and Morrow in the mid–1920s. They are credited with designing San Francisco's first Modern house in Forest Hill in the 1930s, and they consulted on the design of the Golden Gate Bridge.

Besides Gutterson, the architects Masten & Hurd had a large influence on house design in St. Francis Wood. Under contract with Mason-McDuffie as an in-house design office,[50] Masten & Hurd designed a total of ninety-nine St. Francis Wood homes from 1917 to 1940, the great majority built during the 1920s. Their homes were described as being for those "without unlimited means at their disposal" and demonstrated, "excellent taste and a quiet dignity, with good scale and proportion."[51]

Charles F. Masten (1886–1973) was born in Nebraska and raised in San Francisco. He graduated from University of California, Berkeley, and received his architecture license in 1920. He worked on his own until 1924, when he joined Lester W. Hurd (1894–1967), an East Bay native who attended the École des Beaux Arts and received his architecture license in 1922. Masten & Hurd are best known for their work with Ernest J. Kump on the campus of Foothill, Cabrillo, and De Anza Colleges in the early 1960s.

One of the widely known architects to practice in St. Francis Wood was Julia Morgan (1872–1957), the first woman to be formally admitted to the École des Beaux-Arts. She worked for John Galen Howard and then opened her own practice in 1905. Morgan, best known for her work on Hearst Castle at San Simeon, California, designed more than seven hundred buildings, including three houses in St Francis Wood. Morga's style is characterized by Arts and Crafts attributes, including exposed support beams; horizontal lines that blended with the landscape; and extensive use of shingles, California Redwood, and earth tones.

Historian Richard Longstreth observed:

> Morgan was eminently practical in her use of form, space, and structure. She rejected the pursuit of innovation when a good, feasible solution was already available, concentrating on adapting and refining it to the specific needs of the situation. Morgan felt that most buildings should read as unobtrusive elements in the landscape and refrained from the use of particularly assertive form or detail. At the same time, volumes are rendered with forthright simplicity and clarity of form; the major elements are crisply delineated and carefully balanced.[52]

In designing individual houses in St. Francis Wood, architects were faced with a number of constraints. The topography rises gently east of Junipero Serra Boulevard and then more steeply east of Santa Clara Avenue. Streets in St. Francis Wood generally follow the terrain and avoid steep grades. As a result, there are many irregularly shaped lots that vary in size. Lots can be wide and shallow or narrow and long. They vary from about 3,400 to 25,000 square feet. Houses also vary in size, from two-bedroom cottages to seven-bedroom houses with servants' quarters.

Architects also were conscious of producing designs compatible with neighboring houses in terms of scale, massing, and context. Along a particular street, the houses had to work together harmoniously. However, due to the variety in lot shapes and sizes, house styles, and the terrain, the streetscapes in St. Francis Wood are not uniform. Sometimes the houses present similar block faces, such as along San Pablo Avenue or Santa Clara Avenue. Other streets exhibit a regular pattern, such as asymmetrical entries, symmetrical porticos, formal stairways or—conversely—meandering, casual paths. Houses on some streets have entrances at the front, while others have entrances at the side. Corner buildings play a stronger role in defining space, notably around the fountain on Santa Ana Avenue and St. Francis Boulevard.

As befitting a garden community, everything was tied together by the landscaping. The Olmsteds' hierarchy of street trees provided a visual framework for the neighborhood. Large species were planted along the major axis, St. Francis Boulevard, and the major cross streets, Santa Clara and Santa Ana avenues. On the narrower cross streets, trees were planted so their canopies would gradually rise, moving east. At the street level, ample planting beds between sidewalks and the street and the lush front gardens that were open to the sidewalk created the impression of a garden path. These features, plus the limitation on fences between houses, helped protect the garden setting and encourages a feeling of community and neighborly interaction.

The frequent droughts in California prompted the Olmsteds to select drought-resistant plants, reduce the extent of lawns, and use low-growing ground covers intermingled with brightly flowering shrubs. Since this policy was not strictly followed, irrigation was provided for lawn and plants. The Olmsteds wrote with a hint of resignation, "Californians, like all Americans, still retain that English passion for green lawns which is clearly one of our national traits.... people display [a fondness] for a type of horticulture which has been derived from a moister and more northern climate."[53]

St. Francis Wood Over the Years

Perhaps the greatest physical change to affect St. Francis Wood was the 1950s widening of Portola Drive, which forms the western border of St. Francis Wood. During the 1920s Portola Drive was widened and curves were straightened out. The St. Francis Home Association successfully opposed further widening of Portola Drive in 1930 and again in 1933.[54] But the city persisted and began buying property and removing houses as early as 1941.[55] Portola Drive was finally widened under the 1954–1959 Trafficways Program.[56] Fifteen houses in St. Francis Wood were either were moved to new locations, lifted and pushed to the rear of their lots, or demolished. Afterward, new houses, some built by the Twin Peaks Development Company, were shoehorned onto the smaller lots that remained as a result of the street widening.

For some time after Gutterson's death in 1954, the supervision of house designs relaxed. Several house additions violated the original restrictions. Some houses added modern, two-car garage doors facing the street. Residents preferring more privacy installed fences and walls around their gardens that were inconsistent with the design intent. Some contemporary houses were built that violated setbacks and other requirements. Homeowner dues did not keep up with inflation and the need to repair and maintain fountains, structures, and irrigation pipes. Some homeowners had introduced inappropriate plants, altered the parkways, or planted many unsuitable trees.

Efforts began during the 1980s to increase the assessments and empower the homeowner association to compel payments to pay for repairs. The desired changes were put into effect in 1990.[57] The association adopted a set of architectural guidelines that it still uses to review proposed changes to houses and landscaping for conformity with the traditional architecture of St. Francis Wood and the Olmsteds' landscaping design. St. Francis Wood retains architectural supervision, which is provided by the association. These changes, coupled with significant fundraising efforts on the part of the residents, allowed the association to undertake a large-scale restoration effort in the 1990s.

St. Francis Wood was McDuffie's only real estate project in San Francisco. His firm carried on for many years as a regional real estate developer after his death in 1951.[58] But other developers, including another East Bay developer, launched residence parks concurrently with McDuffie.

7

Newell-Murdoch, Lang Realty

In 1912, about the same time the Residential Development Company (RDC) accepted Duncan McDuffie's bid to create St. Francis Wood, it also accepted an offer from Newell-Murdoch for a piece of Rancho San Miguel. Newell-Murdoch, like Duncan McDuffie, was an East Bay real estate firm with a proven track record of developing residence parks in Berkeley and Oakland. The Newell-Murdoch Realty Company picked a hilly and tree-covered site across from the Alms House (Laguna Honda Hospital) to create Forest Hill. In 1920, Newell-Murdoch launched Balboa Terrace residence park adjacent to St. Francis Wood. However, Newell-Murdoch left the real estate business in 1921.[1] Other firms took over the development of Forest Hill and Balboa Terrace.

Newell-Murdoch Company

The Newell-Murdoch Realty Company was a partnership of Robert C. Newell and William C. Murdoch. Robert C. Newell (1878–1963) was born in Iowa and moved to California in the 1890s, settling in Piedmont. In 1897 he became an organist for St. Paul's Episcopal Church in Oakland and was a director in the musical group, Oakland Orpheus. He traveled widely as a musician around the turn of the century and helped organize the Bohemian Club's orchestra. William C. Murdoch, Jr. (1884–1968), was a banker who invested in the Republic Saving and Investment Company and was elected cashier (a senior position) in Western National Bank in 1906 before entering real estate with Newell.[2]

In 1909 Newell and Murdoch began marketing the Thousand Oaks neighborhood in Berkeley on behalf of John Hopkins Spring. Spring was a major landowner and developer in Berkeley and was one of the investors in the Forest Hills Company, which created Forest Hill Extension residence park (see Forest Hill Extension section later in this chapter). Newell and Murdoch were sons-in-law of John Spring.

Mark Daniels

Spring hired landscape engineer Mark Daniels to lay out Thousand Oaks. Mark Roy Daniels was born in 1881 in Spring Arbor, Michigan. He graduated from University of California, Berkeley, in 1905, with a BS in civil engineering. He claimed an impressive resume: superintendent of a mine in Plumas County; an engineer with Southern Pacific Railroad; the chief engineer of the Monterey, Fresno, & Eastern Railroad; an engineer for Weyerhaeuser Lumber Company; and the assistant city engineer in Potlatch, Idaho. In 1907 Daniels opened an office with U.C. Berkeley alumni George P. Dillman and Samuel P. Eastman as Daniels & Dillman. In 1909 Daniels brought in Vance C. Osmont, a Berkeley engineer with expertise in volcanic rock, to handle the rock outcroppings on the Thousand Oaks site. The firm became Daniels & Osmont.

John Spring was an important client for Daniels. Spring subdivided a succession of tracts on the Berkeley hills: Thousand Oaks (1909), Arlington Villa Sites (1910), Arlington Heights (1911), Arlington Oaks (1912), and Thousand Oaks Heights (1912). Mark Daniels and Osmont laid out these tracts with streets that undulated with the hills, sweeping vistas, generous lots, and walking paths. World War I delayed the start of building, but the tracts were built out during the 1920s when Berkeley's population ballooned from 56,000 to 83,000.[3]

The Newell-Murdoch Realty Company retained Mark Daniels, who lived next door to the partners, for several projects. In 1912, Newell-Murdoch and the Wickham Havens Company opened Haddon Hill Park in Oakland, California, on a hill on the east shore of Lake Merritt. James C. Jordan, developer of Jordan Park residence park, had purchased the Oakland property around 1892 but left it undeveloped. His wife sold the land after his death in 1910.[4]

Daniels had divided the site into villa-sized lots that were wider than they were deep. He used a semicircular street layout, curved streets, and statuary by Sari Studies, features he would duplicate in other residence parks. The *San Francisco Call* called the street layout an innovation:

> This is in accord with the new theory of the proper arrangement of home parks. It is the idea of Mark Daniels, the landscape engineer, that the narrow, deep lot was the outcome of the necessity for a place in which to locate barn and stables, but with the advent of the motor vehicle the necessity of this area has been eliminated, and the lot of wide frontage and comparatively shallow depth … eliminates the usually unsightly back yard, and gives for the same money a frontage that permits the erection of a spacious dwelling, not crowded close to the adjoining residences, but with liberal areas of lawn on all sides.[5]

Forest Hill

When Baldwin & Howell announced the development of "a vast residential park—a 'city beautiful'—an ideal community of artistic homes and the real showplace of San Francisco," they had in mind the kind of work done by Newell-Murdoch and Mark Daniels. Baldwin & Howell awarded development rights of approximately 225 acres to Newell-Murdoch Realty Company, which again turned again to Mark Daniels to design the tract named *Forest Hill*. Newell-Murdoch promised to incorporate the best features of residence parks in Chicago, Cleveland, Detroit, Boston, and New York, as well as artistic features from England and the Riviera.[6]

Forest Hill was a challenging site. The parcel was in effect a steep hill, carpeted with trees whose dense growth made it difficult even to reconnoiter the terrain. The idea was to maintain as many of the trees as possible to convey a feeling of living in a park, while providing streets that could reach as many lots as could be carved out of the forest.

Daniels laid out Forest Hill in a curvilinear street design that responds to the hilly

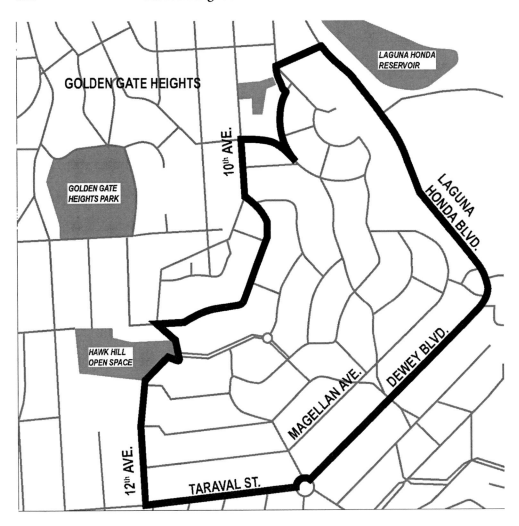

Forest Hill is located across from Laguna Honda Hospital (map by Kushal Lachhwani, 2019).

topography and is quite different from the street grid in the surrounding neighborhoods. The main entrance to Forest Hill is at Pacheco Street and Dewey Boulevard, where a large triangular planting bed sits at the base of the grand staircase that leads up the hillside. Decorative urns were designed by the Sarsi studios.[7] Sarsi studios manufactured cast and artificial stone mantels and garden furniture that were used in many residence parks.[8] Orestes Stefano Sarsi was born in Florence, Italy in 1868 and studied at the Academy of Fine Arts in Florence. By 1910 he had settled in San Francisco. He assisted Bernard Maybeck in designing the Palace of Fine Arts.[9]

A second entrance to Forest Hill is at Pacheco Street and Ninth Avenue and is marked by a gateway, also designed by Mark Daniels. Each side of this structure consists of a tall pillar next to the street and a curved freestanding bench that frames the sidewalk. Within Forest Hill, houses are set back from the street at a uniform distance. Due to the steep topography and narrow streets, some of the streets are divided into upper and lower lanes separated by a median or retaining wall. A network of concrete stairs cuts through steeply sloped blocks.

The main entrance to Forest Hill at Pacheco Street with sidewalk benches, curving streets, the urn by Sarsi Studios, and grand staircase. Pacheco Street curves to the right and runs through the tract (photograph by author, 2016).

When asked in 1912 about his work on Forest Hill, Daniels stated: "It became evident some five or six years ago that the mere cutting up of property into rectangular blocks without regard to grades, scenic effects, and other natural advantages which the property might have, was rapidly becoming a thing of the past."[10] Four years later, Daniels wrote at length about his design approach for Forest Hill and how he balanced his artistic vision with business necessities:

> Streets, sidewalks, sewers there had to be, and arranged as to give the maximum of selling and salable frontage. This much was laid down as law by owners. No experiments were to be made with irregularly shaped lots, inner courts, back lot parks, and group houses. Genuine, orthodox, hand-to-hand subdividing was to be done with a uniform lot as a unit … since no parks of size or other unique features were to be introduced, the problem resolved itself into how to secure a park-like effect … all effects would have to be secured by the streets themselves and the vistas which they would open up, so that a passage along the street would have the effect of a ride in a park.[11]

Daniels acknowledged that the winding streets were confusing to visitors but countered that the residents had no objections. Two arteries, Pacheco and Magellan, were provided with winding secondary streets, adding a picturesque effect to the benefit of slowing traffic. Daniels designed footpaths to give pedestrian shortcuts, an amenity he said was seldom provided in residence parks (although they are also found in Ashbury Park, Ashbury Terrace, Balboa Terrace, St. Francis Wood, and Claremont Court—some of these predate Forest Hill). (For more about Mark Daniels, see Chapter 13.)

Newell-Murdoch heavily advertised Forest Hill, which has become one of San Francisco's better-known residence parks. The developers produced an illustrated brochure and Forest Hill was featured in a local publication, *Homes and Gardens* magazine.

The Twin Peaks streetcar tunnel runs under the site, and Newell-Murdoch donated eighteen lots for the streetcar station and an adjacent commercial strip. The station was named Laguna Honda Station, but city engineer O'Shaughnessy suggested changing the name to *Forest Hill* to reflect the developers' land donation.[12] (The building is still inscribed with the earlier name, but the station is officially called Forest Hill Station.) The commercial buildings were supposed to have a classically inspired design to match the streetcar station, but this was not carried out.[13]

Forest Hill restrictions were similar to those in other residence parks that allowed only single-family houses; house costing at least $4,000; houses with a 15-foot setback from the street; houses containing no more than two stories; and no "Japanese, Chinese, or Negroes."[14]

Newell-Murdoch did not provide for children's playgrounds or tennis courts, pointing out that Golden Gate Park was only eight blocks away.[15] (Actually, eight blocks is at the closet point; other lots would be farther away on steep streets, so getting to Golden Gate Park was not convenient.) A more likely reason for the omission of playgrounds and tennis courts is that Newell-Murdoch wasn't inclined to give away more lots for recreation after donating twenty-one lots for the transit station and shopping district. The firm donated another four lots for the clubhouse designed by Bernard Maybeck.

Forest Hill underground streetcar station and Laguna Honda Boulevard in 1919 looking north. Forest Hill is to the left and Laguna Honda Hospital is to the right. The city widened Laguna Honda Boulevard in 1929 (OpenSFHistory wnp36.02646).

The Forest Hill Clubhouse designed by Bernard Maybeck. It is used for meetings of the home-owner's association and can be rented (photograph by author, 2018).

Newell believed residence parks should be large enough so residents could walk to the streetcar stop without having to see "undesirable things such as saloons, a livery stable, or a Chinese laundry."[16] He said that large tracts, such as Forest Hill (230 acres) and St. Francis Wood (175 acres), were just the right size for residence parks and disputed claims that tracts containing more than 30 acres would glut the market.

By March 1919, the residents of Forest Hill were so dissatisfied with Newell-Murdoch's oversight of the tract that they took over the management of streets, sewers, and lighting from the company.[17] The following year, the Lang Realty Company began planning, financing, and constructing houses in Forest Hill.[18]

Newell-Murdoch began with a large tract (650 houses) and an ambitious and sophisticated design for Forest Hill: hiring a prominent landscape designer to plan curvilinear streets on a hilly site; installing formidable (and expensive) sculptures and stairways; and donating land for a streetcar station, community shopping center, and clubhouse. But after eight years the principals at Newell-Murdoch soured on Forest Hill and left real estate. Newell moved into brokerage and insurance, serving as a director and vice president of the Title Insurance and Guaranty.[19] Murdoch joined a stock brokerage business.[20]

It is not clear why Newell and Murdoch changed careers, but a combination of factors—resident complaints and slow sales because of a recession after World War I—might have contributed to the break. In 1922, after constructing a few houses in Balboa Terrace residence park, they sold their interest in that development too.

Lang Realty

In contrast to Robert Newell and William Murdoch, the principals in the Lang Realty Company had a long-term commitment to the real estate business. The prolific, family-run company was active in the Bay Area from 1915 through the 1950s. Throughout the 1920s, Lang Realty used Forest Hill to highlight its work, opening a "San Francisco Model House" in the tract to showcase design features.

Lang Realty was founded by August J. Lang (1865–1955) in 1915. He came to San Francisco in 1878 and opened a butcher shop and brewery before establishing a real-estate firm. Lang Realty consisted of August Lang and his sons August Jr., William, and Rudolph.[21] Several members of the Lang family had previous experience in the building industry, working as managers and salesmen at major construction and sales firms, including Fernando Nelson and Sons, and Oscar Heyman and Brothers. Lang Realty handled real estate, insurance, and home building and acted as the sales agents for Forest Hill, Claremont Court, and Balboa Terrace. Lang would also "build to order" throughout the West of Twin Peaks area. In the 1920s the Lang Realty Company took over Charles A. Hawkins' Laguna Honda Park, adjacent to Forest Hill Extension. Lang also built 200 bungalows in the Parkside District.

By 1930 the firm had twelve sales offices and had expanded to the Sherwood Forest development adjacent to St. Francis Wood. By 1937 operation of the firm had passed to August Lang's three sons, including William, who was also president of the San Francisco Board of Realtors. In 1939 Lang Realty had a headquarters downtown and branch offices near Sherwood Forest, West Portal, San Anselmo, and Burlingame. Lang Realty moved its headquarters to 19th and Ocean avenues in 1949 and claimed to have built more than two thousand houses over a thirty-year period. At the time, the firm was planning a $12 million building program in Sherwood Forest, Merced Gardens, and Laurel Village in San Francisco; and Sleepy Hollow and San Anselmo in Marin County.

Forest Hill's houses were initially designed by individually commissioned architects in a variety of period revival styles. For example, the idiosyncratic and highly influential Bernard Maybeck designed three houses—270 Castenada Avenue, 51 Sotelo Avenue, and 275 Pacheco Street—and the clubhouse at 381 Magellan Avenue.[22] The Forest Hill Clubhouse was built in 1919 by paid laborers. Urban legend says the residents built the clubhouse, but that is not true.[23] By early 1920, the cost of labor had increased, and the foreman of the construction crew was allowed to live in the uncompleted clubhouse with his family instead of receiving a higher payment.[24] The residents paid the estimated cost of $8,500.

Architect Harold Stoner designed houses in Forest Hill and introduced picturesque and Storybook designs. In 1927, he designed a Flemish cottage that became one of four model homes commissioned and opened for tours "under the auspices of the [San Francisco] Chronicle."[25] He also was the Langs' in-house architect for a later development (Balboa Terrace), but it is not known if he worked under this capacity in Forest Hill. One decidedly not period revival house was what many consider to be San Francisco's first Modern (International) Style house at 171 San Marcos Avenue was designed by Morrow and Morrow.

Forest Hill Extension

The name *Forest Hill Extension* is slightly misleading because it was not a later extension of Forest Hill. The two residence parks were laid out by Mark Daniels, but they had

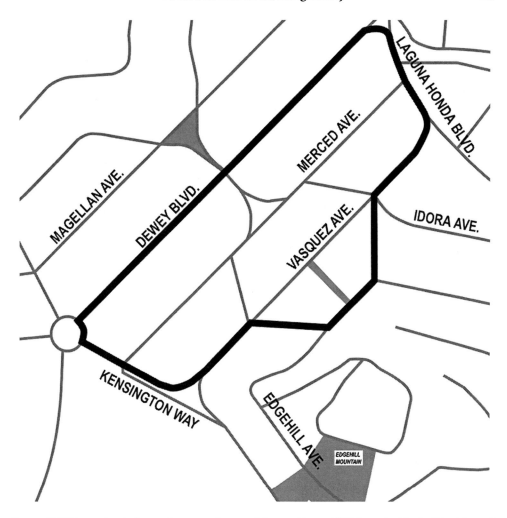

Forest Hill Extension is located next to the much larger Forest Hill (map by Kushal Lachhwani, 2019).

different owners.[26] Forest Hill Extension is less than 1/6 the size of Forest Hill, with only ninety-four lots as originally laid out. Forest Hill Extension lies southeast of Dewey Boulevard and the streets are nearly flat until they run up against a promontory known as Edgehill Mountain. Forest Hill Extension sits next to Laguna Honda Park and Claremont Court residence parks.

Dewey Boulevard is the dividing line between Forest Hill and Forest Hill Extension. Dewey Boulevard was a dirt road for many years before the tracts were laid out and it remained unpaved for some time. Usually, the developer of a residence park paved the streets, but none of the people involved with developing Forest Hill and Forest Hill Extension did so. The residents were responsible for maintaining the streets because the city refused to be responsible for their upkeep, as the streets did not meet city standards. Residents refused to pay for paving Dewey until the 1930s, the city assumed the responsibility for maintaining the streets in the 1970s.[27]

The land for Forest Hill Extension was bought by John H. Spring, Alfred Meyerstein, and Charles A. Hawkins, and building began on May 8, 1913. It is not clear how

The staircase in Forest Hill Extension is more modest than the staircase in Forest Hill (photograph by author, 2019).

much involvement the men had in developing Forest Hill Extension. Spring was actively engaged in the East Bay, and the other two men had their own residence parks to worry about (Meyerstein, Claremont Court; Hawkins, El Por-tal Park). While "Forest Hill" was heavily promoted, few mentions of "Forest Hill Extension" appeared in the newspapers. Firms such as Buckbee, Thorne & Co., and the O.A. Brown Building Company handled the marketing and much of the early building activity in Forest Hill Extension.

The main entrance to Forest Hill Extension is on Pacheco Street at Dewey Boulevard, across the street from Forest Hill. The features of the entrance to Forest Hill Extension mirror those at the entrance to Forest Hill, except that the staircase is smaller and the terrain not as steep. Forest Hill Extension was filled in with a mix of large and more modest-sized houses, built during the 1920s.

Balboa Terrace

Balboa Terrace had a protracted development. In 1912 the Balboa Terrace Company bought 15 acres from the Residential Development Company and supposedly installed street improvements, gas lines, and water mains.[28] Little is known about the Balboa Terrace Company. Balboa Terrace is shown on John M. Punnett's 1914 plat map of new neighborhoods planned by the RDC, but the 1915 Sanborn map shows no houses in the tract. The Balboa Terrace Company sold the entire property to Newell-Murdoch in May 1918.[29]

Punnett and Parez designed the plat map for Balboa Terrace in 1920, and John Rosenfeld's Sons Company, a realty company, filed the map with the City of San Francisco. Four houses were under construction by October 1920.[30] In 1922, with the Lang Realty Company acting as broker, Newell-Murdoch sold the property to Ernest C. and Oscar

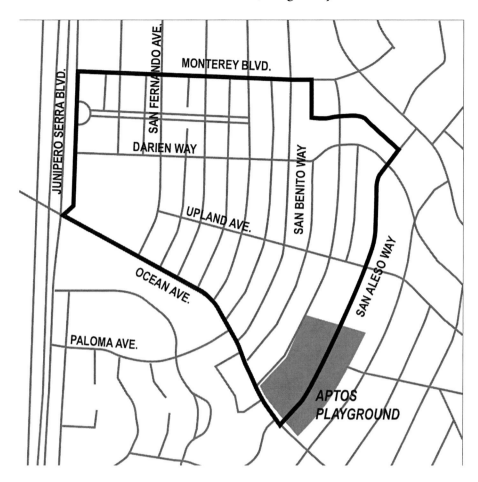

Balboa Terrace is adjacent to St. Francis Wood to the north (map by Kushal Lachhwani, 2019).

M. Hueter.[31] The Heuter brothers came from a wealthy family and were part of the city's business elite. Their father, Ernest L. Heuter, was owner of Bass-Heuter Paint Company, which had 600 dealers, and was vice president of the California Ink Company.[32] He also was a member of the Commercial, Olympic, California Golf, and Mill Valley Country Clubs.[33] Son Ernest Claus Heuter was a vice president of the Bass-Heuter Paint Company, secretary of the California Ink Company, a partner in the San Francisco Pioneer Varnish Work, and vice president of the Balboa Securities Company. He was a prominent member of the Shriners and was one of the founders of the Shriners East-West Game and the Shriners Hospital for Crippled Children.[34]

With so many business and civic interests, the Hueter Brothers entrusted the Balboa Terrace development to Lang Realty, in-house architect Harold Stoner, and builder Walter Zweig of Boxton & Zeig. The Hueter Brothers' deed restrictions were similar to those in other residence parks at the time: minimum construction prices, required setbacks, lots reserved for residential use only, and ownership and occupancy limited to Caucasians.

In 1924 the Hueters expanded the tract by purchasing 36 acres east of Balboa Terrace from Charles W. Sutro for $325,000. Balboa Terrace eventually reached the east side of San Aleso Avenue, employing a street pattern that subtly bends with the hillside as it runs down to Ocean Avenue.[35] The topography slopes down gradually from east to west, into a series of terraces that gradually decreases in elevation. As a result, the houses fronting on the east side of the street are at a higher elevation than those fronting on the west side.

Contrary to other residence parks, Balboa Terrace has a pedestrian, not automobile, ceremonial entrance. Located at the west end of the greenway facing Junipero Serra Boulevard, the entrance is an elaborate multi-level structure, designed by civil engineers Punnett & Parez in 1920. Each side of the greenway is framed by a curved seat wall. Concrete stairs extend across the base of this entrance. The concrete sidewalks and paving in this area have inlays of red brick edging and decorative details. A stucco-clad bus shelter with a red tile roof is located near the front entrance across the frontage street on Junipero Serra Boulevard.

By the early 1920s, it was clear that developers could profit from subdivision development only by mass-produced construction. This is a theme that appears in several tracts. An article in *Homes and Gardens* explains the building process:

> That is when an entire block or avenue is built up, activity moves to the next street. Pavement and walks are laid, ornamental lighting installed, and the new street is built up in units of homes in types that vary from the villas of the Italian Renaissance to the English Cottage type. However, the majority are, by popular demand, of Italian and Spanish design.... One might call it a symphony of architectural types.[36]

Author Jacquie Proctor, in her book *Bay Area Beauty,* estimates that at least 60 percent of the houses in Balboa Terrace were designed by Harold Stoner.[37] Harold Stoner arrived in San Francisco from England in 1914 and began working for architect George Dixon. Stoner saw combat in the U.S. Army in France during World War I. After being discharged from the army in 1919, Stoner's first commission was to design houses in Ingleside Terraces for Joseph Leonard's Urban Realty Improvement Company. Many of the houses designed by Harold Stoner in Balboa Terrace were in the Storybook style, which

Balboa Terrace's pedestrian entrance off Junipero Serra Boulevard. The transit shelter was used by streetcars until 1929 when the tracks were relocated to a private right of way in the center of the street (photograph by author, 2020).

An example of Harold Stoner's Storybook style (photograph by author, 2019).

included Tudor and English garden cottages. As development stretched further into the 1920s, however, Stoner began to design larger Spanish Colonial and Italian Renaissance Revival buildings. Most of the houses are one or two story and clad in stucco.

Developers of residence parks in San Francisco did not make allowances for schools, churches, or other institutions and services. As the population grew, the need to provide services was up to the city's school board or religious congregations to secure locations for schools and churches. Balboa Terrace is unusual for a residence park in that it abuts two public schools and two churches. These buildings are not part of Balboa Terrace.

A junior high (now middle) school, Aptos, was built in 1931 on several lots that were part of Balboa Terrace.[38] The school has the distinction that one of its graduates was the late Broadway legend Carol Channing. An elementary school, Commodore Sloat School, sits on the corner of Ocean Avenue and Junipero Serra Boulevard.[39] This location was the site of previous schools dating back to a one-room schoolhouse in 1865.[40] The St. Francis Episcopal Church was built (1928) on San Fernando Way and Ocean Avenue. Henry Gutterson designed the Ninth Church of Christ, Scientist Church (1941) on Junipero Serra on the site of an earlier church built in 1921.[41]

8

Claremont Court, Merritt Terrace, El Por-tal Park, Arden Wood I and II and Laguna Honda Park

After selling to professional real estate companies Mason-McDuffie and Newell-Murdoch, the Residential Development Company (RDC) turned to novices for the next phase in the subdivision of Rancho San Miguel. During 1912–13, RDC sold an area bounded by what is now Dewey, Woodside, Portola, Ulloa, and Lenox to a partnership consisting of Alfred Meyerstein, Charles Hawkins, and John H. Spring.

The men were bankers and officers in the same bank. Meyerstein was president and Spring and Hawkins were vice-presidents of the Merchants National Bank of San Francisco. Meyerstein and Spring also had controlling interest in the People's Savings Bank in Santa Cruz and were co-owners of a three-story concrete building on Market Street.[1]

In 1912 the men formed the Forest Hill Realty Company, with Spring as president and Hawkins as vice president. Spring was a veteran real estate developer in the East Bay, but the others had limited experience in real estate and none with residence parks. Spring did not take an active part in developing San Francisco residence parks, while Alfred Meyerstein launched Claremont Court and Charles Hawkins launched El Por-tal Park. A fourth man, George Merritt, also a banker and real estate novice, was brought into the partnership and he launched Merritt Terrace. The four men divided the land into what they thought were equal lot values: i.e., not necessarily equal number of lots. Lots that were closer to the Twin Peaks Tunnel entrance were thought to be more valuable that those farther away.

A number of building and racial restrictions would run with the land. Only residential buildings were allowed; the minimum cost of a house was to be $3,000; each building would have a 15-foot front setback and a 2-foot side setback; and no stores, salons, groceries, spirits or malt [beer] would be permitted. In addition, the developments would have no flats or apartment houses, only one building per lot, buildings with no more than two stories, and no fence greater than 6 feet. No persons of "African, Asiatic, or Mongolian descent" could purchase, own, or lease property.

Mark Daniels, who had laid out the streets for the adjacent residence parks (Forest Hill and Forest Hill Extension), also laid out the streets for Claremont Court, using gentle curves. Merritt, Meyerstein, and Hawkins paid to widen Portola Drive from 60 to 70 feet and to construct concrete curbs, with the understanding that the City of San Francisco would pay for street paving.[2]

Although Meyerstein and Merritt may have intended to create residence parks, they soon gave up and sold out to merchant builders, including Fernando Nelson and the Meyer Brothers. Hawkins put his project on hold for several years and then rebranded it as Laguna Honda Park. Hawkins also tried twice unsuccessfully to build a residence park called Arden Wood on land he owned nearby.

Alfred Meyerstein—Claremont Court

On April 1, 1914, Claremont Court was announced in the *San Francisco Chronicle* offering improved lots, underground utilities, sidewalks, and views of the Pacific Ocean and Lake Merced. The westerly portal of the Twin Peaks streetcar tunnel was located in Claremont Court, and the time to get to downtown was advertised as only seventeen minutes.

Alfred Meyerstein entered real estate via his father, Louis Meyerstein, who had immigrated from Germany in the early 1850s. Louis founded the men's clothing firm L. Meyerstein & Son. The firm was successful, Louis became wealthy, and in 1896 he incorporated the company with a capital of $500,000. The firm occupied a five-story building at the corner of Bush and Battery streets and operated a factory on Stevenson Street, employing two hundred people. As Louis Meyerstein became rich, he started to dabble in real estate.[3]

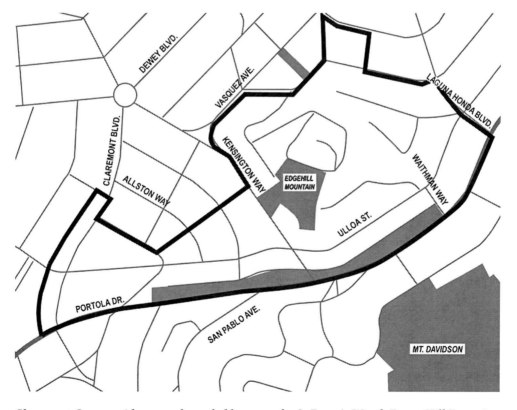

Claremont Court residence park nestled between the St Francis Wood, Forest Hill Extension and Merritt Terrace residence parks (map by Kushal Lachhwani, 2019).

Alfred Meyerstein was a member of San Francisco's business elite. He resided in San Francisco but also maintained a country estate in Woodside for many years.[4] Meyerstein was a member of the committee for the Panama-Pacific International Exposition.[5] He also was a member of an exclusive group called *The Cabinet* that met for "luncheon in the Palace Hotel every day." The Cabinet included the city's top business leaders, including M.H. de Young, John D. Spreckels, Jr., E.D. Coblentz, and Samuel M. Shortridge.[6]

In 1916 Meyerstein retained a young architect, Emile Peter Antonovich, to be the supervising architect for Claremont Court. Antonovich was born in San Francisco on January 6, 1884, to Florio and Mary Antonovich. His father had arrived in San Francisco from Konavlje, Dalmatia, Croatia in 1851 as a crew member on the clipper ship, *Flying Cloud*.[7] Young Emile Antonovich became fairly well-connected. He acquired his architectural license in 1907 and taught architecture and drafting at night school. He was an officer in the United Ancient Order of Druids and a member of the Elks and the Knickerbockers. In 1911, he married Miss Margareta Law, a member of a prominent eastern family.[8] Antonovich had a number of high profile commissions, including the winning submission for a city hall in Redwood City,[9] the Druids' Hall on Page Street between Franklin and Gough, a reinforced concrete building at 731 Sansome for the Pacific Coast Syrup Company (extant), and a nine-story hotel.[10]

Antonovich may have made the acquaintance of Josiah Howell of Baldwin & Howell when they both served in the California National Guard. Antonovich was a sergeant in Company B, Signal Corps, the same unit where Josiah Howell was a colonel.[11] This connection may have led to an introduction to Meyerstein and could have helped Antonovich receive other commissions. Antonovich is known to have worked in the Clover Heights residence park in Eureka Valley, where he designed the entrance gates and ten houses (see Chapter 12).

Antonovich's job in Claremont Court was to "harmonize" all house designs. It is unclear what this meant. The only known restrictions were that houses were supposed to be of the "villa" type (meaning large), cost from $7,500 to $12,500, and sit on generous lots set back 30 feet from the curb line. However, the houses that were built varied in size and were set back no more than 15–20 feet instead of 30 feet. And, while they are detached, the houses are not widely spaced. The promised park with a playground and tennis courts was not constructed.[12] It's doubtful whether Antonovich did much in Claremont Court; he enlisted in the Quartermaster Corps during World War I and remained in the army until he retired as a colonel in 1944.[13]

Meyerstein turned to society architect E.E. Young to design some houses, although it appears that Young was not the tract architect. He did design a pair of Claremont Court houses, which Meyerstein featured in advertisements for the tract.

Edward Eyestone (E.E.) Young arrived in San Francisco in 1902 at the age of thirty-two. Within three years he had obtained an architecture license. In 1907, he designed his own house in the prestigious Presidio Terrace residence park. Young worked for several high-profile builders, often designing houses in small groups in stylish neighborhoods such as Pacific Heights and Presidio Heights.[14]

However, Meyerstein lost interest in Claremont Court, probably as a result of the economic depression during World War I. In 1916, he sold $250,000 worth of lots to W.A. Rudgear who had already bought part of Claremont Court.[15] Another factor in Meyerstein's decision to sell might have been the unfavorable publicity he received from his ownership of a quarry in Claremont Court, at the base of Edgehill Mountain

Meyerstein hired a prestigious architect, E. E. Young, to design twin houses at 677 Ulloa Street (left) and 683 Ulloa (right). The house on the right was completed first in 1915 and was advertised as having a marine view and a "dancing" room. The price was $7,850 (*San Francisco Chronicle*, February 26, 1916) (photograph by author, 2019).

(where Waithman Street and the New Life Church of the Nazarene are now located). Dynamite stored in the quarry may have been used in the July 1916 Preparedness Parade bomb explosion that killed ten people and wounded forty. Detectives traced the explosives to a batch stolen from the Claremont Quarries, the State Highway Commission, or both. "A. L. Meyerstein, owner of the Claremont Quarries, admitted last night that a quantity of dynamite was stolen about two months ago. Meyerstein was not communicative. He said he did not know whether the police had investigated the disappearance of the explosive or whether anyone connected with the bomb suspects had worked in his quarries."[16]

Although Meyerstein had sold part or all of Claremont Court, he maintained his interest in the Forest Hill Realty Company. In 1918 he commissioned a speculative house in Claremont Court, 185 Dorchester Way, designed by architect Samuel Heiman.[17] However, during the 1920s, Meyerstein became increasingly involved in the oil business.[18] He died on March 4, 1937.[19]

With Meyerstein out of the real estate business and no supervising architect, many other architects and builders became active in Claremont Court, including the ubiquitous Charles F. Strothoff. He designed five buildings (781, 775, 769, 763, 750 Ulloa) but there are undoubtedly more. Also, buildings were constructed that are incompatible with a residence park, such as gasoline stations on the corners of Claremont and Ulloa and commercial buildings along the west side of Claremont near Ulloa. A row of houses in Claremont Court along Portola Drive were removed during the 1950s, when the street was widened from Withham to Dorchester Way.

George Noble Merritt—Merritt Terrace

A cattle rancher and banker from Yolo County launched Merritt Terrace, named after himself. George Noble Merritt was the son of Hiram Merritt, an 1850 pioneer and cattleman who became one of Yolo County's wealthiest and most influential citizens.[20] George Merritt married in 1872 and settled in Woodland, California, in 1902. By 1906 he owned 22,000 acres in Trinity and Mendocino Counties and a 400-acre ranch west of Woodland.[21] He was also vice president of the Bank of Yolo.[22]

Merritt owned land on both sides of the entrance to the Twin Peaks tunnel. In 1916, he filed a subdivision map by John Punnett for the land east of the tunnel after Alfred Meyerstein launched Claremont Court. Punnett continued the curving street design established by Mark Daniels. Interestingly, the street names were imports from Berkeley: Claremont Boulevard, Kensington, Grafton (renamed Granville), Allston, and Dwight (renamed Dorchester). The names perhaps reflected the influence of Daniels, who lived and worked in Berkeley. One change Punnett made was to place 10-foot automobile alleys behind the houses in Merritt Terrace to avoid cutting driveways in front of houses.

Merritt apparently had little involvement in his residence park, and he sold the land west of the tunnel to the Meyer Brothers. In 1925 the Meyer Brothers filed a subdivision map called *Merritt Terrace Addition*. The lots north of Verdun Alley (presumably named

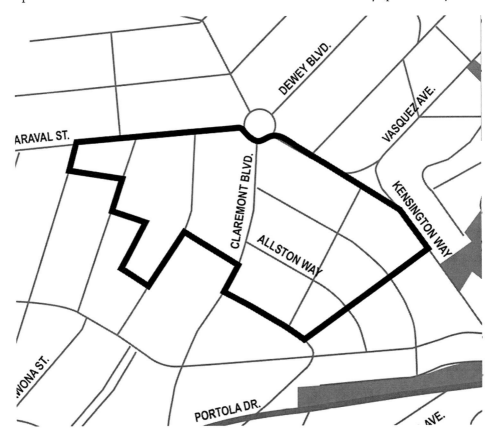

Merritt Terrace residence park (map by Kushal Lachhwani, 2019).

This postcard, postmarked October 2, 1916, from real estate agent George Holden to F. E. Moorhouse shows 81 Allston Street. It reads in part "New Attractive 6 room residence with breakfast room and sleeping porch. In restricted Merritt Terrace at the Westerly portal of the new Twin Peaks Tunnel. The residence has a garage (reached from a rear alley), furnace, hardwood floors, Southern gum interior finish. The price includes tunnel assessment paid in full, bitumen streets accepted by the city, sewer, water, gas, and electric light service, wise restrictions that are a protection to buyers. Price $7200, $1700 cash, balance like rent" (author's collection).

West Portal Elementary School circa 1940. This one, designed by city architect John Reid, opened in 1927 with one wing on the left. An auditorium (not visible) and second wing (right not extant) were added in 1931. The Twin Peaks tunnel runs under the building and caused the wing on the right to settle so unevenly that it was demolished in 1976 (OpenSFHistory/ wnp26.1927).

Dozens of mass-produced houses on Lenox Way in a section of Merritt Terrace in 1926 (OpenSFHistory wnp36.03408).

after the World War I battle in France) were purchased by the City of San Francisco for West Portal Elementary School, which opened on January 31, 1927.[23]

During the 1920s, the Meyer Brothers constructed rows of identical houses on the remaining lots. The Meyer Brothers, Theodore and Roland, were merchant builders who constructed thousands of houses to nearly identical designs. Theodore Meyer began as a carpenter in the 1910s and became a contractor circa 1919. He teamed with his brother as the Meyer Brothers in the 1920s. One of their biggest projects was Miraloma Park on Mount Davidson.

Neither Claremont Court nor Merritt Terrace were developed as residence parks. By 1925, the names *Claremont Court* and *Merritt Terrace* fell out of use. An advertisement by the George Holden Realty Company offered houses on Granville Way and Claremont Boulevard in what had been Claremont Court or Merritt Terrace, but he did not mention those names.[24] Both subdivisions are considered part of the West Portal neighborhood.

Charles A. Hawkins; El Por-tal, Arden Wood and Laguna Honda Park

The third member of the original group that formed the Forest Hill Realty Company was Charles A. Hawkins, who received part of Rancho San Miguel bounded by what is now Dewey, Woodside, Portola, and Laguna Honda Boulevard. Hawkins tried three times unsuccessfully to create residence parks before finally developing Laguna Honda Park in the 1920s.

Hawkins was a little-known pioneer of the West of Twin Peaks. Charles Albert Hawkins was born on April 13, 1871, in Fort Scott, Kansas. He had a colorful early life. He was a self-made man who had many careers during the first half of the twentieth century: sewing machine salesman, truck and auto executive, munitions maker, inventor, banker, and real estate developer. He ended his life as a fig grower in Fresno. Before he turned 18, he tried and failed at railroad construction, successfully hustled pool, moved to Texas and sold Singer sewing machines, quit and joined the Texas Rangers, was fired for getting into a fight, and rejoined Singer as a trouble shooter and salesman. He was promoted and moved to Portland, Oregon, as a reward for inventing a better sewing machine belt. He intended to go to Alaska for the Gold Rush but instead accepted an offer from the White Sewing Machine Company and moved to San Francisco. His first wife, Grace Prideaux, bore him a son named Charles Ernest in 1897, but he and Grace later separated. He met his second wife, Mable, who bore four children: Sidney, June 2, 1903; John Norris Albert, July 25, 1907; Anne Wendela, June 23, 1912; and Jean Mary, October 17, 1917.[25]

According to the family, Hawkins was not a good salesman; he was too aggressive and talked too much. He was a good organizer but not a long-term administrator because of his hot temper. But he was a valuable trouble-shooter and inventor. When the White Sewing Machine Company expanded into the automotive truck and steam-powered car business as White Automotive, Hawkins hit his stride. He invented a stronger truck axle that gave White trucks an advantage over the competition for many years.[26]

Hawkins lived on Clay Street just before the 1906 earthquake and fire, after which he bought property in western San Francisco, including the northeast corner of 19th Avenue and Sloat Boulevard, bounded approximately by 19th Avenue, Sloat Boulevard, Wawona Street, 15th Avenue, and West Portal Avenue. On 19th Avenue he constructed a large house, which was under construction at the time of the 1906 earthquake. It sustained damage, and the family camped on the grounds until the house was repaired. This part of San Francisco was very much in the country. The grounds were a family estate for many years, with a gardener's cottage, a barn for horses, and another barn for cows.[27]

El Por-tal Park

In 1914 Charles Hawkins entered the real estate business by launching El Por-tal Park residence park. The area was next to Forest Hill Extension, roughly bounded by today's Vasquez Avenue, Woodside Drive, Portola Drive, and Laguna Honda Boulevard. Hawkins named El Por-tal after Laguna Honda (Forest Hill) Station, which he called the "first" portal of the soon-to-be-built Twin Peaks tunnel. The streetcar stop at Forest Hill Station is 60 feet below ground. Conventionally, the term *portal* refers to an actual door or opening and not to something 60 feet below ground. Earlier ideas contemplated a shorter Twin Peaks tunnel that ended at grade level at what is now Forest Hill Station, so perhaps Hawkins had this in mind when he named his tract.

Hawkins announced the opening of El Por-tal, a "restricted residence park" with an ad that touted the advantages of buying a lot either to build a home or as a speculative investment that would increase in value by three to six times when the tunnel was completed. The ad said that El Por-tal would have restrictions against "undesirable business buildings, Africans and Orientals."[28]

Hawkins knew he was competing with other residence parks such as St. Francis Wood and Forest Hill, so he called for impressive features for El Por-tal. The main street, Laguna Honda Boulevard, would be 80 feet wide with a 22-foot-wide strip lined with palms, lawn, and red gera-niums. Yellowish-beige colored entrance gates made of concrete pressed brick would be installed at both entrances, at the intersections of Laguna Honda Boulevard and Corbett Road (now Por-tola Drive) and at Laguna Honda Boulevard at Dewey Boulevard. Two 20-foot diameter urns, 7-feet high, designed by the Sarsi studio, and sim-ilar to those at Forest Hill, would grace the circu-lar junctions of Laguna Honda Boulevard with Vasquez Avenue and Ulloa Street. The urns would be

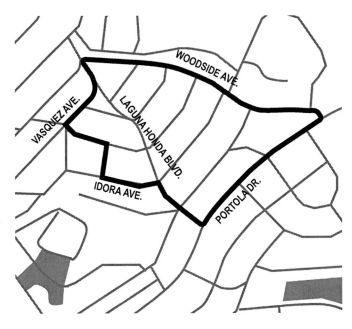

El Por-tal Residence Park (map by Kushal Lachhwani, 2019).

The design for El Por-tal was advertised with huge urns designed by the Sarsi studio, similar to those at Forest Hill. This design was not realized (San Francisco History Center, San Francisco Public Library SFW-0180. Image quality enhanced by Kushal Lachhwani, 2019).

filled with brightly colored flowers set on a lawn and a bed of red geraniums. Mark Daniels would lay out the streets to create a picturesque effect, as he had in Forest Hill.[29]

Hawkins promised to invest $100,000 on these amenities, and he assured buyers that the lots would increase in value by 200 to 500 percent once the Twin Peaks Tunnel opened. (This is less than the three to six times he had claimed earlier, but developers frequently made extravagant claims for property appreciation.)

Sales started well but slowed with the start of World War I on July 28, 1914. Even though the United States would not declare war until April 1917, the war's effects were dramatic. Hawkins wrote, "lots were selling fast and at high prices, but the bottom dropped out of sales and values fell with the European war." Hawkins said his land was worth $306,000, but during 1914 and 1915 he sold only $19,675 worth of lots.[30] At that rate, it would take Hawkins thirty years to unload his property. So, after less than two years, Hawkins abandoned El Por-tal Park. None of the streets were laid out, Mark Daniels was not involved, none of the statuary was installed, and no houses were built.[31] Hawkins decided to cut his losses in real estate because he "saw a great opportunity in the war munitions business."[32]

During 1916, Hawkins took out a $250,000 mortgage on El Por-tal from the RDC and created the Hawkins Improvement Company with Rollin H. White (son of the founder of the White Sewing Machine Company). This was a holding action. Hawkins convinced J. Pierpont Morgan and Co. in New York to lend him $21 million to produce war materiel in Cleveland, where Hawkins moved the family. He supposedly made $700,00 profit in a week.[33] In 1917, he came back to the Bay Area and joined the C.L. Best Gas Traction Company of San Leandro as president. He was partially responsible for the invention of the Best tractor and many of the company's patents, but he also was alleged to have committed fraud. He was fired in 1921 but received a $122,000 settlement for libel.[34] The firm became the Caterpillar Tractor Company in 1925.

With the war over, and no longer working for the C.L. Best Gas Traction Company, Hawkins returned to real estate. This must have been an easy decision because the real estate market was hot during the 1920s. Hawkins had two properties for possible development, the family estate at 19th Avenue and El Por-tal. As it happened, he started projects on both parcels around the same time.

Hawkins Rebrands El Por-tal Park as Laguna Honda Park

Charles Hawkins rebranded the moribund El Por-tal Park into Laguna Honda Park. In 1923 he filed a plat with 128 lots laid out by engineers Punnett and Paez. The plan eliminated the features envisioned in the 1914 plan; there were no entrance gates, urns, or 22-foot-wide planting strips. By August 1926, Hawkins was advertising twenty model homes were ready for purchase in the "restricted" Laguna Honda Park. But it appears that Hawkins let other realtors and builders build and sell houses in his tract. It is difficult to trace in the newspaper accounts who was responsible for what. For example, an ad in 1927 said that the builder R. Leon Lawrence and agents Davis and Williams were the "developers of Laguna Honda Park." A year later the "developer" was C.V. Campbell, who offered to sell complete houses or build to order. It could be that various players were involved from time to time.

By 1928, about one-third of Laguna Honda Park had been completed. Then, with bad

The residents have maintained the city-owned park for decades and are embarking on a new effort as this was being written. The deteriorated fountain top was removed for safety after this photograph was taken (photograph by author, 2018).

timing, the Hawkins Improvement Company announced the completion of six houses on October 26, 1929, two days after the "Black Thursday" stock market sell-off that triggered the Great Depression. In spite of the Depression, Laguna Honda Park was mostly built out by 1938, except for the blocks near Portola Drive.

Hawkins did not provide parks or statuary, but in 1937 residents persuaded the city to purchase a triangular shaped parcel at the intersection of Vasquez Avenue and Laguna Honda Boulevard for use as a park. The city agreed to provide free irrigation water, but the residents were required to do the maintenance. In 1942 a flagpole was installed and later Dr. Joseph Roger, a resident, built a fountain in honor of his son, Paul D. Roger (Private First Class, 2nd Marine Division), killed in action October 21, 1942, on Guadalcanal. Paul, a graduate of George Washington High School, enlisted in the Marines at age eighteen, 11 days after Pearl Harbor.[35]

Arden Wood

In late 1924, as he was launching Laguna Honda Park, Charles Hawkins formed the Arden Wood Corporation and engaged Mudd, White and Holt to build a residence park with one hundred bungalows on his holdings at 19th Avenue and Sloat Boulevard. The site was heavily forested and featured a deep ravine in the center of the parcel. The 19-acre tract would have two curving boulevards at the edges of the ravine and English-Colonial–style houses with views of the Pacific Ocean. Two tennis courts, plus a school, playground, community clubhouse, and a stadium seating 2,600 people rounded out the plan. This was far more ambitious than any other residence park in San Francisco.

But Hawkins changed his mind. In early 1925, after four houses were built (100, 112, 124, 136 Sloat) to designs by architect Joseph J. Rankin, Hawkins hired Bernard Maybeck to lay out one hundred homesites and create a "high grade residence park" in the wooded land-scape. Bernard Maybeck is perhaps the Bay Area's most widely admired architect, and at that time he was an architect of distinction best known for his Palace of Fine Arts building at the 1915 Panama-Pacific Interna-tional Exposition. He had also designed the club-house and other houses in Forest Hill. Hawkins wanted the cachet that Maybeck would bring to Arden Wood (sometimes called Ardenwood).

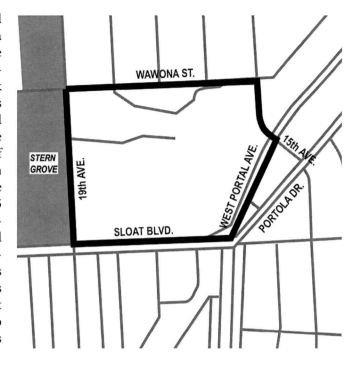

Boundaries of Arden Wood residence park. Charles Hawkins tried twice to develop the property using the same boundaries (map by Kushal Lachhwani, 2019).

Little is known about Maybeck's involvement with the plan but a time-sheet at the University of California Environmental Design Archives shows that Maybeck logged six hours for Hawkins on January 7, 8, and 9, 1925. Also, in a letter dated February 16, 1925, Mrs. Elizabeth Gerberding wrote she was "delighted to learn of [Maybeck's] connection with the Arden Wood colony" where she frequently visited the Hawkins. She asked May-beck to refer prospective buyers to her, as Hawkins had agreed to let her become a sales agent.[36]

Gerberding's connection with Maybeck stemmed from her long-term efforts to pre-serve the Palace of Fine Arts. Elizabeth Bates had married Albert Gerberding in 1894. After her husband's death she became a noted author, civic leader, and women's club leader. She successfully fought for the Hetch Hetchy water project and for the takeover of Spring Valley Water Company by the City of San Francisco. She died in 1937.[37]

Had Arden Wood been completed, it would have resulted in the greatest collec-tion of Maybeck residential designs. But, for reasons unknown, Hawkins abandoned this scheme. In 1927 Hawkins sold some of the land to the Christian Scientists for their retire-ment home. The Standard Building Company in 1932 announced the building of what they called a restricted home park of fifty-one houses named Arden Wood off Sloat Bou-levard and south of the Christian Scientists retirement home. They built twenty-three houses on a dead-end street called Ardenwood Way. The area does not resemble a resi-dence park.[38]

As part of divorce proceedings, Hawkins' wife, Mabel, had received the house at 19th Avenue. In 1940, Mabel tried to rezone her property so that a gasoline station could be constructed. Successfully opposing her were the two residence parks, St. Francis Homes

Association and Balboa Homes Association, as well as other groups, including the Lakeside Home Owners Association, Merced Manor Property Owners Association, and E.L. Stoneson (a prolific builder who wanted to keep the area as peaceful and non-commercial as possible). The area is now occupied by the Scottish Rite Masonic Center, and The Grove condominium complex.

In 1936, Hawkins moved to Fresno, where he established himself as a prominent cotton and fruit rancher. He died in 1952.[39] According to his descendants, Hawkins was a millionaire three times over. He made money as an inventor and lost it in conservative investments and real estate.

If the accounts of Alfred Meyerstein, George Merritt, and Charles Hawkins say anything about building residence parks, it's that brains, money, and connections were not enough to be successful. The following chapters show how other qualities, such as practical experience, technical knowledge, judgment, and flexibility were important in the creation of residence parks.

Allen & Company

Harry B. Allen (1889–1966) of Allen & Company was a major builder responsible for three residential parks in San Francisco, from the most prestigious Sea Cliff, to the least known Windsor Terrace and Fourth Avenue and Fulton tract. He also was a prominent member of the real estate profession and served as president of the San Francisco Real Estate and the California Real Estate Associations, a director and vice-president of the National Association of Real Estate Boards, and a member of the American Institute of Real Estate Appraisers.

Harry Beckwith Allen was born on November 7, 1889, to Gertrude (Beckwith) and David H. Allen.[1] His father was in the liquor business, but soon after the 1906 earthquake and fire he entered the real estate business. One of his father's rental ads said, "For rent … a well and completely furnished flat, including piano, silverware, bed and table linen; ready for immediate occupancy; a bargain and must be seen to be appreciated; not damaged by earthquake; also furnished houses and rooms and office suitable for doctor or dentist with separate entrance; running hot and cold water."[2] In 1910, twenty-one-year-old Harry and his brother Laurence had founded Allen & Co with their father.

Windsor Terrace

Harry Allen's first foray into the residence park market was Windsor Terrace, launched in 1914. Windsor Terrace is a puzzle to many people who see the entrance pillars but have no idea what they signify.

This small tract was part of the Sunset District grid. Windsor Terrace is located between Lawton and Moraga streets, on both sides of Eighth Avenue and the east side of Ninth Avenue. The land rises noticeably from Lawton to Moraga. Eighth Avenue borders the edge of a canyon. Nearby ran the No. 6 streetcar that went downtown.[3]

To set off the tract, Allen constructed red brick pillars at Lawton and

Windsor Terrace in the Sunset district was a small tract (map by Kushal Lachhwani, 2019).

Entrance pillars at Eighth Avenue and Lawton (photograph by the author).

Moraga streets. He built an alley behind the houses to park automobiles and to avoid cutting driveways into front yards. The houses and sidewalks on the city block between Eighth and Ninth avenues sit several feet higher than the street, and red brick stairs lead from the sidewalk to the street.

Allen built houses to suit buyers and also built speculative houses using the services of the distinguished architect, Albert Farr.[4] Architect Farr might have designed at least ten houses in the tract.[5] The earliest announcement advertising the tract implies that Albert Farr would design all the houses in the English style.[6] An article titled, "Windsor Terrace Beautiful Park: Elevated Tract in Sunset Is Distinguished by Artistic Plan and Treatment," noted: "The English scheme of arrangement and architecture has been carried out in every detail, with multi-stone and brick gateways, red brick streets, terraced walks and trees and shrubs to beautify the terrace." Advertisements for the houses in Windsor Terrace listed servants' rooms, garages, wood floors, tiled bathrooms, unobstructed views, and sleeping decks.[7]

Albert L. Farr spent most of his childhood in Japan and moved to the Bay Area in 1891. He apprenticed with the prominent local architects Clinton Day and the Reid Brothers. In 1897, he opened his own practice, and in 1901 he obtained his state architecture licenses. In 1909 Farr moved his office to 68 Post Street, where he remained for the rest of his career. Farr is often associated with the Craftsman style and the English Arts and Crafts movement. His work can be seen in many Bay Area communities, especially Belvedere and Piedmont. His most famous project was for author Jack London: Wolf House (Glen Ellen, Sonoma County), which burned in 1913, shortly before construction

Windsor Terrace in 1921 with few houses built. The road at the bottom of the hill is Seventh Avenue which becomes Laguna Honda Boulevard (to the left.) Visible halfway up the hill is the rear driveway for cars. Lawton Street runs up the hill (OpenSFHistory wnp 26.001).

Looking uphill on Eighth Avenue in 1915. Note that houses on the right are higher than the street or sidewalks (OpenSFHistory wnp36.00796).

was finished. In 1922 Farr took on a Joseph Francis Ward as associate architect, ultimately making him a partner in the firm of Farr & Ward. They designed a number of houses in Russian Hill, Sea Cliff, and St. Francis Wood. Albert Farr died on July 12, 1947.[8]

In 1916, with only sixteen houses built on the eighty-two lots,[9] Allen took on a much more ambitious project in Sea Cliff.

Sea Cliff

Although San Francisco is a city surrounded by water on three sides, Sea Cliff (sometimes Seacliff) is the only place where houses are located right on the edge of the water. While some houses in the Sunset District are located along the ocean, they are several hundred feet away from the beach and separated by an embankment and the four-lane Great Highway. Other developers talked about marine views, but that term usually referred to distant views of the ocean that were obscured later by developments and trees. Only Sea Cliff has some houses nestled on the ocean cliffs, making it an extraordinary location for a residence park.

Sea Cliff (map by Kushal Lachhwani, 2019).

Sea Cliff Avenue looking toward the Golden Gate before the bridge was built. The photograph is undated, but the house on the left (308 Sea Cliff Avenue) was constructed in 1922 (courtesy of the Sonoma County Library Digital Collections).

Sea Cliff was part of Rancho Punto de los Lobos, granted free to Benito Diaz by the Mexican government in April 1845. The rancho encompassed approximately two leagues that included the current neighborhoods of the Richmond, Pacific Heights, and the Marina.[10] In September 1846, Diaz sold the rancho to General Thomas O. Larkin of Monterey, who later sold most of it to Bethuel Phelps and Dexter Wright when land prices skyrocketed during the Gold Rush. Larkin and Phelps intended to subdivide the rancho but failed to secure title after the annexation of California to the United States in 1850.[11]

By 1863, the current Sea Cliff area was part of the Baker Tract. On June 1, 1874, Maria Baker Batchelder (widow of Edwin Dickinson Baker) mortgaged the tract to John Brickell. Batchelder defaulted on taxes, giving Brickell the right to foreclose. By the 1890s, Brickell had acquired the Baker Tract after approximately twenty years of court battles.[12] The tract retained the name *Baker* and the cove of a popular bathing spot was called Baker Beach. The John Brickell Company had extensive land holdings in San Francisco and did not develop its remote holdings during the nineteenth century.[13] As a result, the area around Sea Cliff remained sand dunes and thickets for a long time.

In September 1907, George F. Lyon and Edgar L. Hoag laid out lots along 32nd Avenue (see Chapter 10). That success, coupled with Presidio Terrace in 1905 and West Clay Park in 1910, led the John Brickell Company to launch Sea Cliff in 1913.[14]

The original plan was to install gates at four streets—25th, 26th, 27th, and 28th avenues where they cross El Camino del Mar—to create an exclusive residence park similar to Presidio Terrace. This would have cut off public access to Baker Beach. The Richmond Federation of Improvement Clubs opposed the move, arguing that while the streets were not officially dedicated to the city, people had used them for decades to reach the beach.

Opponents wanted the city to condemn Brickell's land, dedicate it for public use, buy a strip of land along the buff, and link it with Lincoln Park.[15] Although the city did not do any of these things, Brickell relented, and only pillars, not fenced gates, were used to mark the tract. Sea Cliff has rough-cut stone pillars as gateway features to define the entrances to Sea Cliff along the boundaries that intersect with the broader street system. Access to Baker Beach remains open.

In 1913, the Brickell Company commissioned William B. Hoag to survey and record Sea Cliff Subdivision #1, which covered the parcels between 25th and 27th avenues, north of West Clay Street (El Camino Del Mar) overlooking the Golden Gate and the Marin Headlands.[16] By 1916, Allen and Company was managing the development of Sea Cliff as exclusive sales agents. A second subdivision opened, bounded by California Street, McLaren Avenue, Lake Street, and 28th and 29th avenues. This section contained a group of moderately priced homes for the "average buyer."[17] In 1923, a third subdivision opened north of El Camino Del Mar, Sea Cliff Avenue to the west and north, and 27th Avenue to the east. A large building program on Lake Street from 30th Avenue to El Camino Del Mar was underway by 1926.[18] The fourth and last subdivision was completed in 1928.

The houses throughout Sea Cliff are set back from the street to create a band of shallow front yards along both sides of the street. Six-foot-wide concrete sidewalks, with rectangular planting strips, are located between the front yards and the streets. Most of the blocks have internal service roads or alleys that provide access to the garages. The blocks along the northern and western boundaries lack the internal road system and have driveways in front of the houses.

Pillars at El Camino Del Mar and 26th Avenue (photograph by author, 2012).

Sea Cliff incorporates the existing grid street pattern system around the southern edges and then becomes more curvilinear in the interior and along the seaside portions, where the topography is more varied. This curvilinear arrangement distinguishes the arrangement of Sea Cliff streets and lots from the surrounding outer Richmond neighborhood. In 1916, Allen & Company took over the tract, and he later claimed to have built 500 houses.[19]

To preserve as much of the marine view as possible, Hoag terraced parts of Sea Cliff (e.g., along the 600 block of El Camino Del Mar) and sited roads to preserve marine views. Hoag claimed to have graded thousands of cubic yards of sand in order to endow as many lots as possible with a marine view.[20] Although some sources credit Mark Daniels for the roads or landscaping in Sea Cliff, his only known work occurred in 1915 when he designed a terraced garden down the seaside cliffs of the Doble residence.[21]

Sea Cliff had the advantages of being close to transportation and the beach. Public transportation was provided by the Municipal Railway's C-line streetcar along California Street and the Market Street Railway's Sutter and Clement Street line. The John Brickell Company donated an 80-foot-wide strip of land to build El Camino Del Mar Boulevard, linking the Presidio with Lincoln Park through Sea Cliff.

The idea of building this boulevard had many proponents. It is shown on Daniel Burnham's Plan in 1905. In the 1910s the superintendent of city parks envisioned a scenic boulevard that would connect the site of the upcoming Panama-Pacific International Exposition (PPIE)—in today's Marina District—with Ocean Beach.[22] The Richmond Federation of Improvement Clubs wanted Lake Street, which ended at 33rd Avenue, to be

Lake Street and El Camino Del Mar are divided into upper and lower lanes separated by 14-foot-wide landscaped medians. The medians have red brick retaining walls and public stairs that link the upper and lower lanes (photograph by author, 2011).

cut through to Lincoln Park to create a scenic drive.[23] City Engineer Michael O'Shaughnessy was another proponent of building a scenic boulevard. All parties cooperated by
creating El Camino Del Mar that also became the terminus of the Lincoln Highway. Construction began in 1915, and the road was extended to Sutro Heights in 1924. Landslides
plagued the road for decades, and it was closed in the 1950s.

Although Sea Cliff did not have an official tract architect, Carl Bertz designed so
many houses that advertisements credited him for creating the "spirit of Sea Cliff." Bertz
began working with John Brickell in 1918 and shortly thereafter joined forces with Harry
B. Allen.

Earle Baldwin Bertz was born in San Francisco on September 7, 1885. He attended
Pacific Heights Elementary and then high school at the California School of Mechani-
cal Arts (now Lick-Wilmerding), where he was a star athlete and captained the football
team in 1903. After graduation, he apprenticed as a draftsman under architect Albert Farr.
While apprenticing with Farr, Bertz was assigned to Jack London's Wolf House in Sonoma.
In August 1914, Bertz passed the state architecture license examination. In 1918 he opened
an office in the Foxcroft Building at 68 Post Street (the same building as Farr) and began
working with real estate developer and insurance broker John Brickell. Shortly thereafter,
he joined forces with realtor Harry B. Allen.[24] Between 1916 and 1925, Bertz designed more
than thirty houses in Sea Cliff, including Allen's home at 290 Sea Cliff Avenue.

Bertz was best known for his work in Sea Cliff, but he also designed residences in
the Richmond District, St. Francis Wood, Russian Hill, and Forest Hill for Allen & Co.
He was a director of the San Francisco chapter of the American Institute of Architects. In
1927, he partnered with two of his draftsmen—Albert H. Winter and Charles F. Maury—
as Bertz, Winter & Maury. After the partnership dissolved in 1935, Bertz began working
with San Francisco real estate developer Martin Stelling, Jr., and also designed several
commercial buildings in Burlingame and San Francisco. He spent the duration of World
War II working on U.S. Government projects and died in 1948.

Sea Cliff's proximity to the Golden Gate and the ability to bathe in the ocean was
stressed in early advertising.[25] A sandy beach runs from the Presidio to Lincoln Park.
Sea Cliff is on a bluff and provides direct access to China Beach, which was a popular swimming spot for decades. (China Beach takes its name from Chinese fisherman
who were thought to have worked there in the 1800s, although there is little evidence
that they did.) In 1933, the State of California bought the beach and named it after former mayor James D. Phelan, who donated $50,000 for the purchase. In 1954, a concrete
drive was constructed from Sea Cliff to a city-owned beach house.[26] Access to the beach
is through the streets in Sea Cliff. Sea Cliff has become home to many multimillionaires
who share the streets with hundreds of beach goers who drive past mansions on the way
to the beach.

Fourth and Fulton Street Tract

The Fourth and Fulton tract is unrecognizable as a residence park. In 1921, with
Sea Cliff well underway, Allen launched this small restricted tract in the Richmond
District on the existing street grid bordering Golden Gate Park. It has modest two-story
houses designed by Bertz.[27] He used a standardized floor plan with either an "English"
entrance (i.e., vestibule) or an exterior stairway. Except at the block corners, the houses

are attached and are nearly identical inside, although Bertz varied their façades to prevent monotony. Attached houses are unusual in residence parks.[28]

The Fourth and Fulton tract can be seen as an attempt by Allen to capitalize on his reputation with Sea Cliff and construct houses that were modestly priced (and perhaps easier to sell) when inflation and other costs were at their peak. The standard design played to Allen's advantage. By the early 1920s, Allen & Company was a large real estate and building company employing twenty-nine salesmen, an architectural department, and one hundred construction workers. In an article for *The National Real Estate Journal*, Harry Allen said:

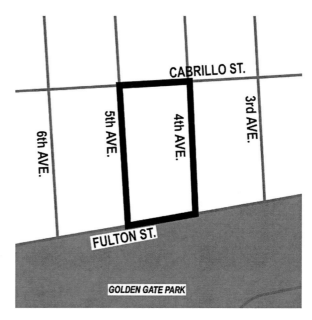

Fourth Avenue and Fulton was a small tract in the Richmond District across the street from Golden Gate Park (map by Kushal Lachhwani, 2019).

It is always gratifying to see one's business enterprise grow, and we take added pleasure in our growth because we realize that such has been possible only because we have been able to serve the community. Indeed, service is the secret of our splendid development—a willingness and a constant endeavor on the

Former tract office on the corner of Fourth Avenue and Fulton Street. The original multiple pane windows have been replaced, a porch between the end gables on the second story has been enclosed, and faux Tudor style trim has been added (photograph by author, 2019).

part of everyone in any manner connected with our company to render useful and timely service to the city of San Francisco…. We have sought to learn and minister to the needs of San Francisco from the standpoint of new subdivisions and homes, and we have not hesitated to pioneer in this regard when such seemed necessary.[29]

In 1935, with mature projects like Windsor Terrace, 4th and Fulton, and Sea Cliff, Allen bought the Belvedere Land Company and began to development Belvedere and its lagoon in Marin County, a project that would take some twenty years to complete.[30] Nonetheless, Allen considered Sea Cliff to be his personal monument.[31]

10

Lyon & Hoag

The Lyon & Hoag real estate firm was a major actor in developing and promoting residence parks in San Francisco and south in San Mateo County. The firm Lyon & Hoag was created in 1898 when George F. Lyon and Edgar L. Hoag became partners in real estate, insurance, and rent collections. Lyon was president and Hoag was vice president of the firm. Later, Lyon & Hoag merged with Cranston, Belvel and Dwyer (Fred A. Dwyer was a developer in the city of San Carlos) but kept the name Lyon & Hoag.[1]

George F. Lyon

George F. Lyon (1868–1937) was born in San Francisco to George and Julia M. (Cowling) Lyon. His father, a native of Germany, came to San Francisco to try his hand at gold mining and then started a retail business on Clay Street. Son George attended public school in San Francisco and worked as an elevator boy for the White House department store at age twelve. He attended night school, took a commercial course at the Lincoln School, and finished one year of high school. In 1884 he joined the C.W. Beach & Company, where he learned the fundamentals of real estate. He then worked at McAfee Brothers under A.S. Baldwin. In 1893 George, age 25, visited the 1893 Columbian Exposition or the "White City" in Chicago. The exposition's effect on Lyon is not recorded but it may have influenced his later efforts to create residence parks.

By 1897, Lyon was sufficiently wealthy to become an investor in the newly incorporated Baldwin & Howell.[2] Lyon, along with George D. Toy, organized the San Francisco Real Estate Board.[3] In 1904 Lyon was one of two hundred shareholders behind a new bank, Mechanics Saving Bank, created for the purpose of making real estate loans, where he served on the board of directors and as a vice president. When the bank merged with the Bank of Italy (Bank of America), he was given a seat on the board of directors.[4] He remained a banker until his death in 1937, his obituary calling him "the father of Burlingame."[5]

Edgar Hoag (1873–1929) was well connected and prominent in real estate. He, along with George Lyon and Josiah Howell (of Baldwin & Howell), served on an advisory committee to assess property for taxes after the 1906 earthquake and fire.[6] Hoag served as president of the San Francisco Real Estate Board and was active with its efforts related to reconstruction after the earthquake.[7] With D.P. Fullerton and A.P. Giannini (founder of the Bank of Italy, later Bank of America), Hoag served on a Board of Trade committee that secured $200,000 in highway bonds for building the El Camino Real state highway through San Mateo.[8]

Edgar Hoag had business dealings with several prominent businessmen in San Mateo County. In 1905 he, George F. Lyon, William H. Crocker, and others incorporated the Burlingame Realty Company.[9] Lyon and Hoag were the first directors of the Bank of Burlingame in 1909.[10] They also founded and owned the Burlingame Water Company with a stock value of $100,000.[11] A syndicate of Edgar Hoag, George Lyon, Fred Dreyer, and George A. Turner paid $400,000 for 3,200 acres of agriculture land on Union Island near Tracy.[12] After Hoag's San Francisco home was destroyed in the 1906 earthquake, he moved to the exclusive town of Hillsborough, built a large estate called "Tuckaway," and helped the town to incorporate.[13] In 1906, Lyon & Hoag launched a subdivision in Burlingame that still bears their names. Edgar died on April 13, 1929, following an operation for appendicitis.[14] George Lyon and the builder S.A. Born were pallbearers at his funeral.[15]

Walter Rockwell Hoag

Edgar Hoag's older brother, Walter Hoag (1871–1945), maintained his own real estate practice as W.R. Hoag & Co. and spent most of his effort in San Mateo County. It's not clear how much interaction he had with his other three brothers. He graduated from Berkeley High School in 1890 and began working for Charles A. Bailey in the real estate business in Berkeley.[16] In 1894 Walter was hired by the McAfee brothers, the predecessor to Baldwin & Howell, and in 1904 managed the firm after the McAfee brothers retired.[17] He partnered with Philip M. Landsdale, and conducted business in the Hawaiian Islands as Hoag & Lansdale.

Walter Hoag was mistakenly listed as a member of Lyon & Hoag upon returning from a trip to the 1905 Portland Exposition. The exposition must have had a big impact on Walter because the *Chronicle* noted that he was "much changed in appearance."[18] After the 1906 earthquake and fire, Walter Hoag was a director of the City Reconstruction Company.[19] Walter Hoag explained his business operation in 1915:

> As a part of our business, we have been engaged in the purchase and sale of real estate in the City and County of San Francisco, on a commission basis, and also purchasing tracts and subdividing them. Some of the tracts in the city that I have been interested in are tracts along Bakers Beach; the Presidio line; different tracts along Golden Gate Park.... About fifteen years ago (circa 1900) I first became interested in real estate in San Mateo County.... I have bought and sold property there.... Hillsborough Heights, Highland Park, El Cerrito Park.... I was interested in the Hoag & Lansdale Subdivision of San Mateo.... I have been employed by institutions to appraise the values of properties in San Mateo, but most of my appraisals have been for friends that I have had in the institutions. I have appraised for the Hibernia Bank, for the Bank of Italy, for the First National Bank of San Mateo, for the Bank of Burlingame, for the Crocker Bank, and for several building and loan societies.[20]

William Burnham Hoag

Edgar Hoag's younger brother, William B. Hoag (1876–1955) worked as a civil engineer for his brother's firm, Lyon & Hoag, and for other clients. According to his World War I draft card he was a self-employed civil engineer and does not appear to have been an employee of Lyon & Hoag. William graduated from University of California, Berkeley, in 1899 with a BA in history of jurisprudence.[21] In June 1899 he placed an ad in *Mining and Scientific Press,* seeking a position as assayer and bookkeeper, listing references as Abbot A. Hanks and Baldwin & Howell.[22] His relationship with Baldwin & Howell is not known; perhaps he worked at the firm during college. After graduation he worked in Alaska, returning to the Bay Area in 1907.[23] William married Jessica Smitten, the sister of George F. Lyon's wife.[24] The couple were married at the Lyons' Hillsborough home.[25]

William Hoag worked as an engineer or surveyor on a variety of projects, including West Clay Park for his brother Edgar (see below), Sea Cliff for Allen & Co., the Aptos Beach & Country Club, a subdivision in San Carlos, and Millbrae Highlands.[26] William Hoag described his work in Millbrae Highlands: "In line with my usual custom in my developments down the peninsula [south of San Francisco], I have planned this tract, taking full advantage of the wonderful view and location which it enjoys."[27]

Baker's Beach[28] Land Company

In 1908, George F. Lyon, as president of the Boston Investment Company, filed a subdivision map ("Lyon & Hoag Subdivision of the Property of the Baker's Beach Land Company") on a north/south strip of land along 32nd Avenue, north of California Street. (The strip of land ended in a cul-de-sac at West Clay Street.) West Clay Street was later renamed *El Camino Del Mar*. Thirty-second Avenue has since been cut through to connect with El Camino Del Mar. This area was not marketed as a residence park, but deed restrictions were imposed, requiring only single-family dwellings, a minimum $5,000 cost of construction, setbacks,

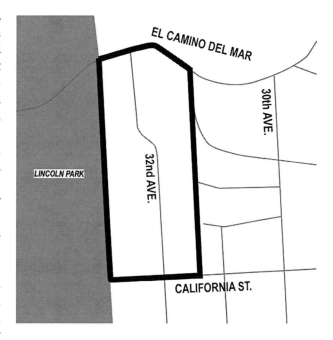

Baker's Beach (map by Kushal Lachhwani).

and fences limited to 5 feet high. A number of Craftsman, Shingle, and Edwardian style houses were quickly erected. This may have set the tone for subsequent residence park projects.

West Clay Park

West Clay Park is not well known now, but during the 1910s it was a role model for residence parks. Lyon & Hoag, acting through the Boston Investment Company, had

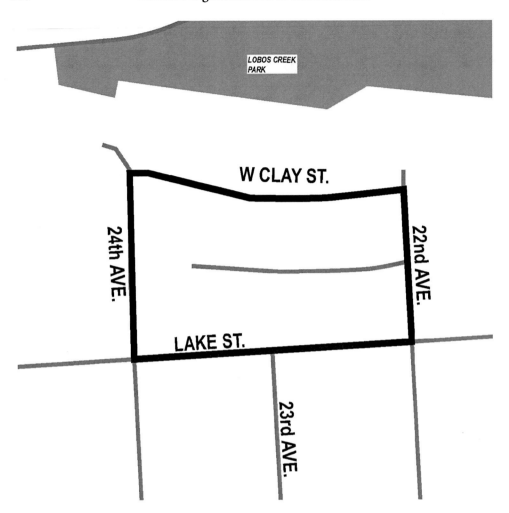

West Clay Park is located at the edge of the Presidio (map by Kushal Lachhwani, 2019).

purchased the land from the Pope & Talbot Land Company earlier that year.[29] On March 30, 1910, Lyon & Hoag's Boston Investment Company filed a subdivision map for West Clay Park, drawn by Hoag's engineer brother, William.[30]

Lyon & Hoag had several dealings with Pope & Talbot over the years including selling property in the Richmond District on Pope & Talbot's behalf. Later Lyon & Hoag developed the Ashbury Terrace residence park on land owned by Pope & Talbot. The Pope & Talbot Land Company was a subsidiary of the Pope & Talbot Lumber Company, founded in 1850 by Andrew Jackson Pope and William Talbot. The firm grew into a major enterprise with lumber mills and timber holdings in the Pacific Northwest. They had a lumber yard at Third and Berry streets and a wharf on Channel Street, as well as other real estate in San Francisco.[31]

West Clay Park is located north of Lake Street between 24th and 26th avenues in the Richmond District, next to the Presidio. The fifty lots range from 26 feet to 60 feet wide and 90 to 120 feet deep. The site slopes downward from Lake Street to Lobos Creek. In 1910 it had unobstructed views of the Presidio and the Golden Gate. The developers elected to terrace the land so that each house could enjoy the view, although today the tree canopy obscures it. The terracing involved grading thousands of cubic yards to create three terraces, each 25 to 35 feet high.[32]

The name *West Clay Park* referred to a new one-block-long street, West Clay, created by the developers that ran through the subdivision. Clay Street runs from the bay through several neighborhoods, including the prestigious Presidio Heights, and stops at Arguello (then First Avenue), twenty-two blocks east of the tract. Naming the new street *West Clay* was probably chosen to perpetuate an association with Clay Street and Presidio Heights, even though there is no connection.

Lyon & Hoag touted the features of West Clay Park: houses costing at least $5,000; no flats or other "objectionable features"; graded lots; paved and curbed streets; underground utilities; ornamental stone gates; many trees, scrubs (bushes), and flowers; and close to the electric streetcar to downtown.[33] In less than a year, half the lots were sold and six houses erected. Lyon & Hoag soon claimed that West Clay Park was "the Most Successful Real Estate Sale of 1910" in a newspaper article.[34] By March 1911, only fourteen of the original fifty lots were left. The 1915 Sanborn map shows thirty-five houses, although it appears that some of the lots had been subdivided. Many of the houses in West Clay Park were constructed by the S.A. Born Building Company. Lyon and Hoag worked with Born on several projects. According to the late architect and historian Patrick McGrew:

Stephan A. Born (c.1859–1927) was a native of Decatur, Illinois, who moved to San Francisco in 1879. He acquired a knowledge of the carpenter's trade in George Doring's shop and later developed his business skills in the firm Martin & McGuire. In 1890 he founded his eponymous building company, constructing and selling homes. For thirty-seven years, "Born Built" was his trademark. His company was among the earliest in San Francisco to import the residential park style of real estate development, and among his projects were West Clay Park, Sea Cliff, Ashbury Terrace, and Lincoln Manor. Following his initial success in San Francisco, Born relocated his headquarters in San Mateo to be near the developing San Francisco and Monterey Peninsulas.[35]

This undated photograph shows the pillars to West Clay Park at 24th Avenue with a view of the Golden Gate (before the bridge) and the Marin headlands, now obscured by houses and vegetation (courtesy Western Neighborhoods Project and Chuck Barnhouse).

Born started as a carpenter who lived at 2719 Folsom at 23rd Street before moving to Noe Valley. He became a contractor and was active in various parts of the city. By the turn of the century he was acquiring larger parcels, such as the property on Union Street from the estate of Amelia V.R. Pixley.[36] Born expanded his business by teaming up with W.B. Pringle and one of the most wealthy and powerful men in the city, Charles H. Crocker (of the Crocker Estate Company), to create a special-purpose realty company, the Real Estate Improvement Company. In 1903 the company purchased the block bounded by Haight, Page, Ashbury streets, and Masonic Avenue from a Veronica Baird for $105,000. Lyon & Hoag were the sale agents. The plan was to subdivide the block into thirty-seven lots to be offered at auction by Lyon & Hoag.[37] This interaction between Lyon & Hoag and Stephan Born might have led to their later collaboration.

Business was good and Born spent $25,000 on a brick house for himself at 99 Divisadero.[38] He offered to sell complete houses, such as a $15,000 residence on Steiner Street, and other houses on "terms no more expensive than rent" (a universal sales pitch). He also offered to build to suit "vacant lots in different parts of city on which I will build homes, flats or stores to suit purchaser."[39] Born was one of the first builders in West Clay Park.[40]

As a child Ansel Adams (1902–84), the famed landscape photographer known for his black-and-white images of the American West, met Born during the building of West Clay Park. The Adams family owned a house on 24th Avenue that predated the development. In his 1985 autobiography, Ansel Adams recalled Born favorably:

Mr. S.A. Born was one of the more dependable and prosperous contractors and the one who developed the lands surrounding our home. His houses were contractor designed, put together without compromise, and have lasted with a stern dowager quality for many decades. He was very kind to me, allowing me to visit his field office and observe his draftsmen. His patience passeth understanding. From him I learned how to draw a straight line and a ninety-degree angle. I drew up some plans for houses, forgetting to provide for stairs and closets.

Words fail to convey my total experience in that office: the smell of pinewood, ink, and sweat, the all-pervading sand on tables, chairs, paper, and between teeth, the hot afternoon light coming through the small, dusty, spider-hazed windows, and the sound of wind and surf invading the room every time the door was opened. There were rolls and rolls of plans, pale blue and frayed at the edges, stacked on frames and on the floor, bearing incomprehensible hieroglyphics of plumbing, wiring, and framing details. The master carpenter would come in, loudly arguing with gusty profanity some point, then exit in slam-the-door wrath only to reappear, sanguine, an hour later....

Most of his houses were completed at close to the same time and they were quickly sold and inhabited. We became an instant neighborhood, a part of San Francisco, no longer loners on the sandy outskirts. Most thought it progress; I wistfully remembered the sand, sea, grass, and lupines.[41]

West Clay Park quickly achieved local prominence. Years later, R.C. Newell, the developer of Forest Hill, said that West Clay Park and Presidio Terrace were the models for others to come.[42] Realtors in San Mateo County used West Clay Park as an exemplary example of a residence park.[43] Lyon & Hoag themselves called Ashbury Terrace, their next development, "Another West Clay Park."[44]

Ashbury Terrace

In June 1912, the Pope-Talbot Lumber Company retained Lyon & Hoag to plat and market a residence park with forty-nine lots on a sloping site on Buena Vista Heights and

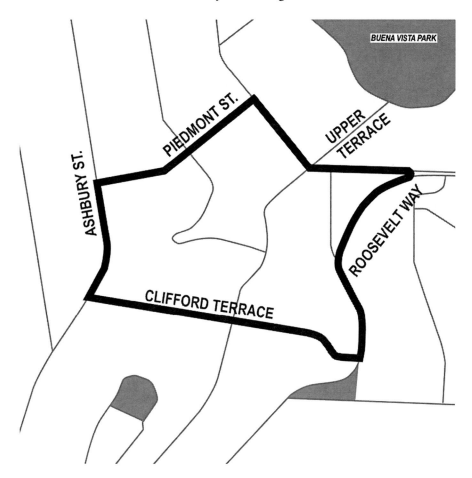

Ashbury Terrace (map by Kushal Lachhwani, 2019).

Mt. Olympus.[45] They called it *Ashbury Terrace*. The name was taken from the street called Ashbury Terrace, which runs through the tract. This development is not to be confused with another tract called Ashbury Park, initially marketed by Lyon & Hoag in 1908 (see Chapter 12). Perhaps to prevent confusion, the street Ashbury Terrace was renamed *Delmar* in 1914 (as it is a continuation of Delmar Street) but was quickly changed back due to objections from residents.[46]

Most of the houses were built on speculation by the builders S.A. Born Building Company or W.W. Rednall. Architects included Edward G. Bolles, Charles Strothoff, E.E. Young, and William Koenig, who were also working in West Clay Park. Architect J.W. Dolliver designed the entrance portals flanked by urns on Ashbury Street and a public staircase on the interior of the development.[47] Building restrictions were justified as a protection for unobstructed marine views and to guarantee homes of a high-class character.[48]

A 1913 newspaper article described the development:

The future of Ashbury Terrace is now assured by the fact that W.W. Rednall has started this week in the erection of six beautiful residences which will represent values from $12,000 to $15,000. Mr. Rednall is known to thousands as an artistic and clever builder. Ashbury Terrace is destined to become a beauty spot in [the] city. Its magnificent views, winding roads and central location are all in its favor. It … can

Entrance pillars to Ashbury Terrace in 1941. In 1962, the *San Francisco News-Call Bulletin* quoted Martin J. O'Dea, who resided at 75 Piedmont Street, saying "Now they've become an eyesore." In 1990 the pillars were restored with larger size lettering than seen in this photograph (OpenSFHistory wnp14.12207).

Staircase on Ashbury Terrace Street (photograph by author, 2019).

Other residence parks promised marine views, but Ashbury Terrace actually had them. The tract sits on one of the tallest in hills in San Francisco, Mt. Sutro, 908-foot elevation (photograph by author, 2019).

be reached easily from the business center. It is located in the fashionable Ashbury Heights District, and the entrance gates on Ashbury Street are only two- and one-half blocks from Haight Street and only one block from Masonic Avenue car line at Frederick and Ashbury streets.[49]

Lincoln Manor

On January 19, 1914, Lyon & Hoag filed a subdivision map for another residence park, Lincoln Manor, again under the company name Boston Investment Company. This was Lyon & Hoag's fourth subdivision in six years in San Francisco.

Lincoln Manor is located in the northern tip of the Richmond

Lincoln Manor lies south of the municipal Lincoln Park (map by Kushal Lachhwani, 2019).

District, between 36th and 38th avenues, bordering Clement Street on the north, and Geary Boulevard on the south. Thirty-seventh Avenue runs halfway into the tract, where it intersects with Shore View Avenue. The land slopes slightly uphill toward Clement Street, which borders Lincoln Park. The elevation provides the lots on the tract with views toward the Pacific Ocean.

The main street, Shore View Avenue, bisects the compact tract much the same way as West Clay Street does in West Clay Park. Shore View Avenue (a not-so-subtle reminder of the marine views) has a slightly curved alignment, broad planting strips, and red brick for many of the stairs and retaining walls. Two alleys provided automobile access to garages set at the rear of the lots. This feature also recalls West Clay Park. The subdivision is a little larger than West Clay Park with seventy-two lots. Most of the lots are 33 feet to 34 feet wide and 100 feet to 117 feet deep, except for smaller lots near Geary Boulevard.

Lincoln Manor was created after the San Francisco Board of Supervisors turned approximately 150 acres of former cemetery land north of West Clay Park over to the Parks Commission to become Lincoln Park, in honor of President Lincoln. Construction of a golf course began in 1909, and the links were open to the public in 1912.[50] Thus, Lincoln Manor, like Presidio Terrace, could boast of having a golf course nearby.

Lincoln Manor was advertised as having the same features as Lyon & Hoag's West Clay Park (marine views, building restrictions, large lots, curved streets, and imposing entrance gates) for one-third the price: $90 per front foot versus $200–$300 in West Clay Park.[51]

Lot sales proceeded quickly. In 1914, the contractor L.T. Pockman and Company

Entrance to Lincoln Manor at 37th Avenue and Geary Boulevard. The name reflects its proximity to Lincoln Park, north of the tract (photograph by author, 2019).

bought fifteen lots on both frontages of 37th Avenue, intending to build houses costing from $8,000 to $12,000. Architect Theo S. Boehm designed eleven houses for Pockman.

Architect Theophile "Theo" Sigismund Boehm was born in Pasadena on January 4, 1889, to French-born parents. The family moved to San Francisco, where Theo's father worked as a carpenter. At age eighteen, Theo became a draftsman for architect David C. Coleman and later worked for German architect/builder William Koenig before striking out on his own. One of his first designs—at 1550 Lake Street—in 1912 brought Boehm in contact with L.T. Pockman. Boehm was an architect who had served with distinction in the U.S. Army in World War I, achieving the rank of sergeant first class, a senior non-commissioned officer.[52]

Seventeen more lot purchases were made in 1914, making about half of the lots sold during the first few months.[53] In April 1914 E.A. Janessen & Company, formerly of Oakland, purchased five lots.[54] In 1916 the S.A. Born Company began building houses in Lincoln Manor. The company purchased more than twenty lots comprising the entire northern frontage of Shore View Avenue, as well as the frontage on 38th Avenue between Clement Street and Shore View Avenue. Lyon & Hoag prominently advertised the purchase, highlighting that the S.A. Born Building Company, "the noted builders of West Clay Park and Sea Cliff," were building Lincoln Manor homes similar to houses in the other parks at half the price: i.e., $8,000 to $12,500.[55]

Born hired architect Ida McCain to design some of the houses in Lincoln Manor.[56]

Houses along Clement Street in Lincoln Manor facing Lincoln Park. Most of the houses in Lincoln Manor are two stories and detached, built in a variety of architectural styles (photograph by author, 2019).

She designed several houses on 38th Avenue, including personal houses for Born at 414 38th Avenue and William Hoag at 420 38th Avenue, as well as houses at 400 and 428 38th Avenue. She also designed 88 Shoreview Avenue.

Ida Florence McCain was born on August 27, 1884, in Fort Collins, Colorado. She enrolled at the Colorado State Agricultural College in 1899, the only woman in the college's new architecture program. She moved to Los Angeles after graduation in 1903 and was hired as a draftsman in the firm of L.B. Valk & Son. The firm built a reputation designing Craftsman bungalows. McCain moved to San Francisco in 1915 and soon earned a reputation for designing homes in the bungalow style. As mentioned earlier she was hired by Baldwin & Howell to supervise architectural work in Westwood Park.[57]

While Lyon & Hoag promised that Lincoln Manor would have the same features as in their other residence parks, water supply proved to be a problem. In 1918, residents filed a complaint with the Railroad Commission to declare the Lyon & Hoag water system a public utility. This was a ruse to force the Spring Valley Water Company to make good on its promise to take over the system.[58] In 1920, the Lincoln Manor Improvement Association asked the San Francisco Board of Supervisors to increase the water pressure in the tract. The association claimed there was no water for firefighting north of Geary Boulevard. It's not known when the issue was resolved.

Sutro Heights Park

Over the years, a total of three proposals were made to turn Sutro Heights into a residence park. As discussed earlier, in 1910 A.S. Baldwin proposed one plan that was not implemented. Lyon & Hoag launched another plan, but World War I stymied their efforts. The Lang Realty Company took over part of the tract during the 1920s and constructed houses and apartment buildings but not a residence park. During the 1930s, another developer launched what he called a "restricted park" on land adjacent to the Lyon & Hoag tract.

In 1915, Lyon & Hoag launched the tract with the name *Sutro Heights Park*. This was located on the Richmond District street grid between 44th and 46th avenues and Geary and Anza. This land was slightly east of the residence park

The proposed Sutro Heights Park overlooked the Pacific Ocean (map by Kushal Lachhwani, 2019).

Baldwin had proposed in 1910. Sutro Heights Park was advertised as having restrictions similar to West Clay Park, but it is not clear if there were in fact *any* deed restrictions. There are 12- to 15-feet-tall pillars at 45th Avenue and Geary and smaller pillars at the corners and mid-blocks from 44th Avenue to 46th Avenue along Anza and Geary. The blocks from 44th and 45th avenues between Geary and Anza have a rear auto alley. The compact nature of the tract, the pillars, and automobile alley recall features Lyon & Hoag employed in West Clay Park and Lincoln Manor.

In 1916, Lyon & Hoag advertised houses for $5,500, conceding that this was a low price for residence parks. They were still trying to sell lots after World War I, when George Lyon said that the increased use of automobiles made the tract more accessible: "Not many years ago property in the Sutro Heights District was considered a long way out and only the invertebrate lover of marine views would consider living beyond 5th or 6th Avenue. The automobile and the electric car have changed this condition." He advised people to see the area during stormy weather so they could see the worst (which he insisted was not that bad).[59] But the aftermath of World War I depressed sales, and little was accomplished. Lyon & Hoag sold the property to Lang Realty who changed the name to *Sutro Heights Marine View Property*—not a residence park.[60] Lang Realty proceeded to build attached houses and a few apartment buildings with the result that the tract did not reflect residence-park planning principles.

Pillars at 45th and Geary mark Lyon & Hoag's Sutro Heights. Light standards were once installed on the top of the pillars. The color and design of brick pillars are similar to those at Lyon & Hoag's Lincoln Manor residence park at a few blocks away (photograph by author, 2019).

Vista Del Mar

Many years after Lyon & Hoag abandoned their attempt at creating a residence park at Sutro Heights, others tried during the Great Depression to create a "restricted" tract in the same area. In 1931 a restricted tract called Vista Del Mar went on the market on land that had been part of or adjacent to Lyon & Hoag's original residence park. (The precise boundaries of these tracts overlap and are not clear.) Vista Del Mar extended from 45th to 48th Avenue, Anza to Clement.

The land was still owned by the Sutro heirs who sold the land to Keirnan & O'Brien in August 1930.[61] A model home opened to the public on December 5, 1931, with Mayor Rossi and Sutro's daughter, Emma Merritt, officiating. It was unusual for the mayor to appear at the opening of a housing tract, but that may have been due to the effects of the Depression, which was precipitated by the stock market crash of 1929. In a reference to the onset of the Depression, the developers of Sutro Heights said they were beginning construction in the winter instead of waiting for the spring "to give work to men who would otherwise be unemployed."[62]

The adage of the real estate industry is always "now is the best time to buy," but Richard J. O'Brien of Kiernan & O'Brien said in 1932 that now was the best time to buy, depression or no depression: "Building of new homes practically stopped in 1927, two years before the stock market crash of 1929. That means that real estate has had a five-year

The Casa Cordoza model home on the 8000 block of Geary Boulevard. On Geary between 44th Avenue and 48th Avenue houses are set back with a 10-foot planning strip and a front yard, unheard of in the Richmond District (photograph by author, 2019).

cycle of depression—and that is the longest that any depression has lasted. The supply of new homes has dwindled to the vanishing point—and demand is gaining."[63] Of course O'Brien couldn't know that the Depression was to last seven more years.

The model homes in the restricted tract were given romantic names: *Del Mar*, *La Belle Normandy*, *Casa Cordoza*, and *La Florentine*. Buyers were assured the tract was "fully restricted against houses of poor construction and inappropriate design" and that the neighbors would be "eligible for your own social circle."[64]

A year later, at the depths of the Depression, Kiernan & O'Brien sold their Vista Del Mar property to the Marian Realty Company. Founded in 1922, the Marian Realty Company was led by Arthur Rousseau and his younger brother Oliver. These architects had designed and constructed large apartment buildings, hotels, and office buildings in San Francisco. In the 1930s, large-scale projects had dried up during the Depression, so the brothers took on the single-family market. Arthur focused on financing, while Oliver designed in a picturesque Storybook style. In the early 1930s, the Marian Realty Company partnered with the Whitney Investment Company to construct about two hundred houses in the Sunset District.[65]

In taking over the Vista Del Mar project, the Rousseaus said they intended to quickly dispose of six existing houses by Kiernan & O'Brien, build thirty-two more, sell lots to other developers, and otherwise dispose of the property within a year. However, mounting debts forced the Marian Realty Company to declare bankruptcy at the close of 1933.[66] At that time, the firm's liabilities were listed at more than $6 million, with debts owed to banks, insurance companies, and mortgage firms. Arthur Rousseau also declared personal bankruptcy. In April 1934, Oliver Rousseau formed a solo real estate and brokerage firm called "Rousseau & Company," which focused on in-fill development.[67]

In 1939, another builder took on the remaining lots in Vista Del Mar. Jesse Horn, president of the Arco Building Company, announced it was building twenty-two houses in the Vista Del Mar tract. No mention was made of building restrictions or amenities, only that the rising prices due to the war in Europe (World War II) made it, once again, the best time to buy.[68]

11

Joseph Leonard and
Fernando Nelson & Sons

Two successful nineteenth-century builders got caught up with residence parks fever when they were approaching retirement. Veteran architect and builder Joseph Leonard designed and constructed the first houses in Jordan Park for real estate investor James Jordan, and then had a rancorous business break up. Leonard went on to develop his own residence park, one of the largest residence parks in San Francisco—Ingleside Terraces—and was the first to feature curved-street design. Another builder, Fernando Nelson, a Victorian carpenter who became a wealthy developer by the early twentieth century, launched Parkway Terrace and West Portal Park with his sons. Nelson didn't use the words "residence park," but he was trying to imitate that model. He did so successfully in Parkway Terrace but less so in West Portal Park.

Jordan Park

Jordan Park started as a typical speculative subdivision called Jordan Tract, not as a residence park. James Clarke Jordan, the eldest son of the founder of Jordan, Marsh and Company of Boston, the largest retail organization in New England, arrived in San Francisco in 1890 and bought eight blocks that once were part of Laurel Hill Cemetery. Despite having no previous real estate experience, he bought 50 acres adjacent to the Laurel Hill Cemetery for $410,000. The tract was bounded by Point Lobos Avenue (now Geary), First Avenue (now

Jordan Park (map by Kushal Lachhwani, 2019).

152

Arguello), California Street, and Williamson Street (now Parker Avenue) platted on the western edge of the Western Addition grid.[1] The parcel had not been used for burials, but it was adjacent to cemeteries, crematoriums, and Children's Hospital (built in 1887, now California Pacific Medical Center).

In 1891, Jordan partnered with George F. Macomber and contracted with the Carnall-Fitzhugh-Hopkins Company to grade the site, install sewers, and macadamize (pave) the streets at a cost of $185,000.[2] Jordan and Macomber thought the costs to improve the lots would be more than repaid after the Sutter Street cable car line was extended and Post Street was cut through the cemetery to the tract. Neither happened.

During the 1890s the land remained unsold. A recession began in 1893, Jordan was preoccupied with other business interests, and he could not get along with his business partners. Macomber filed a lawsuit claiming Jordan had abrogated the agreement with the Carnall Company and then Jordan left the state.[3] It is not clear how this litigation was resolved, but in 1895, Jordan was sued by his attorney, James P. McElroy, who claimed non-payment for handling Jordan's legal affairs, including disputes over the Jordan tract.[4]

At this time, Jordan was preoccupied with other businesses, including purchasing Haddock Hill near Oakland's Lake Merritt. Jordan was also president of the Jordan Bituminous Rock and Paving Company, with an office in the prestigious Chronicle Building, San Francisco's first high-rise, designed by Burnham and Root in 1889.[5] The company carried rock in its own ships from a crushing plant in Pismo Beach (near San Luis Obispo, California) to San Francisco. In 1898, during the Spanish-American War, Jordan let the U.S. Army set up a field hospital on the Jordan Tract; there were serious outbreaks of communicable diseases, probably due to the inadequate sewers Jordan had installed.[6] By the turn of the century, the economy had recovered, but the entire tract was still vacant.

In 1903, in an attempt to kick-start sales, Jordan created a special purpose company

Jordan Tract looking south at camp of the 51st Iowa Volunteer Infantry Regiment. Lone Mountain cemetery is in the background (OpenSFHistory wnp27.4987).

to develop the tract, the San Francisco and Suburban Home Building Society, with Jordan as head. The Home Building Society would sell the lots, insure the buildings, finance purchases, and design and construct the houses.[7] In 1905, Jordan retained real-estate agents Lyon & Hoag to sell the Jordan tract (which he owned) to the San Francisco and Suburban Home Building Society (probably at a profit).

In the meantime, in 1905 Baldwin & Howell had opened Presidio Terrace residence park, which was a few blocks away. Seeing the publicity and initial success of Presidio Terrace, Jordan recast his "tract" as a "park." The same year, the tract was being referred to as "Jordan Park," with the kind of building restrictions found in residence parks. Lots were a minimum width of 33 feet. Houses would be set back 12 feet from the sidewalk and separated from one another by 7 feet. Sidewalks were to be 6 feet wide with 4½ feet between the sidewalk and the street for landscaping. Palms "or other attractive trees" would be planted.[8] Jordan Park was advertised as the only place of suburban homes in San Francisco with wide, well paved streets, green lawns and flower gardens, and streetlights.[9] The claim ignored the existence of Presidio Terrace, which had all those features.

Joseph A. Leonard

In 1906 Jordan hired architect and builder Joseph A. Leonard to be the general manager of the San Francisco and Suburban Home Building Society. Leonard, who had thirty

The former sales office of the San Francisco and Suburban Home Building Society on Euclid Street (photograph by author, 2016).

years of experience as an architect, salesman, and builder, would design and construct the houses and share in the profits.

Joseph Argyle Leonard was born near Dallas, Texas, in 1850. He studied at Eastman's National Business College in Poughkeepsie, New York, and then apprenticed as a contractor. He moved to Philadelphia and studied architecture before returning to Dallas to begin his career building homes. Leonard and his wife moved to San Francisco in 1883 and then to Alameda in 1887, when the town was becoming a ferry commuter suburb.

Leonard achieved success and local fame in Alameda. Between 1889 and 1896, he built sixty-six houses in Alameda on the existing street grid with sidewalk planting strips and front and side setbacks. Most of the houses had two stories and were built in the Queen Anne style. In April 1890, the *Argos* newspaper stated, "J. A. Leonard is building so many houses that it is impossible to keep track of them," and this development became known as "Leonardville."[10] He also designed an ornate clubhouse on the end of a pier for the Encinal Yacht Club, where he raced, and he also built houses in Berkeley. The Leonard family prospered until the recession of the 1890s, whereupon Leonard tried gold mining in the Alaska gold rush. He failed at mining, returned to the Bay Area, and consulted on (but didn't design) a temple for the Vedanta Society of Northern California (extant). During the city's recovery from the 1906 earthquake and fire, Leonard and his son, George, built small cottages to house refugees.[11]

During 1906 Leonard started designing and constructing houses in the Craftsman style in Jordan Park. The layout of Jordan Park resembled that of Alameda with detached, two-story houses on a grid with setbacks. In this sense, Jordan Park resembled some other residence parks. But, unlike other residence parks in San Francisco, Jordan Park allowed or even encouraged the building of flats and other multiple-family buildings. Leonard spoke of a "group of double duplexes" on one wide (unspecified) avenue with a private park. These residences were to be sold to "small families who could not fill one of the stylish and spacious residences and to those who prefer to dwell beneath the same roof with relatives and still have separate apartments."[12]

An advertisement in 1907 mentioned that no stores or businesses would be allowed "in the residential section" of Jordan Park and that no house could be more than two stories, except on the "main avenue."[13] Saying there was a "residential section" implied that there would be a "non-residential section" as well, although no further details have surfaced. This was unusual, as other residence parks in San Francisco prohibited commercial activities. Although a 1909 article mentioned that flats and apartments were prohibited in Jordan Park, the following year saw many ads for rental flats in Jordan Park.[14] This change revealed some confusion on Jordan's part. Was Jordan Park going to be exclusively for single families or a mix of multi-families? One inference is that Jordan was trying to appeal to a larger audience with lower incomes.

In fact, multiple-family buildings make up a significant part of Jordan Park. The 1915 Sanborn map show 32 flats located on Palm and Parker avenues, comprising 21 percent of Jordan Park's 153 buildings at the time (32 flats and 121 single-family dwellings). Large apartment buildings were also constructed. In 1919 architect E.E. Young announced plans to build a three-story apartment building.[15] The percentage of multiple-family buildings increased over the years, and the 1950 Sanborn map shows 89 flats or apartment buildings (34 percent) and 172 single-family dwellings.

Leonard's tenure was short-lived. During 1907 a dispute erupted over Jordan's attempt to terminate the contract with Leonard and to sell vacant lots, instead of houses designed and built by Leonard. Leonard quit (or was fired), and he later sued Jordan for lost income and damages.[16] Leonard almost certainly designed and built the homes constructed through 1908 (and possibly later), and he may have been responsible for establishing the building set-back restrictions and the overall look and feel of Jordan Park. After all, he had laid out his houses in Alameda much the same way, and Charles Jordan had no building experience.

Perhaps Leonard was better off leaving when he did. The new residents were discovering problems, and they formed the Jordan Park Improvement Club to fix them. One problem was Jordan's decision to purchase land adjacent to cemeteries. The club wanted the city to remove the cemeteries and to ban cremations, whose smoke wafted to their houses. They also wanted better sidewalks, streets, streetlights, sewers, and public transportation.

After Jordan's death in 1910, the tract passed through several hands.[17] In May 1911, the southern portion was sold to Fred A. Bull, the former sales agent for Jordan Park. M. Fisher was the builder, with Baldwin & Howell acting as the sales agent.[18] In 1914, L.V. Kiddle, general sales agent for the Parkside Realty Company, is quoted as saying that the Parkside Realty Company was selling lots and building houses in Jordan Park. In spite of continued complaints about the fumes from the Odd Fellows Cemetery crematorium[19] and the continued inadequacy of the sewers, by 1914 two-thirds of the lots had been sold.[20] In 1915, the park was placed in the hands of Kane and Co.[21]

Jordan Park saw various changes over the years. According the *San Francisco Call*, "a palm tree was planted along the sidewalk in front of each house," but today the only surviving palms from that era are the ten on Palm Avenue. This *Call* article also stated that clinker brick pillars framed the "end of each street."[22] Pillars were located at the ends of

Looking south on Commonwealth Avenue circa 1925. The U.S. Army camped there in 1898. In the distance stand Lone Mountain and Saint Ignatius Church (dedicated in 1914). The Oddfellows Cemetery is at the end of the street (OpenSFHistory wnp26.1319).

Palm, Commonwealth, and Jordan streets but were later removed. One pillar ended up at 41 Commonwealth Avenue. Seven buildings on Palm Avenue (four flats, a four-unit apartment building, and two single-family dwellings) were removed to expand the playground at Roosevelt Junior High School (now Roosevelt Middle School) sometime after 1950, according to Sanborn maps. Residences stood along the north side of Geary Boulevard in 1925, but they were replaced in later years by commercial buildings. The house at 70 Commonwealth was used as a nursery school from 1942 to 1954.[23] St. Gregory the Illuminator Armenian Apostolic Church was constructed in 1965 at 51 Commonwealth Avenue.[24]

View of Children's Hospital and Jordan Park circa 1970 looking north. Jordan Park is in the lower section of the photograph (author's collection).

Jordan took sole credit, not only for Jordan Park, but also for being (falsely) the first person to conceive of the idea of a residence park in San Francisco. He claimed he had a vision of a new kind of development when he saw San Francisco's narrow lots. He compared those lots with the spacious lots on Commonwealth Avenue in Boston and vowed to create something similar in San Francisco.[25] He had purchased the land with no intention of creating a residence park, was stymied from developing it for fifteen years, and then rebranded it as a residence park. Given Jordan's lack of real estate training and experience, erratic dealings with business partners, firing of Joseph Leonard, and the convoluted evolution of the tract's development, it is clear that Jordan was making it up as he went along.

Joseph Leonard

After falling out with James Jordan, Joseph Leonard worked for a short time during 1908–09 with another architect, Clarence Russell, as Leonard & Russell. They designed and constructed houses on California Street between 8th and 9th avenues.[26] In 1910 Leonard decided to take control of his future by creating his own house-building

This house was designed by Leonard in Richmond Heights at the northeast corner of 10th Avenue and Balboa Street. This 1912 photograph also shows Leonard's Urban Realty Improvement Co. sales office at the far right. Leonard designed unusually large and complex houses for the area (OpenSFHistory wnp37.02702).

company, the Urban Realty Improvement Company (URICo) with Charles A. Murdock, James Brownell, and Thomas Magee.[27] His son, George L. Leonard, acted as assistant manager. The company's approach was to bring all aspects of property development in-house, from purchasing the land through designing, constructing, and selling houses. URICo hired its own carpenters, ran its own lumber mill, and financed house sales.

URICo's first project was in what was called Richmond Heights, from 9th to 11th avenues between Anza and Balboa streets on the existing city grid. The site has 104 lots, although some were further subdivided, and houses sold from $5,000 to $15,000. This was not a residence park, although the lots, at 33⅓ feet, were wider than usual, and building restrictions, such as 12-foot front setbacks and 7 feet between houses (the same as Jordan Park), were put in place.[28]

Leonard designed and built single-family detached homes in the Craftsman style, including some with picturesque detailing "for people of ordinary means but possessing intelligence and refinement." To ensure his homes were not adversely affected by later development on adjacent lots, he developed a list of restrictions. As the *Call* proclaimed in 1913, "Richmond Heights became noted throughout the city for its magnificent homes, and property there [was] held at a premium."

Ingleside Terraces[29]

The success of Richmond Heights encouraged Leonard to purchase land for his only residence park, Ingleside Terraces. The 148-acre site is located in a valley between the

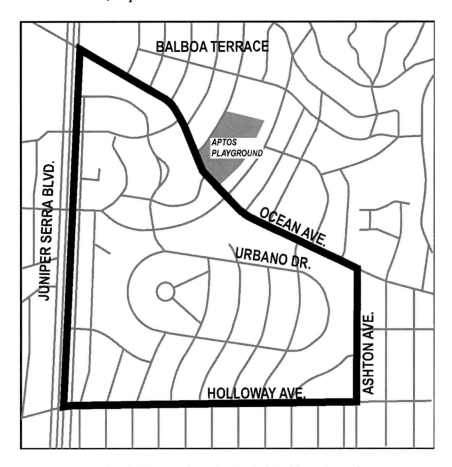

Ingleside Terraces (map by Kushal Lachhwani, 2019).

western face of Mount Davidson and the ridgeline of Merced Heights. It had been a part of Adolph Sutro's Rancho San Miguel, but he sold it in 1894 to a syndicate who built the Ingleside Racetrack. Before he became city engineer, Michael O'Shaughnessy picked the location and oversaw the grading of 191,000 cubic yards of soil and rock to create an oval track and ancillary buildings. The track opened in 1895 and was used for horse racing until 1905.

After the 1906 earthquake and fire, the racetrack owner, Thomas Williams, offered the land as an earthquake refugee camp, which was in operation until January 1908. Periodic bicycle and automobile races were held on the racetrack after the camp's closure. In January 1910 Williams announced his intention to build a residence park on the site, saying, "There will be no square blocks or straight streets in the tract. The whole area will be laid out in the highest style of the landscape gardener's art. There will be winding boulevards bordered with lawns, trees, and flowers."[30] A month later Williams sold the land to Leonard for $400,000 and had no further involvement with it.

Leonard announced the opening of Ingleside Terraces for sale on November 11, 1911, with this promise: "I frankly and unhesitatingly say that I shall make this tract the very best residence park, not only in San Francisco, but in the state of California, not excepting the beautiful residence parks in Los Angeles and Pasadena." Lots were from 50- to 150-feet wide, with "marine views that can never be obstructed."[31] (Later housing developments, the Stonestown shopping mall, and trees eventually eliminated many of the views.)

In April 1912, Leonard filed for city approval of a 792-parcel subdivision designed by engineer Edward J. Morser with curving streets. This was the first time a developer of a residence park tried to use curvilinear or curved streets.[32] Morser's design was initially rejected as "contrary to established customs and ordinances" (i.e., not using the grid). Leonard also wanted to use concrete street curbs instead of the costlier granite which was required at the time.[33]

Morser should have anticipated this rejection because he was a retired chief assistant city engineer, well acquainted with San Francisco's policies.[34] Leonard presumably instructed Morser to use a curved-street design because Leonard had argued that the grid ruined large parts of San Francisco for building purposes. Straight streets made it impossible to live on hilly sections without a cable car line on every block. Leonard was able to convince the city to approve the curving street plan by arguing that successful developments in Oakland and Berkeley followed the contours of the hills.[35]

However, URICo did not strictly follow the contours of the land as it graded 300,000 yards of soil to create a series of terraces that gradually decreased in elevation from east to west, providing striking views of the ocean.

The entrances along Junipero Serra Boulevard—including the main entrance at Mercedes Way and secondary entrances at Moncada Way, Paloma Avenue, Estero Avenue, and Holloway Avenue—are framed by large stone pillars constructed of rough-cut, gray Colusa sandstone. The original ironwork archways that spanned the streets and connected the pillars were removed in the 1950s. The entrances along Ocean Avenue—at Paloma, Cedro, Cerritos, and Victoria avenues—are framed by large stone pillars that are similar in appearance and materials to those along Junipero Serra Boulevard.

Ingleside Terraces entry gate at Junipero Serra Boulevard and Mercedes Way, circa 1912. The iron work was later removed (OpenSFHistory wnp15.644).

One of the most distinctive aspects of the tract is Urbano Drive, a large oval that traces the inner racetrack.[36] The tract also has a number of internal parks or medians. The Moncada Way Park, or landscaped median, consists of a crescent-shaped area (approximately 225 feet long by 65 feet wide) in the curve of Moncada Way between Paloma and Cedro avenues, dividing the road into two lanes. Corona Street has an oval-shaped planting area covered with grass and several trees.

To create excitement and add drama to the development, Leonard built a concrete sundial, approximately 30 feet long by 17 feet high, at the center of a park. Four columns with Doric, Ionic, Corinthian, and Tuscan columns are sited around the sundial. Leonard also used the former racetrack clubhouse at 85 Cerritos Avenue as an office before it became a clubhouse for the residents for several years.[37]

Leonard assembled a team of architects, as well as a group of managers and overseers. To standardize work, he set up a planning mill, cabinet shop, paint shop, plumbing shop, and lumberyard on the site. Leonard became increasingly frustrated with the slow pace of bureaucratic red tape in securing approval to move the project forward. To keep construction on track, he installed water mains and electrical and gas lines, instead of waiting for the public utility companies.

Leonard also implemented restrictions similar to those he had used in Richmond Heights: no lot could be less than 50 feet wide, houses had to be at least 14 feet apart and set back 12 feet from the front line, only single-family houses were allowed, and houses could had to be no taller than two stories and cost at least $3,000. Lodgers and borders were prohibited; fences were limited to the rear of the houses and could be no higher

Ingleside Terraces sundial (photograph by author, 2019).

than 6 feet and house plans had to be approved by the URICo board of directors. People of "African, Japanese, Chinese, or any Mongolian descent" were barred from owning or leasing.[38]

By July 1912 the north end of the tract was completed, and the tract had sewers, gas, and water mains. By the end of the year, thirty-eight houses were built or under construction. The initial houses built during the 1910s were generally large Craftsman or Edwardians. Unfortunately, however, public transportation to the tract was poor. The United Railroads' #12 streetcar line on Ocean Avenue had opened in 1895, but service was slow and infrequent. Prodding from URICo and other property owners improved the frequency, but transportation was still not adequate or fast. When the Twin Peaks tunnel finally opened, it provided the only streetcar service with travel times quick enough to make the tract attractive to buyers.

Development in Ingleside Terraces progressed, but World War I stalled sales. When the long-anticipated Twin Peaks tunnel opened in February 1918, Leonard, aged sixty-eight, was nearing retirement. His son, George L. Leonard, was managing much of the business. Joseph Leonard did retire in 1921, with 80 percent of the lots still vacant. He turned construction over to W.C. Duncan, with sales by Duncan and R.D. McElroy. The firm of Morrison and Holt took over exclusive sales management. A year later, George Leonard bought out Morrison, and the company became Leonard and Holt, with George's son, Joseph, as vice president.[39] By 1924 the firm had subdivisions underway in Redwood City, Burlingame, Tamalpais Valley, and Fairfax.

The cul-de-sac was marketed in 1927 as a picturesque Spanish village, "El Plazuela," a small plaza or square in Spanish (photograph by author, 2016).

Leonard and Holt designed and constructed houses during the 1920s, including fourteen two-story houses on an "L" shaped cul-de-sac named *El Plazuela* off Junipero Serra Boulevard. The firm marketed El Plazuela as a picturesque Spanish village, although this was just advertising hype. Leonard and Holt also built smaller bungalows and stucco-clad Mediterranean-style houses. They designed and marketed these houses to people of moderate incomes who bought houses along Ocean Avenue for $4,000, paying $75 a month. But Leonard and Holt sold pieces of the tract to other firms such as John R. Lindsey and Gordon W. Morris. C.S. Allred designed and constructed two hundred houses (25 percent of the total) during the 1920s, including houses on Corona and most of Lunado. By the end of the 1920s, Ingleside Terraces was about 75 percent complete, with more than six hundred houses built.

When Joseph Leonard retired, he and his wife moved to Ukiah, California, although they split their time between Ukiah and San Francisco. Joseph took out an advertisement in the *Ukiah Republican Press*, announcing himself as, "Joseph A. Leonard, Ukiah, Designer and Builder, Home Building a Specialty."[40] By the time of Joseph Leonard's death in 1929, the family businesses included Leonard & Holt, Inc.; Lenoit National Securities Company, a mortgage company; Union Building and Loan Association; and Lenoit Hotel Properties Company. Leonard's estate was worth $5 million.[41]

Fernando Nelson—Parkway Terrace and West Portal Park

Fernando Nelson's career spanned the history of single-family construction in San Francisco. He claimed to have built four thousand houses between 1876 and 1953. He and his sons developed two of what he called "restricted tracts," Parkway Terrace and West Portal Park.[42]

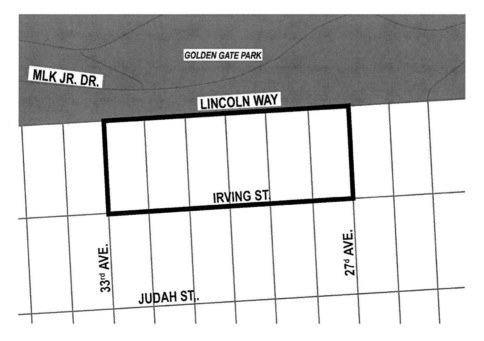

Parkway Terrace (map by Kushal Lachhwani, 2019).

Born in New York in 1860, Fernando Nelson came to San Francisco with his mother in 1876 and built his first house at age sixteen.[43] During the 1870s and 1880s Fernando progressed from apprentice carpenter to journeyman and finally to contractor, building Victorians in the Mission and Eureka Valley districts. Of 1,500 builders working during the 1890s, he was among the few that rose to the top of his profession.[44] In the twentieth century he became a wealthy developer and brought his three sons into the business. In 1916 they incorporated as Fernando Nelson & Sons. As a major developer his business model was to purchase a tract of land, construct a large house on a corner lot (ostensibly for his personal residence but really as a showcase for the development), sell some lots to buyers with a contract for construction, sell some lots to other contractors, and use vacant lots for a shop and lumber storage.

During the 1880s and 1890s he designed and built modest houses or flats for working-class families in the prevailing tastes of the day. Nelson is said to have carried a card in his pocket with different floor plans from which his clients could choose. A carpenter without architectural training, he freely borrowed ideas from other builders and added a few signature details. His son, George Nelson, explained his father's business practices in a 1974 interview:

> Fernando didn't call the houses he built any style. Words like Stick and Eastlake meant nothing. They built "stud" houses referring to balloon framing. Nothing they did was perfect; they were builders not architects…. He thought that people should pay for their houses according to how far they were from the nearest [transit] line; he said that after a certain distance they [Nelson] should just give them [buyers] the houses.[45]

George Nelson also commented on how frugal Fernando was:

> Nails came in kegs from the East. Some kegs would always be broken, and the nails would be shoveled into open bins. Fernando would go down and buy sacks of nails from the open bins because they cost less. Then he would take the nails home and all of the children would sort them according to size.[46]

Around the turn of the twentieth century, Nelson started working in the sparsely settled Richmond District. The Richmond District was platted on the grid, where builders constructed single-family or two-flat residences of varying heights, with setbacks and detailing. Most builders produced rows of nearly identical buildings on speculation. This method produced uneven streetscapes, often with a building sited on the front property line and the remaining 40 percent of the lot occupied by gardens, a shed, a garage, or, in some cases, a residual windmill or tank house.

In 1902 Nelson bought the site of the old Bay District Race Track, which had served in the late 1890s as Camp Merritt, a staging area for troops awaiting deployment to the Philippines during the Spanish-American War. The property between First Avenue (now Arguello Boulevard) to Third Avenue, and Anza to Cabrillo streets was graded, had water and sewer service, and was near public transportation on Geary Boulevard.

Local historian John Freeman describes the way Nelson worked:

> He didn't build a tract of land as a modern subdivision speculator would today—building mostly identical floor plans, advertising, and hoping for sales. Nelson's methods were more personalized. He built to the customer's specifications and budget. He only started a project when he had a commitment from the client. If a person wanted to buy a lot in his blocks so another contractor could build the home, Nelson had no hesitation in selling it. He also generally left corner lots vacant to be sold at higher prices than those for apartment buildings or commercial space. Nelson's specialty was homes and flats, not apartment houses and stores. Nelson became the consummate developer by acquiring the property, designing and

constructing the building, and even financing the sale; but he always had an eye to customer satisfaction. Nelson's designs provided the average homeowner with an affordable, customized, quality-built, home.[47]

Nelson constructed many houses in the Richmond District after the 1906 earthquake and fire. He also became wealthy and indulged in his passion for automobiles, an expensive hobby. Nelson built a corner home for his newlywed eldest son William at 694 2nd Avenue in the Inner Richmond. He lived two lots away with his wife, three sons, and daughter.

His recurring pattern was to move himself and his sons to a development, live in it for a while, and then move them to the next development. Fernando's daughter-in-law, Mrs. William Nelson, complained to her son, William S. Nelson, Jr., that "they'd build a nice house, you'd get used to it, and then you'd have to sell it. And, also, it wasn't theirs [yours], it was still Fernando's house. They [You] just lived in the house. That's another thing that kind of aggravated my mother. She said, 'Well, why don't we own the house? We live in it.' So, finally, when [Nelson] built the Ulloa Street house [935 Ulloa, built 1919, extant], they owned that house."[48]

In 1909 Nelson bought a double lot in the exclusive Presidio Terrace residence park and commissioned a leading architectural firm, MacDonald and Applegarth, to design a mansion described as "an Elizabethan cottage on a mammoth scale." This move was uncharacteristic for Nelson in two ways; previously, he had moved into his own developments and had not used architects. Perhaps he or his wife desired more comfort and permanence. It probably wasn't to join high society; his son said that his parents stayed home most nights and worked. He cared only about his family, his work, and his automobiles.

In the meantime, in 1910, he launched a project on the old Chutes Amusement grounds in the Richmond District between Cabrillo and Fulton streets and 10th and 11th avenues. Although this was not a residence park, his buildings reflected a more

Fernando Nelson built this house in 1910 at the northeast corner of 10th Avenue and Fulton Street. This is a scaled down version of his house in Presidio Terrace (photograph by author, 2019).

sophisticated styling that he was to bring to his residence parks. Victorians were now passé, and Nelson may have felt the need to produce newer styles to his future developments in order to remain competitive. At the northeast corner of 10th Avenue and Fulton Street, he built a half-timbered home with heavily textured stucco, leaded casement windows, and a rolled roof. It resembled a Cornish thatched cottage, a smaller version of his home in Presidio Terrace. His son lived in this showcase house on an uncharacteristically wide lot; the rest of the development consisted of attached houses on standard 25-foot-wide lots.

Living in Presidio Terrace must have piqued Nelson's interest in the new residence park trend. He later launched two "restricted" developments with names that reflected the residence parks mystique: Parkway Terrace (1915) and West Portal Park (1917). Although newspaper articles used the term "residence park" to describe these tracts, Nelson did not do so in his advertisements. Contrary to other developers of residence parks, Nelson did not employ professional architects. Since he was someone who spent hours sorting nails to save money, perhaps he felt that architects were an unnecessary expense. His son Frank took on the role of in-house designer. According to Frank's brother George Nelson, house designs changed around 1914 when Frank took over designing: "He had little formal training but did take a correspondence course in building design from some school back East. Otherwise, he made everything up in his head."[49]

Parkway Terrace

In 1913, after completing other projects in the Richmond District, Fernando Nelson turned to the Sunset District to develop Parkway Terrace. Although he didn't refer to it as a residence park, it has many features of a residence park such as statuary, setbacks, detached houses, and underground utilities.

Parkway Terrace houses on 29th Avenue designed by Frank Nelson (photograph by author, 2019).

Armed with a $100,000 loan from the German Savings and Loan Society, Nelson bought five blocks between Lincoln Way and Irving Street, from 27th Avenue to 33rd Avenue. Four of the blocks were sold by Michael H. de Young and the fifth by the Boston Investment Company (owned by Lyon & Hoag).[50] Nelson didn't acquire the block between 31st and 32nd avenues; its owner, Alice Hastings, developed it. The site was far from downtown and 15 blocks from the ocean, but a streetcar ran along Lincoln Way.

Nelson set back the houses on top of berms with several steps leading to the first-floor living area of these detached houses. Garages are at street level and dug into the berm. Nelson also widened the middle of the streets by about three feet, perhaps to give a sense of spaciousness, although it is not readily noticeable. Nelson was bound by the rectangular layout of the grid, but he placed curved concrete benches at the intersections with Lincoln Way in order to create a place of distinction.

The lots, varying in width from 25 feet to 40 feet, and mostly 120 feet in depth, sold with the condition that construction would commence within a year. The houses could be designed by Nelson's son Frank or other architects or be built by other contractors. Many designs look similar to the 10th Avenue tract and probably were Frank's creations. Another of Frank's creations was the showcase house built on the corner of 28th Avenue and Lincoln Way. Although it is not clear if Nelson imposed building restrictions on the lots he sold to other builders, he did built houses on 147 of the 213 lots (69 percent) in Parkway Terrace to designs by his son Frank, giving the tract the a kind of de facto architectural supervision that was practiced more formally in other residence parks.[51]

One of Frank's designs at 28th and Lincoln, called the Italian Villa style, betrays the limitations of his architectural training. According to architectural historian James Russiello:

The building copies many of the details from published Aesthetic Movement designs. The Italian Villa theme is reinforced with the stucco material and central pavilion crowned by an overhanging pergola creating the sense of a deep cornice with shadow lines. The stylized balusters are not Italianate or Villa themed but closer to Viennese Secessionist. They feature acute angled, low-weighted quarter-deep balusters with thick necks spanned between deep projecting water tables and coping and between wide block-like or possibly paneled corner piers with wide urn finials. This design feature was typical in New York theatrical scenery. The chimney stack looks like it would or should have been brick with Shavian scroll work, a common feature for the Arts and Crafts Movement. It should normally have ended in a corbelled-

A sketch of an "Italian villa" at 2701 Lincoln Way, designed by Frank Nelson. The house has been altered with some details removed (*San Francisco Chronicle*, February 12, 1916).

out brick chimney cap. The window surrounds are also stylized Arts and Craft style but if they were (likely) done in stucco, it's an odd translation. The whole thing has an uneven level of ornamentation, which makes it read like a catalogue of features that you could put on your custom home: three types of picture windows, a tripartite window, balconies, pergolas, window surrounds, and chimneys.[52]

The largest residences in Parkway Terrace were detached houses on 28th and 29th avenues, with more modest houses, often one-story-over-garage bungalows, from 30th to 32nd avenues. The west side of 27th Avenue and east side of 33rd Avenue contain large attached houses with two stories over garages. World War I hobbled construction, and Nelson offered to finance purchases with only $500 down payments, "the balance like rent."[53] Similar to other residence parks, post-war houses in Parkway Terrace were more modest and smaller than the pre-war residences.

West Portal Park

In 1916, with Parkway Terrace still underway, Fernando Nelson & Sons bought 49 acres from the Residential Development Company (RDC) adjacent to the western entrance or "portal" of the Twin Peaks tunnel. He called his development *West Portal Park*. In advertisements, Nelson referred to West Portal Park as "restricted," but he did not use the term *residence park*; however, newspaper writers frequently conflated the two terms. The name "Park" was an attempt by Nelson to capitalize on the residence-park mystique. Nelson's tract was adjacent to St. Francis Wood, Forest Hill, Claremont Court, and Merritt Terrace, all residence parks that had been launched four to five years earlier.

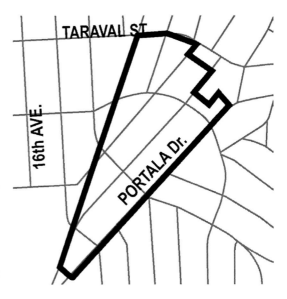

West Portal Park (map by Kushal Lachhwani, 2019).

RDC had withheld this land from sale in order to use it to stage equipment for the construction of the tunnel and as a dump for the tailings. A creek bed was filled in to become the right of way for the streetcars exiting the tunnel. This seasonal creek, called Trocadero on some maps, ran between Edgehill Mountain and Mt. Davidson, along what is now Ulloa Street, turned south roughly at West Portal Avenue, turned west into C.A. Hawkins' Arden Wood property, past the Trocadero Inn (in Sigmund Stern Grove), and finally emptied into Pine Lake.

Nelson paid $300,000, or about $6,000 per acre for the land, two or three times more than other residence parks. Nelson's piece of land was located at the terminus of the Twin Peaks tunnel, where streetcar tracks would run through his property—very unusual for a residence park. While close proximity to transportation was important to the success of residence parks, streetcars typically ran some distance from or at the edge of a residence park, not through it.[54] Why would Fernando Nelson pay top dollar for land with a streetcar line running through it? Maybe he thought the lots along the streetcar right of way would fetch good prices for the businesses that would move in to serve the new residences. (It seems as if everyone involved assumed that a business district would grow up along the tracks.) Or he may have been late to the game, as this was the last parcel RDC offered for sale from the Sutro estate.

Nelson did not construct statues or provide any amenities or special features to establish a visual identity for West Portal Park, as did other residence park developers and what he himself had done in Parkway Terrace. He might have felt that such costs could not be justified at a time when real estate sales were slow. Or he might have felt that the tunnel's Beaux Arts entrance was sufficient to establish a sense of place.

Nelson's first homes, built in 1917 to 1920 on the west side of Portola Drive, mimic the high end, custom houses going up across the street in St. Francis Wood. His houses were two stories, detached, on fairly wide lots, and with front setbacks. But Nelson didn't continue these types of houses in the rest of his tract. Houses built away from Portola are smaller and simpler. Nelson built some houses to designs by his son Frank, such as those along Forest Side Avenue. The 1920s was a period of tremendous variety in architectural styles, with revivals of Colonial, Tudor, Spanish, and Italianate styles. Nelson followed the trends of the day, including some Marina-style homes.

Nelson sold lots to other builders. He also purchased parts of two contiguous residence parks, Merritt Terrace and Claremont Court, blurring the distinction among all three tracts. Today, the former separate residence parks Claremont Court, Merritt Terrace, and West Portal Park are simply known as the West Portal neighborhood.

After West Portal Park, Nelson & Sons developed Mount Davidson Manor in the 1920s and Merced Manor in the 1930s. William Nelson designed many of the houses. He also built houses in other areas in San Francisco until the onset of World War II.

This house at 1520 Portola, built in 1918, has similar architectural elements to those used in Parkway Terrace (OpenSFHistory wnp 37.04220).

Nelson marketed four "restricted" residential tracts during 1916. He also offered "business lots" on the future West Portal Avenue. Park Wood Heights was at First (Arguello) and Parnassus. Most of the houses were torn down for the UCSF Medical Center (*San Francisco Chronicle* October 16, 1916).

Row of houses designed and constructed by Fernando Nelson & Sons along Wawona Street. The San Francisco Planning Department considers this to be a historic district (photograph by author, 2019).

Fernando Nelson died in 1953 at the age of 93. One of his grandsons, William Nelson Jr., summed up the family business by saying:

> It was a very close family run business … my grandfather had a safe and if my father or any the uncles wanted to do any shopping, they'd just reach in there and grab a handful of gold coins. That was their bookkeeping. That was probably through the 1920s. I think they got a little more organized in the 1930s. Had they been well organized they'd probably be multi-millionaires…. If they were better organized, they could have gone much further. This is what my mother use to tell me.[55]

Joseph Leonard and Fernando Nelson illustrate how family-run companies could successfully compete with other developers. However, the houses and tracts designed by Leonard, a trained and experienced architect, appear more cohesive than do those designed by Fernando's son Frank, who had minimal training and who tried to work with an architectural vocabulary he wasn't familiar with.

12

Ashbury Park,
Twin Peaks Terrace and
Clover Heights

Although most residence parks are located west of Twin Peaks, three residence parks were launched on the eastern slopes of Twin Peaks: Ashbury Park, Twin Peaks Terrace, and Clover Heights. Launched just before World War I, the tracts developed slowly and did not live up to the promise of residence parks.

These developments were built on a subdivision of part of Rancho San Miguel in 1867. The elongated tract ran north to south and extended from approximately today's 18th Street on the north, Douglass Street on the east, Burnett Avenue (then called Lincoln) on the west, and then tapered to a point at today's Diamond Heights Boulevard.

The subdivision was a typical example of nineteenth-century land speculation. No thought was given to making improvements; grading or paving streets; putting in sewers, water, and landscaping; or providing amenities of any kind. The two main "roads" through the subdivision, Ocean Road and Corbett Road, were no more than dirt paths. Ocean Road generally followed today's Grand View Avenue. Corbett Road ran through the middle of the subdivision and merged with the Ocean Road near southern end of the subdivision. Corbett Road was macadamized around 1862 with compacted stone layers, and tolls were charged for its upkeep. The toll was unpopular, and in 1877 the City and County of San Francisco bought the road and abolished tolls.[1] The road quickly reverted to dirt.

The streets conformed to the existing surface to avoid the expense of grading, and the lot sizes varied enormously due to the topography. These were large lots for San Francisco, varying from twice the average size lot to a full city block or more. The smallest lot was 50 × 125 feet and the largest upward to 400 × 500 feet. Three hundred and fifty "suburban villa residence" lots were offered at auction in March 1867. The terms were ⅓ down, ⅓ due in one year, and the remainder due in two years, with an annual interest rate of 13.8 percent.

The site is extremely steep; Burnett Street almost reaches the top of Twin Peaks (922 feet in elevation). Most of the streets laterally traverse the slope, following natural contour lines with alleys or short connecting streets. The streets (Seward, Stanton, Eagle View, Rose, and Short) were steep, twisting, unpaved dirt roads that washed out during winter rains. The alleys on the 1867 map still exist, except one. From north to south on the map they are: Opal (expunged 1909), Iron, Copper, Pearl (now Morgan), Diamond (now Dixie), Silver (now Hopkins/Argent), and Gold (now Golding). While having fantastic views, most of the lots were all but inaccessible, contrary to claims that they were "very easy of access—the Mission cars running to within a few blocks."[2] The Mission cars refer to horsecar lines, but the nearest was ten blocks away, down a steep hillside. Development was sparse throughout the nineteenth century.

From Brick Kiln to Residence Park

In 1900, a group of men from Los Angeles thought a site around Opal Alley high on the hill would be a good spot to quarry rock and make bricks. In May 1900 Edward Simons, Charles E. Fout, Lutie W. Fout, E.W. Simons, and C.F. Simons incorporated the Simons-Fout Brick Company for $100,000 and purchased blocks from the northern edge of the subdivision to Romain Street. The quarry was located above Corbett Road, between today's Graystone Terrace and Villa Terrace, between Opal and Iron alleys. The brick factory straddled Iron Alley and Corbett. It was a 300-foot-long wood and corrugated iron structure with a brick kiln and a 100-foot iron chimney. The plant burned to the ground in 1902, was rebuilt, and closed in 1918.[3]

Ashbury Park

In 1908, the Simons-Fout Brick Company retained Lyon & Hoag to market the property north of the brick factory and quarry as a residence park called *Ashbury Park*. The name comes from the street in front of the tract, which was called *Ashbury Street* before the portion from Corbett to just past 17th Street was renamed *Clayton Street*. The tract is bounded on the west by today's Twin Peaks Boulevard, on the north by Carmel Street, on the east by Clayton Street, and on the south by the Pemberton Place steps. It includes the streets Crown Terrace, Raccoon Drive, Graystone Terrace, and Villa Terrace.

The Pemberton Place staircase was named after William S. Pemberton, secretary-treasurer of the Simons-Fout Brick Company. The staircase provided access to Ashbury Park and is similar in function to the staircase in Forest Hill.

The Park and 18th Street streetcar (today's 33 Muni bus line) ran on Clayton Street on its way from the Mission District over the hill to Frederick Street near Golden Gate Park. The streetcar line was a key advantage of the hilly site that was not otherwise accessible due to the hill's steepness and lack of good streets. The developers deliberately placed Pemberton Place for easy streetcar access; it is north of Opal Alley, which was eliminated. To further open up the site for development, the brick company donated land to create Fout Avenue (now Graystone Terrace), named after one of the owners.[4]

Lyon & Hoag placed the first advertisement for Ashbury Park on May 24, 1908.[5] The ad listed macadamized streets, sewer, gas, and water but did not mention building restrictions. In 1909 ads promised that sidewalks would be installed and that a $2,500 minimum building cost restriction would ensure a "better class of homes."[6] Sales were slow, but Lyon & Hoag could no longer help market the tract, as the company was busy selling its own residence parks: West Clay Park (beginning 1910) and then Ashbury Terrace (beginning 1912).

Ashbury Terrace was close to Ashbury Park, just up over the hill past 17th Street near Mt. Olympus. It's unclear why Lyon & Hoag picked a name so similar to another

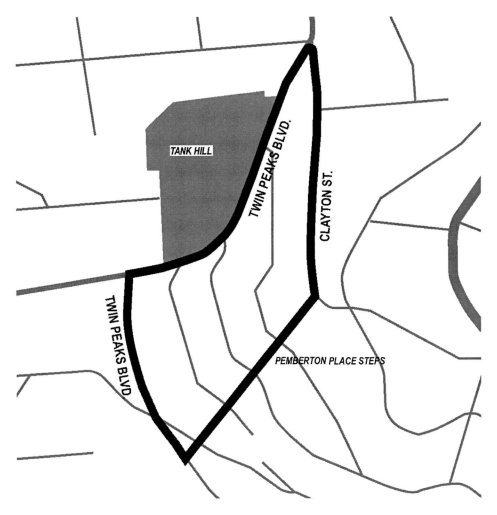

Ashbury Park (map by Kushal Lachhwani, 2019).

residence park. Ashbury Terrace was centered on a street called Ashbury Terrace, but the name must have been confusing to prospective customers.

With few sales and little development, the Simons-Fout Brick Company turned to Edward, Brewster & Clover and D. (David) Coffin to market Ashbury Park. In 1913, they re-launched the tract as a residence park by announcing:

> Ashbury Park is but 20 minutes from the *Call* building by streetcar (3rd and Market). It is located in the neighborhood of the Clarendon reservoir, and its lots terrace up the side of the Twin Peaks. From any lot in the tract the entire city, the broad expanse of the bay and the Berkeley hills may be seen without obstruction. This view probably cannot be equaled in San Francisco, and the district has the added advantage of being without fogs or wind. The improvements which have been installed make this residence park one of the most up to date of any in the city. Beautiful stone facades stretch away from the entrance gate, and the winding streets, which have been well improved, are skirted with trees and broad sidewalks. The lots rise up the hillside, one above the other, giving each of the houses to be built a double frontage. The tract has been restricted, with a minimum price for buildings, which ensures an exclusive neighborhood with homes giving the district a distinction that will be a valuable asset.[7]

Edward, Brewster & Clover and Coffin tried to capitalize on the anticipated Twin

Looking up Clayton from Corbett. The entrance to Ashbury Park is through the retaining wall on the left. Only three houses are visible in this 1917 photograph, although the tract went on the market in 1908. The house on the right is not part of Ashbury Park (OpenSFHistory wnp36.01668).

Pemberton Place stairs at Greystone Terrace (photograph by author, 2019).

An ad for this house in the *San Francisco Chronicle* of January 17, 1914, said: "This elegant Ashbury Park Home, just completed, six rooms, hardwood floors, artistic finish, superb location, view unsurpassed, only $5,250." The garage was inserted later (photograph by author, 2019).

Peaks tunnel by saying it would take only ten minutes to get downtown on the Twin Peaks tunnel line, so lot values would double.[8] But no station was anywhere near the tract. The firm marketed Ashbury Park during 1913 and 1914 and then stopped during the real estate slowdown during World War I. But even after the war, development remained sluggish; only about two dozen houses appear on the 1938 aerial illustration of San Francisco.

Twin Peaks Terrace

During 1913, in addition to trying to kickstart sales in Ashbury Park, the Simons-Fout Brick Company filed a subdivision map for Twin Peaks Terrace on land lying adjacent to and south of Ashbury Park. The streets were a legacy of the 1867 subdivision of Rancho San Miguel by Pioche & Robinson. Twin Peaks Terrace ran between Burnett Avenue and Corbett Street, south from Pemberton to where Greystone (Fout Avenue) meets Corbett Avenue. The only transverse streets were Iron and Copper alleys. Edward, Brewster & Clover and D. Coffin marketed both Twin Peaks Terrace and Ashbury Park as restricted tracts during 1914 but then stopped actively marketing Twin Peaks Terrace, again due to the slowdown caused by World War I.

Little more was heard about Twin Peaks Terrace until 1928, when G. Borden Yount announced it as San Francisco's newest restricted residence village of "pure Mediterranean

View from Pemberton steps (photograph by author, 2019).

design." The developer would lay contour streets and terraced houses, preserving the views in the million-dollar project.[9] However, nothing more was heard from Yount, who was a dentist on Geary Street. He owned a house at Pemberton and Villa Terrace but lived in Belmont and was a member of the Peninsula society.[10] Development of Twin Peaks Terrace was slow; only seven houses appear in an aerial illustration taken in 1938.

Twin Peaks Terrace circa 1920s. No houses are visible between Corbett (left) and Burnett Avenue (right). The building in the middle of the photograph was the Twin Peaks Elementary School at Iron Alley and Corbett Street, built in 1917. It was demolished in 1997 and was replaced with the Rooftop School's Mayeda Campus (OpenSFHistory wnp37.03257).

Clover Heights

The D. Coffin & Company (without Edward, Brewster & Clover) marketed another residence park, Clover Heights, about the same time as Ashbury Park and Twin Peaks Terrace. Laid out on a nearly square-shaped parcel owned by the Anglo-American Land Co., this site was down the hill from the other two tracts, and between Douglass, Yukon, Caselli, and 19th streets. The site rises steeply to the southwest and incorporates Clover Lane, a pedestrian alley. Unlike Ashbury Park and Twin Peaks Terrace, Clover Heights was located in an older and built-up part of Eureka Valley.

A newspaper notice said Clover Heights had two hundred lots, but a brochure by

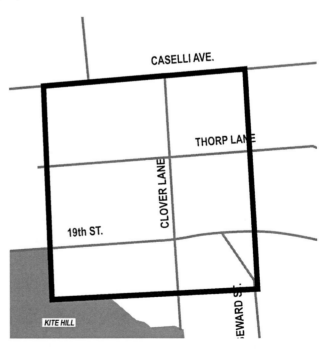

Clover Heights (map by Kushal Lachhwani, 2019).

Houses on Caselli Avenue closely resemble those shown in the newspaper article. Built 1916–19 (photograph by author, 2019).

the company shows sixty-two lots, mostly 25- or 30-feet wide by 100- or 110-feet long on the grid.[11] This was an ambitious project. The project sponsors hired architect E.P. Antonovich who designed arched pedestrian gates and red clay tile roofs on the sidewalks.[12] He also designed a row of two-story houses in the "California Mission architecture" style to match the gates. Antonovich was also engaged at the time as the supervising architect for Claremont Court residence park.

D. Coffin & Company handled sales during 1914, but then advertising fell silent with the slowdown caused by World War I.[13] The houses in Clover Heights were attached with shallow setbacks. The pedestrian gates were not built, and the tract exhibits none of the features of a residence park. A variety of builders was involved, and it is not clear if Clover Heights had or enforced any restrictions. However, the tract was almost completely built out by 1938 because it was not as hilly as the other residence parks and was closer to the built-up parts of Eureka Valley.

Ashbury Park, Twin Peaks Terrace, and Clover Heights did not succeed as residence parks, but they illustrate the popularity of the concept. Brickmakers, dentists, and ordinary real estate firms got caught up in the frenzy but found success elusive.

Mark Daniels,
Landscape Engineer

Landscape engineer and architect Mark Daniels left his mark on many developments in northern and southern California. Ambitious, energetic, and outspoken, Daniels claimed a daunting number of achievements.[1] He got his start in landscape engineering in the East Bay and then worked in San Francisco, Monterey, and southern California. His impact on residence parks in San Francisco ranges from extensive (Forest Hill, Crocker-Amazon) to slight (Claremont Court) to still-born (El Por-tal and Lake Merced). Others projects were partially realized (Presidio Gardens/Marina Gardens), while others have been sometimes erroneously attributed to Daniels (Sea Cliff and St. Mary's Park).

Crocker-Amazon

In 1912, the Crocker Estate Company announced the opening of the Crocker-Amazon tract laid out by Mark Daniels. It was located on San Francisco's southern county line, next to the Excelsior District. This 1,200-acre tract was part of 4,000 acres owned by the Crocker Estate Company and included parts of San Bruno Mountain. The site is nearly flat along Geneva Avenue and rises gently to the south until it climbs up the slopes of San Bruno Mountain. A streetcar ran along Geneva, and the builders promised buyers that with a transfer at Mission Street they could

Crocker-Amazon (map by Kushal Lachhwani, 2019).

reach downtown in 28 minutes, an optimistic promise at best. Crocker-Amazon was described as a restricted tract in early 1913.[2] This large tract was geared for buyers with lower incomes than other residence parks were at the time—only $5 down for a lot.[3] In 1916, after the tract was extended, the name *Crocker-Amazon Tract* was no longer used; it was now Crocker Homes Parks.[4]

Mark Daniels chose a fan-shaped street design "like the old city of Karlsruhe, Germany."[5] It's doubtful that many prospective buyers were familiar with the layout of Karlsruhe, but Daniels may have believed that a semi-circular–shaped street design conveyed a special feeling to the otherwise featureless site. It also allowed him to follow more or less the contours of the slopes without a lot of grading. Such designs were popular in Beaux Arts city planning, and Daniels would rely on them again in other projects.

In Crocker-Amazon, Mark Daniels designed a pergola, called a *civic center*, at the entrance to the tract on Naples Street, which was widened to accommodate it. The purpose was to give the tract a mark of distinction. The pergola was made of wood, less costly than the stone or brick pillars, staircases, or fountains used in other residence parks but more in keeping with the lower lot prices in Crocker-Amazon. The pergola existed until at least 1928 but was removed sometime before 1938.

By 1915, the Crocker Estate Company claimed that 205 houses had been constructed,[6] most of them detached bungalows or Craftsman-style houses. With the slowdown of housing during World War I, Crocker encouraged residents to plant vegetables on the vacant lots.[7] Presumably this effort was part of the National War Garden movement (later called "Victory Gardens") that encouraged people to grow fruits and vegetables using idle

View of Crocker-Amazon in 1925. The view looks south at the San Bruno Mountains. San Francisco Bay is to the left (OpenSFHistory wnp27.4598).

Boys posing at the Crocker-Amazon pergola (called "civic center") on Naples Street between Geneva Avenue and Rolph Street in 1928. The structure at that time needed repairs. The pergola was removed sometime before 1938. In 2010, the city installed a landscaped median in its place (OpenSFHistory wnp27.0517).

land so that more food could be exported to help feed Europe.[8] After World War I, in a bid to spur sales, the Crocker Estate Company announced a $100,000 fund to help working men buy houses.[9] By 1924, the company was building modest houses with identical designs on an assembly-line basis. These were usually attached row houses clad in stucco.

After laying out Crocker-Amazon, Daniels closed his practice and decided to spend a year (1913) at Harvard University taking courses in city planning and landscape architecture. In 1914 he was appointed general superintendent and landscape engineer for the National Park Service. This assignment lasted only a couple of years (1914 and 1915). During this time he reopened his landscape practice with a new partner, U.C. Berkeley alumnus, George H. Wilhelm, under the name Daniels, Osmont & Wilhelm.[10] Daniels was hired to lay out two other residence parks in San Francisco: Claremont Court for Alfred Meyerstein and El Por-tal Park for Charles A. Hawkins. Daniels apparently did little on Claremont Court and nothing on El Por-tal Park (see Chapter 8).

Lake Merced

In 1914, Daniels was commissioned to design a subdivision for Lake Merced, a large lake near the Pacific Ocean in the southwest corner of San Francisco. Lake Merced had been part of the 2,000-acre Laguna de la Merced Rancho.[11] In 1835, the Mexican government granted the land to Jose Antonio Galindo, who sold it two years later to Don Francisco de Haro.[12] De Haro's sons lived on the rancho and raised crops and cattle. Apparently, the land was not very valuable for agriculture, being described as "almost worthless" in 1867.[13] But it was far and away the largest lake in San Francisco.

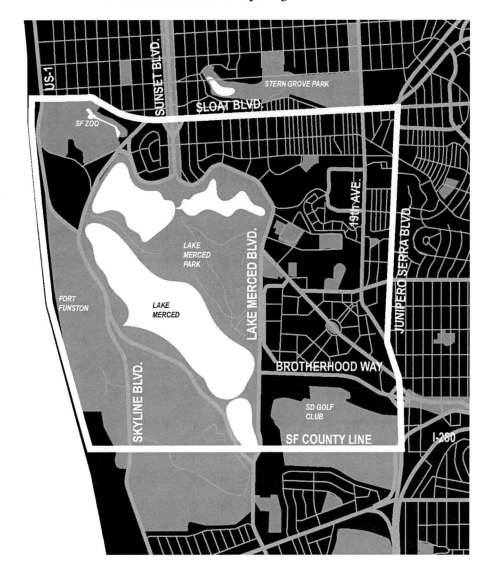

Lake Merced proposed residence park. Boundaries are Pacific Ocean (left), Sloat Boulevard (top), Junipero Serra Boulevard (right) and the San Mateo County line (bottom) (map by Kushal Lachhwani, 2019).

In 1868 the Spring Valley Water Company paid $150,000 to purchase the water rights to Lake Merced and in 1877 began purchasing land encircling the lake to protect the watershed feeding it. By the turn of the twentieth century, Spring Valley owned 2,000 acres from the San Mateo County line north to Sloat Boulevard and from Junipero Serra Boulevard to the ocean.[14] Spring Valley Water Company was a monopoly that owned land throughout the San Francisco Bay Area. It was once headed by the leading capitalists of the day, including Leland Stanford, Collis P. Huntington, Mark Hopkins, and Charles Crocker (the Big Four of the Central Pacific railroad), as well as William Ralston of the Bank of California, Darius O. Mills, and later by other wealthy individuals.[15] Over the years, Spring Valley began to sell off its land holdings around Lake Merced. Ultimately, several residential tract developments, golf courses, and the San Francisco Zoo were built on former Spring Valley land.[16]

Lake Merced and the Pacific Ocean in 1910. The building was the Ingleside Golf Club Clubhouse and would be used as a clubhouse in Joseph Leonard's Ingleside Terraces development (Open SFHistory wnp15.639).

Daniels' design for Lake Merced was a Beaux Arts extravagance. A long street running on a diagonal would cross the site from southwest to northeast, with a bridge over the lower lake. This street would bisect a large section laid out in a semicircle. The rest of the site would be filled with smaller semi-circular sections or curved streets. A young Gardiner Daily, who later became an important architect, drew the plan. Daniels offered to provide additional services, such as determining grades, designing sidewalk curbs, and subdividing blocks into lots.[17] Little else is known about the planned—but never built—project.

Presidio Gardens/Marina Gardens

In 1916 Mark Daniels was asked to lay out a residence park on the former fairgrounds of the 1915 Panama-Pacific International Exposition (PPIE). The site was on the north side of town on the bay between the Presidio and Fort Mason. During the nineteenth century the area was home to Italian truck farmers, Chinese shrimp fishermen shacks, dairies, and a lagoon. When the exposition company leased the land, it evicted hundreds of people, cleared existing buildings, and filled in the lagoon with bay sand and mud. Then the PPIE company erected Beaux-Arts–style temporary buildings along the lines of the 1893 Columbian Exposition. After the PPIE closed in December 1915, many proposals were made for the use of the 330-acre site. Daniels recounted:

Opposite top: "A Plan for the subdivision of the Property of the Spring Valley Water Company Lake Merced, prepared under the supervision of Mark Daniels, Landscape Engineer, drawn by Gardiner Dailey Scheme Number 1," no date. Dailey later became noted architect and served as a San Francisco City Planning Commissioner. Boundaries are Pacific Ocean (top), Sloat Boulevard (right), Junipero Serra Boulevard (bottom) and Daly City in San Mateo County (left). The Lake Merced site contained a freshwater dual lake system and two golf courses (drawn by Kushal Lachhwani, 2019 based on an image in the Bancroft Library).

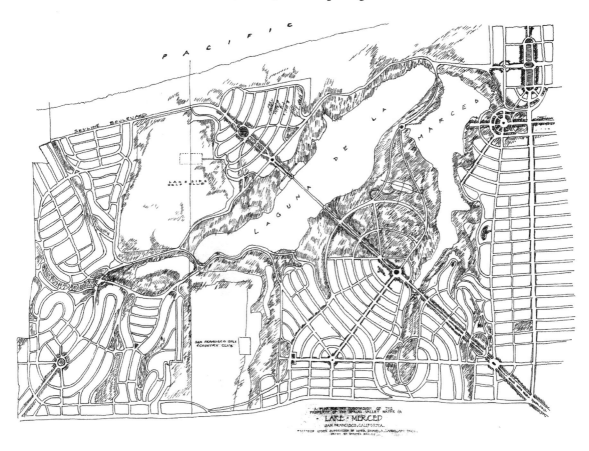

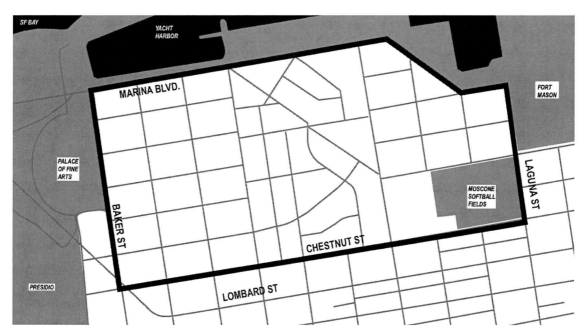

Presidio Gardens (map by Kushal Lachhwani, 2019).

For the past ten years, … San Francisco has been arguing … first to make this site, formerly known as Harbor View, into a manufacturing district, next into a home for wandering warehouses, then into massive shipyards, a wholesale district, freight-yards, and, in fact, almost every possible purpose except that to which geographical condition and the trend of city development point, namely a beautiful residence park…. The hills and slopes in the northern district command a view of the Bay, the Golden Gate, and the Pacific Ocean, that can be surpassed in few cities in the world.[18]

Residents in the exclusive Pacific Heights neighborhood south of the site agreed with Daniels and organized the "Exposition Preservation League" to preserve some of the PPIE buildings, require only high-quality residential development, and build a yacht harbor (rather than commercial docks) on the bay. They opposed relocating the wholesale produce market from downtown to the site. The league hired architect and city planner Charles H. Cheney to argue the case for zoning to restrict land use to "high-quality" residential development.[19] The league ultimately got the yacht harbor and residential development, but only one PPIE building—the Palace of Fine Arts—was ultimately saved.

Mark Daniels designed two versions of a residence park. His first plan was another Beaux Arts extravagance with a large semicircular street pattern and diagonal streets. The diagonals converged on three features that were desired to be preserved from the exposition: the Column of Progress, California Building, and Palace of Fine Arts. Daniels called this plan "Presidio Gardens."[20]

Daniels' design expressed a tenet of the City Beautiful Movement by providing a processional route leading to major landmarks or vistas. City Beautiful planning was fused with classical and Baroque architecture and the movement of individuals through the space, with buildings and monuments sited so as to become the terminal vistas of long, converging, diagonal axes. Daniels explained how the axial streets took advantage of the surviving monuments from the fair and made them the focus of attention:

The main north and south axis of the plan is approximately in the center of the property and is terminated to the north by the Column of Progress, one of the monuments left as a heritage of the Exposition. The two main diagonals also lie on axis with the Column of Progress…. The axis of the

The Preservation League hoped to save the Palace of Fine Arts (left), the 185-foot Column of Progress (center), and the California Counties Building (right). Only the Place of Fine Arts was saved. Photograph taken in 1918 (OpenSFHistory wnp36.01917).

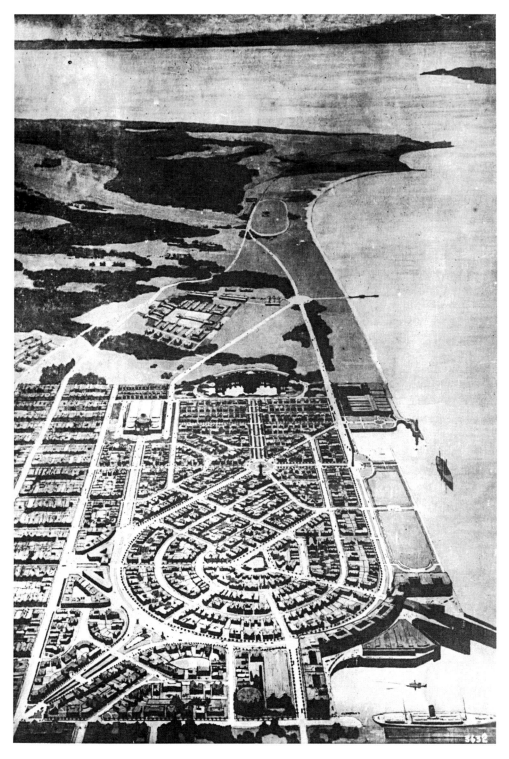

Plan number 1 for "Presidio Gardens" by Mark Daniels 1916. Looking west toward the Presidio, the bay is to the right. Note the grand axial boulevard converging on the Palace of Fine Arts (drawn by Chesley K. Bonestell. OpenSFHistory 36.01379).

main east and west thoroughfare through the property centers on the dome of the Palace of Fine Arts, that wonderful conception of Bernard H. Maybeck, which the people of San Francisco have wisely determined to preserve to posterity. The eastern end of this axis terminates in a plaza formed by its junction with the circle drive.

Daniels believed that his plan for diagonal streets in Presidio Gardens also solved the problem of winds blowing off the bay:

> The diagonals gave an excellent opportunity for disrupting and changing the directions of the streets, thus making it possible to avoid the long streets of continuous direction which seem to invite those winds which so annoy the stranger, while they become the joy of the resident of the city…. The prevailing winds of the district are from the water, or from the west and north. It has been demonstrated in such modern residence parks as Forest Hill that the winds in San Francisco lose their violence in the streets where the directions of the latter are changed frequently. For this reason, the plan does not incorporate any straight street of considerable length, except where a vista upon some inspiring feature is desired.[21]

Presidio Gardens would have the usual residence park restrictions. Daniels wrote: "It is the intention of the owners to establish building restrictions along most modern lines, not only to assure the general character of the neighborhood, but to preserve a unity of architecture. All utilities, such as light and power lines, will be placed underground and installed before paving is commenced. Buildings will be grouped and restricted as to location so as to provide a maximum of sun, view, and air."[22] Presidio Gardens residence park would have 750 lots with only six houses per acre, plenty of

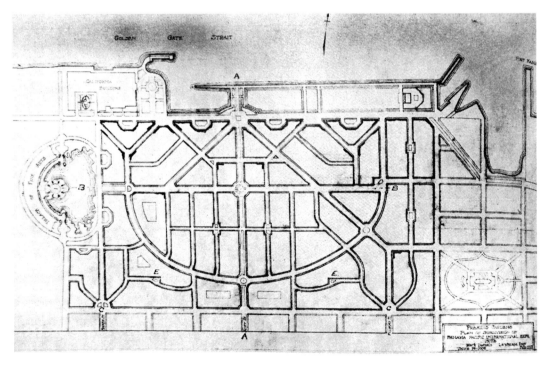

The revised plan retained more rectangular blocks but still called for a monumental approach to the Palace of Fine Arts (left) and a sweeping curved boulevard (Alhambra). Marina Boulevard is north (top), Lyon Street is west (left), Chestnut in south (bottom), and Laguna is east (right) ("A Residence Park on the Site of the Panama-Pacific Exposition" by Mark Daniels, *The Journal of the American Institute of Architects*, Vol. V, No. 4, April 1917. Image quality enhanced by Kushal Lachhwani, 2019).

lawn, and space for children to play. A central heating plant would provide hot water for the houses. Local newspapers announced the plan for Presidio Gardens with great fanfare and it was even covered in Los Angles newspapers.[23] One newspaper labeled it a "Park de Luxe" and compared it to Roland Park in Baltimore and Forest Hills Gardens in New York.[24]

Olivier Charles Stine, head of a real estate firm, was in charge of the project, and he had to secure the approval of the many property owners. Although organizers claimed to have secured the approval of nearly all the Presidio Gardens property owners, this plan was rejected.[25] Daniels was scathing in his comments:

> Plan No. 1 seemed to be the most desirable, but it was found impossible of execution as there were certain owners of property in the district who refused to abandon the idea of the district eventually being used for other purposes than a residential locality.… The property is now subdivided into rectangular blocks with unnecessarily wide streets, and to convince all owners that a change of streets was advisable was, alone, a Herculean task. In some instances, it became necessary to change the plan so as to leave portions of the old streets, if for no other reason than to leave ingress to the stable of the mule whose stubbornness made a change impossible.[26]

This revised plan for Presidio Gardens retained more rectangular bocks and presumably was more amenable to the property owners who had balked at the first design. It still called for a monumental approach to the Palace of Fine Arts and a sweeping curved boulevard with streets located so that the Column of Progress and the California Building would be centers of attention.

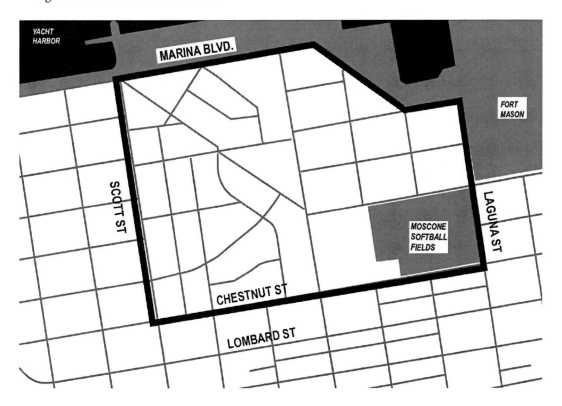

Only about half of the site used Daniels' design, the grid imposed itself west of Scott Street (map by Kushal Lachhwani, 2019).

Plan of the proposed approach on Beach Street to the Golden Gate Bridge by architectural renderer Chesley Bonestell (1934) (Golden Gate Bridge, 1862. Charles Derleth papers, box # 4, folder #32. Special Collections & University Archives, University of California, Riverside).

The adopted plan was renamed *Marina Gardens,* and it used only half of Daniels' design. A subdivision for the map of Marina Gardens, dated April 1917, was recorded on September 13, 1918, and streets were dedicated in November 1918. This subdivision covered the eastern half of the tract, from Scott Street to Fillmore Street. This was supposedly the first phase and would be followed by the rest of the exposition site, from Scott Street to the Presidio, after the war ended.[27]

However, the second phase of the project was never created. Stine, the real estate developer heading up the project, died in January 1918, and Daniels was in France with the Army Corps of Engineers. In any case, he had no further involvement with the project. In 1920, Daniels became consulting engineer for the Del Monte Properties Company.[28] In 1924, he moved to southern California, where he worked for many years. In 1939, Daniels returned to work on designs for the Golden Gate International Exposition to be held on Treasure Island. He died in 1952.[29]

Daniels' design is apparent east of Scott Street, while the grid appears west of Scott Street. Although part of Daniels' street design was maintained, the other elements of a residence park were not. In March 1924, the entire Marina was zoned Second Residential, meaning that apartment buildings were allowed. Evidently, this change was made at the behest of the Marina Corporation, which had purchased the land and planned to subdivide it.

The Marina Corporation was formed by George E. Belvel and the Rothschild Brothers, with J.B. Rothschild as president. They sold parcels to many builders, including the Meyers Brothers (Merritt Terrace), Joseph Arnott & Son, F.W. Varey (St. Mary's Park), and Lang Realty (Forest Hill, Balboa Terrace).[30] Lots were resold and further subdivided by subsequent owners resulting in a dense mix of apartment buildings, flats, and houses. Instead of widely separated houses on wide lots as called for by Daniels, developers put up small contiguous houses on narrow lots with four-story apartment buildings on the street corners. Some of these apartment buildings were badly damaged when their ground floors collapsed during the 1989 Loma Prieta earthquake. Much of the damage to the district might have been avoided if Daniels' plan had been adopted. According to engineering expert Stephen Tobriner, if the tract had "the detached frame houses planned in the original development, with the right foundations and strong wood construction, [they] probably would have been safe in earthquakes."[31]

Daniels idea of a grand axial boulevard converging on the Palace of Fine Arts resurfaced in 1934. Chesley Bonestell was hired to illustrate aspects of the future bridge and he drew a plan for the automobile approach to the Golden Gate Bridge, then in the planning stages.

Chesley Bonestell is known for his illustrations of space flight, futurist worlds, and movies. But he was trained as an architect and had worked for Willis Polk as a young man.[32] He worked for Daniels and drew the plan for Presidio Gardens in 1916. Bonestell's 1930s drawings for the bridge district recalls the design he did for Daniels, with a grand boulevard ending at the Palace of Fine Arts, but this time the boulevard continued around the building on its way to the bridge. Bernard Maybeck, architect of the Palace of Fine Arts, praised the design in a letter to Bonestell:

The drawing of the approach to the Fine Arts building shows the possibility ... of its being a favorite drive. If we can have one road like your painting shows it will give the citizens of San Francisco an idea how S.F. can be made into a city that will attract many people who must and can get away from their homes in the interior of the U.S. when the thermometer reaches 100° and 110° Fahrenheit. We may even cut chunks out of our fogs and sell them to the middle west.[33]

This photograph was taken on Beach Street one block from the Palace of Fine Arts which is almost completely obscured (photograph by author, 2019).

The Palace of Fine Arts (photograph by author, 2019).

Bonestell's route would have required removing houses along Beach and Francisco streets that were only ten years old or less. A less intrusive route was chosen by widening Lombard Street and cutting a new diagonal street, Richardson Avenue, through the southwest corner of the Marina neighborhood.

Unfortunately, the terminal vista of long axes at the Palace of Fine Arts as envisioned by Daniels in 1916 and Bonestell in 1934 was abandoned. Generations of San Franciscans made considerable efforts to save and restore the Palace of Fine Arts, yet it is almost hidden away by an unimaginative grid of narrow streets. It can be approached only from the side on narrow streets. Not what one would expect for such a monumental structure.

14

Accomplishments

Today, few people know about San Francisco's residence parks. That's too bad, because they are quite exceptional for San Francisco. They were also difficult to build. Of the thirty-six projects described in this book, sixteen were either not implemented or did not become residence parks. The developers of residence parks faced the risks inherent in any real estate development. But they also faced additional costs and risks that don't exist today or that can be mitigated.

Developers undertook the entire burden and cost of developing the properties. They were individuals or small partnerships with limited capital. They relied on local banks or their own funds. There was no assistance from the local, state, or federal government, no tax breaks, no enterprise zones, and no public/private partnerships to share or mitigate the risks. Developers paid for most of the infrastructure (utilities, sewers, street paving), donated land for street widening, and paid most of the cost of the Twin Peaks streetcar tunnel. Most developers provided amenities such as landscaping and entry gates; a few constructed sculptures, ceremonial stairs, walkways, or fountains to establish a sense of place. Developers were aware of what others were doing and tried to copy proven strategies, although not all developers were able to do all that they would have liked to do.

Why did some residence parks projects fail? A developer of a residence park needed to be a skillful planner and marketer with the fortitude to stick to his principles, while being flexible and responsive to changing economic trends.

Tremendous differences existed among developers. The successful ones included Baldwin & Howell, Lyon & Hoag, Harry Allen, and Duncan McDuffie. Newell-Murdoch, a two-man partnership who developed successful projects in Oakland, launched Forest Hill and Balboa Terrace but sold out to the family-run Lang Realty Company, which became a large real estate company with projects throughout the Bay Area. Joseph Leonard was an accomplished architect, developer, and builder who launched Ingleside Terraces. The accomplished firm of Fernando Nelson & Sons was successful in realizing residence park features in Parkway Terrace, but much less successful in their West Portal Park project.

Others did not have the knowledge, experience, temperament, or staying power to conceive, plan, and implement a residence park. Examples include the Simons-Fout Brick Company (Ashbury Park) which tried to transform land used for brick making into a residence park. Individual developers called "capitalists" (with enough money [capital] to invest in many business opportunities) were often not able or willing to master the intricacies of residence parks or did not have the means to persevere during difficult times. James Jordan (Jordan Park) tried to take advantage of the cachet of residence parks for his trouble-plagued tract but was quarrelsome and died shortly after the launch of Jordan Park. Others, such as Charles A Hawkins (El Por-tal, Arden Wood), Alfred Meyerstein (Claremont Court), and George Merritt (Merritt Terrace), had checkered or abortive careers as residence park developers.

Differences from Today's Building Environment

The speed with which the developers operated is astounding. They hired engineers, architects and surveyors; purchased land; drew up plans and designed tracts; cleared the land, graded roads, and installed underground utilities; and built houses—all in less than three years. The developers were free to design whatever they thought the market would support (and suffered the consequences if they were wrong).

One reason developers could act so quickly was the lack of regulation. They did not consider social factors, respect civil rights, satisfy modern-city planning goals, or meet other public policy objectives. They didn't conduct public outreach, wait for reviews and approvals, or modify designs to satisfy interest groups. There were no requirements to build affordable or below-market-rate housing. No laws protected the environment or workers. The native plants—California poppies, cowslips, buttercups, wild pansies, baby blue eyes and irises covering the ground that Duncan McDuffie wrote about were plowed up. Developers filled in watersheds, creeks, ponds, marshlands; graded and reshaped the land; displaced wildlife; and planted thirsty and pollen-producing foreign trees and plants.

Yet developers also took care to preserve or take advantage of natural features. They designed their tracts so that residents could enjoy views of the ocean, the bay, and other scenic features. They didn't carve up sites to maximize the number of lots. If they couldn't afford all the features of a residence park, they tried at least to provide detached houses and some landscaping.

Residence parks receded from the scene beginning in the 1920s, as increasingly prescriptive city planning regulations, zoning, and building codes transformed residential development. During the 1930s, the mortgage loan program of the Federal Housing Administration (FHA) had an enormous effect on housing by establishing standards for house design. The FHA program was so large and powerful that it changed the way virtually all houses were financed, designed, and constructed—whether or not they were part of the FHA program. One consequence may have been to standardize some of the features of a residence park in suburban development. For example, newer tracts in San Francisco such as Miraloma Park, Mt. Davidson Manor, Merced Manor, Pine Lake, Lakeside, and Forest Knolls offered detached lots, but they were no longer called residence parks.

Most builders reverted to the mass row housing of the Victorian era. Beginning in the 1920s, accelerating after World War II, and continuing through the 1960s and 1970s, merchant builders, such as Henry Doelger, the Meyer Brothers, Standard Builders, Stoneson Brothers, and Ray Galli, blanketed the Sunset, Richmond, Oceanview, Merced, Ingleside, outer Mission District, Twin Peaks, and other areas with thousands of identical-looking houses that had little or no front or side yards, track landscaping, statuary, or other amenities. These builders provided decent and affordable housing and met the needs of the times, but their work presents a stark contrast to residence parks.

After 100+ years, residence parks look pretty much as they did when they were completed. Some houses have a few unsympathetic additions or alterations, but the streets haven't changed (although traffic is heavier) and land use is unchanged, except for a few churches or schools that were built within or adjacent to some residence parks.

Such longevity was not a forgone conclusion. Cities constantly change, and neighborhoods go in and out of fashion. South Park lost its cachet in less than ten years. In the 1890s, the Western Addition was a prestigious neighborhood with stately Victorians, but it was considered a slum by the 1930s, its old houses viewed as drafty, old-fashioned, and requiring excessive maintenance. Many were demolished during urban renewal in the 1960s and '70s.

Residence parks faced many threats to their physical state. The salt air and foggy conditions in most San Francisco residence parks posed greater maintenance burdens than houses in the warmer Mission or Western Addition districts. The Depression years and then the difficulty of obtaining materials during World War II precluded routine maintenance. Over time, residence parks began to age.

By the 1970s, the houses in residence parks needed repairs as did the pillars, fountains, stairs, statuary, and irrigation pipes dating from the 1910s. Landscaping suffered as increasing labor costs resulted in fewer and fewer gardeners to maintain it. Weeds and ivy had taken over statuary and landscaping. Homeowner dues did not keep up with inflation, and property taxes rose continuously during the 1960s and 70s. Many residents were retired by that time and resisted paying for costly repairs. Some residents preferred greater privacy and installed tall fences and walls that violated design guidelines. Others took advantage of lax oversight and made additions or installed garages that violated setbacks limits. Inexpensive post–World War II materials, such as asbestos-cement shingles, vinyl, aluminum siding, PermaStone, and aluminum sash windows tempted owners to strip decorative features to simplify future maintenance or to create a more modern look.

Yet, residence parks have been resilient. There is little visual evidence that owners used cheap materials or stripped original detailing that plagued Victorian neighborhoods.

View of the Sunset District looking west circa 1958 (Opensfhistory_wnp28.3734).

House additions or remodeling did not alter the overall character of the neighborhoods. Beginning in the 1990s, a renaissance of sorts appeared in some residence parks—more than just individuals fixing their houses. It was a collective response fueled by the recognition that neighborhoods were something special and should be cared for and appreciated. Homeowners have voted to increase dues, establish priorities, and restore and maintain houses and common areas to match the original design intent.

During the first quarter of the twentieth century, a handful of real estate developers created something unusual for San Francisco: spacious and aesthetically designed subdivisions on curvilinear streets with detached houses surrounded by trees, lawns, and landscaping. The architecture of the 1920s with many different styles stand out for their variety and distinction. For one historic period in San Francisco the ideals of Frederick Law Olmsted were realized: "large domestic houses, on ample lots with garden setbacks, enhanced by sidewalk boulevards and plantings that would become luxuriant and graceful to shelter the visitor from the sun [and that would] express the manifestations of a refined domestic life."

Chapter Notes

Preface

1. Richard Brandi, *San Francisco's West Portal Neighborhoods* (Charleston, SC: Arcadia Books, 2005); Richard Brandi, *San Francisco's St. Francis Wood* (San Francisco: Outside Lands Media, 2012).

2. Patrick McGrew, *The Historic Houses of Presidio Terrace* (San Francisco: Friends of the Presidio Terrace Association, 1995).

3. Patrick McGrew, "Neighborhoods and Innovators: An Architect's View of San Francisco's Subdivisions Before 1915," *The Argonaut: Journal of The San Francisco Museum and Historical Society*, 15:2 (Winter 2004).

4. Carolyn S. Loeb in *Entrepreneurial Vernacular: Developers' Subdivisions in the 1920s* (Baltimore: Johns Hopkins University Press, 2001).

5. Woody LaBounty, *Ingleside Terraces: San Francisco Racetrack to Residence Park* (San Francisco: Outside Lands Media, 2012); Jacquie Proctor, *Bay Area Beauty: The Artistry of Harold G. Stoner* (San Francisco: Blurb, 2009); Katherine O. Beitiks, *Westwood Park: Building a Bungalow Neighborhood in San Francisco* (San Francisco: 2017). *See also* Inge Horton, "A Jewel Restored: Fernando Nelson's House in Parkway Terrace," www.outsidelands.org/parkway_terrace_jewel.php; and Inge Schaefer Horton, *Early Women Architects of the San Francisco Bay Area* (Jefferson, NC: McFarland, 2010).

6. See Measuring Worth website, www.measuringworth.com/defining_measures_of_worth.php.

7. Robert Lieber and Sarah Lau, editors, *The Last Great World's Fair: San Francisco's Panama-Pacific International Exposition 1915* (San Francisco: Golden Gate Parks Conservatory, 2004), 20.

Chapter 1

1. John Archer, "Country and City in the American Romantic Suburb," *Journal of the Society of Architectural Historians*, 42:2 (May 1983), 139–156.

2. Robert A.M. Stern, David Fishman, and Jacob Tilove, *Paradise Planned: The Garden Suburb and the Modern City* (New York: The Monacelli Press, 2013), 48.

3. Robert A.M. Stern, David Fishman, and Jacob Tilove, *Paradise Planned: The Garden Suburb and the Modern City* (New York: The Monacelli Press, 2013), 147.

4. Robert M. Fogelson, *Bourgeois Nightmares: Suburbia 1870–1930* (New Haven: Yale University Press, 2005), 63.

5. Richard Walker, "Industry Builds Out the City: The Suburbanization of Manufacturing in San Francisco, 1850–1940." Originally written in 2005 for *The Manufactured Metropolis*, Robert Lewis, ed. (Philadelphia: Temple University Press). http://www.foundsf.org/index.php?title=Industry_Builds_Out_the_City:_The_Suburbanization_of_Manufacturing_in_San_Francisco,_1850-1940.

6. Terrence Young, *Building San Francisco's Parks 1850–1930* (Baltimore: Johns Hopkins University Press, 2004).

7. Frank Soulé quoted in Oscar Lewis, *The Annals of San Francisco* (Berkeley: Howell-North Books, 1966), 163.

8. Randolph Delehanty, *In the Victorian Style* (San Francisco: Chronicle Books, 1991), 43.

9. The Foundation for San Francisco's Architectural Heritage, *Splendid Survivors: San Francisco's Downtown Architectural Heritage* (San Francisco: California Living Books, 1979), 54.

10. James Beach Alexander & James Lee Height, *San Francisco: Building the Dream City* (San Francisco: Scottwall Associates, 2002), 176.

11. Albert Shumate, *Rincon Hill and South Park: San Francisco's Early Fashionable Neighborhoods* (Sausalito: Wingate Press, 1988), 30–35.

12. Peter Booth Wiley, *National Trust Guide/San Francisco* (New York: John Wiley & Sons, 2000), 44.

13. Terence Young, *Building San Francisco's Parks 1850–1930* (Baltimore: Johns Hopkins University Press, 2004), 39.

14. Susan Dinkelspiel Cerny, "Piedmont Way," Berkeley Architectural Heritage Association website. Accessed June 25, 2014. http://berkeleyheritage.com/berkeley_landmarks/piedmont_way.html.

15. "Wellesley Park," Historic American Landscape Survey HALS CA-44, 2005, 6.

16. *Ibid.*

17. Alan Hynding, *From Frontier to Suburb: The Story of the San Mateo Peninsula* (Belmont, CA: Star Publishing Company, 1984), 110–14.

18. *Eden: California Landscape and Garden*

Design History Society Journal, 5:2 (Summer 2002), 5–6.

19. *San Francisco Chronicle*, January 18, 1895.

20. Elizabeth Jo Lampl and Kimberly Prothro Williams, *Chevy Chase, a Home in the Nation's Capital* (Crownsville MD: Maryland Historical Trust Press, 1998), 92–94.

21. Burlingame Historical Society website. Accessed June 26, 2014. http://burlingamehistory.org/history-of-burlingame.

22. Daniel Gregory, *Be It Ever So Humble: The Impact of the Merchant Builder-Land Developer on the Evolution of Housing in the Bay Area, 1850–1979* (Berkeley: University of California, 1979).

23. Richard W. Longstreth, *On the Edge of the World: Four Architects in San Francisco at the Turn of the Century* (Cambridge, MA: MIT Press, 1983), 109.

24. *Ibid.*, 80.

25. Quoted by Harold Kirker in *California's Architectural Frontier* (San Marino, CA: The Henry E. Huntington Library and Art Gallery, 1960; reissued 1970 by Russell & Russell, New York), 106.

26. *The Wave*, 1897, 6. A weekly magazine published in the nineteenth century for which where Polk often wrote.

27. *San Francisco Chronicle,* October 19, 1893; Woodruff Minor, *A Home in Alameda* (Alameda, CA: Alameda Museum, 2009), 60.

28. Richard W. Longstreth, *On the Edge of the World: Four Architects in San Francisco at the Turn of the Century* (Cambridge, MA: MIT Press, 1983), 10, 16, 78.

29. Richard Walker, "Classy City: Residential Realms of the Bay Region," http://geog.berkeley.edu/PeopleHistory/faculty/R_Walker/ClassCity.pdf.

30. Paolo Polledri, Gray Brechin, *Visionary San Francisco* (New York: Prestel Publishing, 1990).

31. *San Francisco Chronicle*, July 22, 1905.

32. A constitutional amendment to merge the towns of the Bay Area with San Francisco to create a "Greater San Francisco" super metropolis was defeated by California voters in 1912.

33. Mel Scott, *The San Francisco Bay Area: A Metropolis in Perspective* (Berkeley: University of California Press, 1959), 9–11.

34. Peter Booth Wiley, *National Trust Guide/San Francisco* (New York: John Wiley & Sons, 2000), 44.

35. Daniel H. Burnham, assisted by Edward H. Bennett, *Report on a Plan for San Francisco* (San Francisco: Sunset Books, 1905); in a facsimile reprint (Berkeley CA: Urban Books, 1971), 35.

36. http://www.encyclopedia.chicagohistory.org/pages/61.html.

37. Terence Young, *Building San Francisco's Parks 1850–1930* (Baltimore: Johns Hopkins University Press, 2004), 185.

38. Daniel H. Burnham, assisted by Edward H. Bennett, *Report on a Plan for San Francisco* (San Francisco: Sunset Books, 1905); in a facsimile reprint (Berkeley CA: Urban Books, 1971), 144, 191.

Chapter 2

1. Jack London, "The Story of an Eyewitness," *Collier's*, May 5, 1906.

2. *The San Francisco Real Estate Board Circular*, November 1910, 1.

3. Mel Scott, *San Francisco Bay Area: A Metropolis in Perspective* (Berkeley: University of California Press, 1959; reprinted 1985), 114.

4. See Thomas S. Hines, *Burnham of Chicago, Architect and Planner* (New York: Oxford University Press, 1974), 174–96.

5. Stephen Tobriner, *Bracing for Disaster: Earthquake-Resistant Architecture and Engineering in San Francisco, 1838–1933* (Berkeley, CA: Heyday Books, 2006), 132–35.

6. *Pacific Coast Architect*, 5:4, July 1913.

7. Stephen Tobriner, *Bracing for Disaster: Earthquake-Resistant Architecture and Engineering in San Francisco, 1838–1933* (Berkeley, CA: Heyday Books, 2006), 182.

8. *Neighborhood Commercial Buildings, Historic Context Statement, 1865–1965*, February 17, 2016.

9. *First Report of the San Francisco Housing Association*, 1911.

10. *Ibid.*

11. *Homes and Grounds,* March 1916, 78.

12. Ownership data is available for houses built in the Bay Station Heritage Area and the Leonardville Heritage Area of the city of Alameda. The author's analysis of the ninety-one houses constructed before 1906 (almost all during the 1890s), shows that sixty-one were sold to people known to have worked in San Francisco. Data taken from Woodruff Minor, *A Home in Alameda* (Alameda, CA: Alameda Museum, 2009).

13. Mark Daniels, "Forest Hill—A Residence Park," *San Francisco Homes & Grounds,* 1:3, March 1916.

14. *Los Angeles Herald*, October 8, 1904.

15. *Los Angeles Herald*, October 13, 1907.

16. *Sacramento Union,* May 5, 1906.

17. Charles Wollenberg, *Berkeley: A City in History* (Berkeley: University of California Press, 2008).

18. http://www.bayareacensus.ca.gov/cities/Oakland40.htm.

19. Joan Draper, "John Galen Howard" in Robert Winter, *Toward a Simpler Way of Life: The Arts and Crafts Architects of California* (Berkeley: University of California Press, 1991), 38.

20. "Northbrae," Berkeley Architectural Heritage Association, 1994.

21. David L. Ames and Linda Flint McClelland, *Historic Residential Suburbs: Guidelines for Evaluation and Documentation for the National Register of Historic Places*, U.S. Department of the Interior, National Park Service, 2002.

22. *History of Public Transit in San Francisco 1850–1948*, Transportation Technical Committee of the Departments of Public Works, Public Utilities, Police and City Planning, City and County of San Francisco, June 1948, 33.

23. San Francisco Planning and Urban research (SPUR) "The Muni Paradox, a Social History of the Municipal Railway," *Urbanist,* June 1, 1999, https://www.spur.org/publications/urbanist-article/1999-06-01/muni-paradox.

24. Roger W. Lotchin, "The Darwinian City: The Politics of Urbanization in San Francisco Between the World Wars," *Pacific Historical Review,* 48:3 August 1979, 357–81.

25. Vincent D. Ring, "Tunnels and Residential Growth in San Francisco, 1910–38," master's thesis, University of San Francisco, 1971, 41, 42.

26. *San Francisco Chronicle,* July 29, 1905. During summer months especially, it's often colder.

27. Richard Brandi and Woody LaBounty, *San Francisco's Parkside District: 1905–57 Historic Context Statement,* 2008.

28. *Ibid.*

29. David Warren Ryder, *Great Citizen: A Biography of William H. Crocker* (San Francisco: Historical Publications, 1962), 110.

30. Vincent D. Ring, *Tunnels and Residential Growth in San Francisco, 1910–1938,* master's thesis, University of San Francisco, 1971.

31. *San Francisco Chronicle,* February 3, 1912.

32. *San Francisco Chronicle,* January 12, 1896.

33. Western Neighborhoods Project, www.outsidelands.org/twin-peaks-tunnel.php.

34. Anthony Perles, *The People's Railway: The History of the Municipal Railway of San Francisco* (Glendale, CA: Interurban Press, 1981), 63–4.

35. Letter to Carl Larsen, November 3, 1913, O'Shaughnessy papers, Bancroft Library, BANC MSS 92/808c, carton 40:8.

36. William Issel and Robert W. Cherny, *San Francisco 1865–1932: Politics, Power and Urban Development* (Berkeley: University of California Press), 1986, 181.

37. *San Francisco Chronicle,* February 2, 1918.

38. In M. M. O'Shaughnessy, *Hetch Hetchy: Its Origin and History* (San Francisco: [s.n.], 1934), http://www.sfmuseum.net/bio/mmo.html.

39. Letter from A.S. Baldwin, August 25, 1913, apparently about the bond issue to create or support the Municipal Railway. MSS 92/808c O'Shaughnessy Papers, BANC Box 1, Folder 7 (Jul–Aug 1913).

40. Letter from O'Shaughnessy August 27, 1913, in reply to A.S. Baldwin. BANC MSS 92/808c O'Shaughnessy Papers, BANC Box 1, Folder 7 (Jul–Aug 1913).

41. Letter from O'Shaughnessy to Mayor Rolph, January 31, 1917, M. M. O'Shaughnessy Papers BANC NMSS 92/808c Box 4 folder 6.

42. Letter from Duncan McDuffie to O'Shaughnessy, December 19, 1917, M. M. O'Shaughnessy Papers, BANC NMSS 92/808c Box 4 folder 10.

43. Mel Scott, *The San Francisco Bay Area: A Metropolis in Perspective* (Berkeley: University of California Press, 1959).

Chapter 3

1. Robert A.M. Stern, David Fishman, and Jacob Tilove, *Paradise Planned: The Garden Suburb and the Modern City* (New York: The Monacelli Press, 2013), 48.

2. First Report of the San Francisco Housing Association, San Francisco, 1911.

3. *San Francisco Call,* October 11, 1912.

4. *San Francisco Call,* editorial, February 11, 1911.

5. Richard W. Longstreth, *On the Edge of the World: Four Architects in San Francisco at the Turn of the Century* (Cambridge, MA: MIT Press, 1983), 145.

6. Elizabeth Jo Lampl, Kimberly Prothro Williams *Chevy Chase; a Home in the Nation's Capital* (Crownsville MD: Maryland Historical Trust Press, 1998), 92–94.

7. M. M. O'Shaughnessy Papers, BANC 92/808c, Carton 7:2.

8. *San Francisco Call,* July 13, 1913.

9. Michael O'Shaughnessy, "Recent Municipal Activities in San Francisco," *Pacific Municipalities,* XXIX, October 1915, 439.

10. *Eden: California Landscape and Garden Design History Society Journal,* 5:2, Summer 2002, 7. No author given.

11. Marc A. Weiss, "The Real Estate Industry and the Politics of Zoning in San Francisco, 1914–28," *Planning Perspectives 3,* September 1988, 311–24.

12. See Robert M. Fogelson, *Bourgeois Nightmares: Suburbia 1870–1930* (New Haven: Yale University Press, 2005), which frequently mentions St. Francis Wood.

13. *San Francisco Chronicle,* November 1, 1912.

14. David L. Ames, Linda Flint McClelland, *Historic Residential Suburbs in the United States, 1830–1960,* National Park Service, September 2002.

15. *San Francisco Chronicle,* July 2, 1926.

16. Marc A. Weiss, "The Real Estate Industry and the Politics of Zoning in San Francisco, 1914–1928," *Planning Perspectives 3,* September 1988, 311–24.

17. https://www.history.com/this-day-in-history/fords-assembly-line-starts-rolling.

18. Model T Forum, http://www.mtfca.com/discus/messages/257047/310623.html. The site now is the John O'Connell School of Technology.

19. Mel Scott, *San Francisco Bay Area: A Metropolis in Perspective* (Berkeley: University of California Press, 1959; reprinted 1985), 68.

20. *San Francisco Chronicle.* February 20, 1915.

21. M. M. O'Shaughnessy *Hetch Hetchy: Its Origin and History* (San Francisco, [s.n.] 1934), http://www.sfmuseum.net/bio/mmo.html.

22. *Ibid.*

23. Charles Wollenberg, "Berkeley: A City in History," 2002: https://bcourses.berkeley.edu/courses/1197829/files/45385994.

24. Mitchell Schwarzer, *Architecture of the San Francisco Bay Area: History and Guide* (San Francisco: William Stout Publishers, 2007), 30.

25. Henry H. Gutterson, *The Building Review* XX:2, San Francisco, CA, August 1921, 24.

26. *The Home Designer and Garden Beautiful,* Oakland, June 1924.

27. Susan L. Klaus, *A Modern Arcadia: Frederick*

Law Olmsted, Jr., and the Plan for Forest Hills Gardens (Amherst: University of Massachusetts Press, 2002), 52.

28. *San Francisco Chronicle* March 13, 1920, according to Baldwin & Howell referring to a report by the National Industrial Conference Board.

29. Bureau of Municipal Research, *Report on Survey of Government of City and County for the San Francisco Real Estate Board* (San Francisco, CA: Rincon Publisher, 1916), 562.

30. Marc A. Weiss, "The Real Estate Industry and the Politics of Zoning in San Francisco, 1914–1928," *Planning Perspectives* 3, September 1988, 311–24.

31. Letter from Michael O'Shaughnessy to Alexander T. Vogelsang, Assistant Secretary of the Interior, September 6, 1917, Bancroft Library BANC MSS 92/808c, Box 4, Folder 9.

32. Duncan McDuffie, "St. Francis Wood," December 11, 1932. A speech delivered to the residents of St. Francis Wood.

33. Philip W. Alexander and Charles P. Hamm, *History of San Mateo County* (Burlingame, CA: Press of Burlingame Pub. Co.,1916), 73–4.

34. *San Francisco Chronicle*, February 2, 1918.

35. San Francisco Real Estate Circular, April 1917; *San Francisco Chronicle*, April 10, 1917.

36. *San Francisco Chronicle*, June 9, 1917.

37. *San Francisco Chronicle*, June 30, 1917.

38. Fukuo Akimoto and Charles H. Cheney, *Planning Perspectives*, 18 (July 2003) 253–75.

39. John L. Tierney, "War Housing: The Emergency Fleet Corporation Experience," *The Journal of Land & Public Utility Economics*, 17:2, 1941, 151–64. doi:10.2307/3158417.

40. *San Francisco Chronicle*, February 2,1918.

41. "Work of Charles Henry Cheney Architect and City Planner," *Architect and Engineer*, LIII:3, June 1918.

42. *The Building Review*, XVII:5, May 1919, 53.

43. Inge Horton, "A Jewel Restored: Fernando Nelson's House in Parkway Terrace," www.outsidelands.org/parkway_terrace_jewel.php.

Chapter 4

1. *San Francisco Chronicle*, May 15, 1920.

2. The occupations of "cashier" and "clerk" refer to an officer in a bank or business, not a sales clerk.

3. This section courtesy of Dennis P. Kelly, "The Political Culture of Western Neighborhood Residence Parks, 1932–1960," *SF West History*, 11:2, 2015.

4. https://www.latimes.com/local/obituaries/archives/la-me-edmund-g-pat-brown-19960217-story.html dated February 17, 1996.

5. Interview with Lillian Strang, daughter of Morris and Minnie Riskin, June 6, 2006.

6. *San Francisco Chronicle*, June 12, 1915.

7. This list comes from newspaper articles of new buyers and cross-referenced with City Directories.

8. Fukuo Akimoto, "California Garden Suburbs:

St. Francis Wood and Palos Verdes," *Journal of Urban Design*, 12:1, February 2007, 43–72.

9. Richard Walker, "Classy City: Residential Realms of the Bay Region," (revised 2002), 12. Accessed at http://geog.berkeley.edu/People History/faculty/R_Walker/ClassCity.pdf.

10. Donna Graves, Page & Turnbull, *San Francisco Japantown Historic Context Statement*, May 2009.

11. *Homes and Grounds,* March 1916, 314.

12. Robert M. Fogelson, *Bourgeois Nightmares: Suburbia 1870–1930* (New Haven: Yale University Press, 2005), 127.

13. *San Francisco Chronicle,* March 28, 1914.

14. Charles Wollenberg, *Berkeley: A City in History*, 2002, https://bcourses.berkeley.edu/courses/1197829/files/45385994.

15. "California Real Estate," California Real Estate Associates, Los Angeles. July 1927, 35.

16. Letter from W.H. Fitchmiller, Santa Monica Realty Board Secretary, March 1, 1927, http://collections.stanford.edu/pdf/10100000000020_0016.pdf.

17. David B. Oppenheimer, "California's Anti-Discrimination Legislation, Proposition 14, and the Constitutional Protection of Minority Rights: The Fiftieth Anniversary of the California Fair Employment and Housing Act." *Golden Gate Law Review*, 40:2, 2010.

18. Deanna Paoli Gumina, *The Italians of San Francisco 1850–1930* (New York: The Center for Migration Studies), 1978.

19. Peter Booth Wiley, *National Trust Guide/San Francisco* (New York: John Wiley and Sons, 2000), 84.

20. www.thesfmarket.org/about-us.

21. *San Francisco Call*, August 13, 1910.

22. Deanna Paoli Gumina, *The Italians of San Francisco 1850–1930* (New York: The Center for Migration Studies, 1978); Sutro Papers, C-B 465 Box 42 v.1 Bancroft Library.

23. *San Francisco Chronicle*, November 4, 1897; various San Francisco City Directories; Municipal Reports, 1894–95, 787.

24. Richard Brandi, "Farms, Fire and Forest: Adolph Sutro and Development 'West of Twin Peaks,'" *The Argonaut*: Journal of the San Francisco Museum and Historical Society, 14:1, Summer 2003.

25. *San Francisco Chronicle,* June 15, 1918.

26. Marion Louis Stireman Dewart, "South San Francisco 75th Anniversary," *Soroptimist International of Northern San Mateo County*, 1983.

27. Unpublished manuscript by Masha Fontes, 1978.

28. Interview with Ed Amanino, 1998.

29. *San Francisco Chronicle,* November 21, 1925, www.infoplease.com/san-francisco-earthquake-1906-census-facts.

Chapter 5

1. *San Francisco Call*, November 26, 1901.

2. *Grass Valley Daily Union*, December 1, 1891.

3. From the dedication program of the Francis Scott Key Monument in 1888, courtesy of Christopher Pollock.

4. *San Francisco Call*, January 9, 1897.

5. Much of this discussion is based on the work of historian Evelyn Rose, PharmD, project director and founder, Glen Park Neighborhoods History Project (www.GlenParkHistory.org) and author of the history blog, "Tramps of San Francisco" (www.trampsofsanfrancisco.com).

6. http://www.foundsf.org/index.php?title= Woodward%27s_Gardens,_c._1860s.

7. *San Francisco Daily Report*, August 7, 1897.

8. *San Francisco Call*, May 18, 1899.

9. *San Francisco Chronicle,* August 4, 1901.

10. *San Francisco Chronicle*, August 27, 1904; *San Francisco Examiner*, November 25, 1906.

11. Correspondence with historian Evelyn Rose.

12. Joan Levy in *The Daily Journal*, August 27, 2007.

13. "San Francisco Landmark 109," https://noehill.com/sf/landmarks/sf109.asp.

14. *San Francisco Chronicle*, October 9, 1961.

15. *San Francisco Chronicle*, June 22, 1890.

16. *San Francisco Call*, September 28, 1905; *San Francisco Call*, August 27, 1906.

17. Patrick McGrew, "Neighborhoods and Innovators: An Architect's View of San Francisco's Subdivisions Before 1915," *The Argonaut: Journal of the San Francisco Museum and Historical Society*, 15:2 (Winter 2004).

18. Patrick McGrew, *The Historic Houses of Presidio Terrace* (San Francisco: Friends of Presidio Terrace Association, 1995).

19. *San Francisco Chronicle*, August 27, 1905.

20. https://sf.curbed.com/2018/1/10/16874056/-presidio-terrace-lawsuit-gofundme-wealthy-rich-residents.

21. *San Francisco Call*, September 12, 1906.

22. *San Francisco Call*, September 18, 1906.

23. *San Francisco Call,* September 28, 1906.

24. *San Francisco Chronicle*, August 7, 1907.

25. *Ibid.*, 9–14. See also *San Francisco Call,* June 5, 1909; October 3, 1909; and July 22, 1911; *The Argonaut: Journal of the San Francisco Museum and Historical Society,* May 22, 1905; and *San Francisco Chronicle,* February 8, 1913.

26. *San Francisco Chronicle*, April 23, 1910.

27. *San Francisco Chronicle*, April 23, 1910.

28. *San Francisco Chronicle*, March 28, 1915; *San Francisco Chronicle*, April 12, 1916; *San Francisco Chronicle*, May 24, 1953; Joan Levy in *The Daily Journal*, August 27, 2007.

29. *San Francisco Chronicle,* February 18, 1911; March 15, 1911; August 12, 1911; September 2, 1911.

30. *San Francisco Chronicle,* July 8, 1912.

31. *San Francisco Chronicle,* February 28, 1920.

32. *San Francisco Chronicle*, March 27, 1920.

33. New Mission Terrace Association, www.nmtiasf.com/uploads/1/2/2/7/1227634/nmtia_history.pdf.

34. Robert E. Stewart, Jr., and Mary Frances Stewart, *Adolph Sutro: A Biography* (Berkeley, CA: Howell-North, 1962), 171. See also Mae Silver, *Rancho San Miguel* (San Francisco: Ord Street Press, 2001), 59–76.

35. Robert E. Stewart, Jr., and Mary Frances Stewart, *Adolph Sutro, a Biography*, 52.

36. "Executrix of Will of Sutro and Report of Management of Estate," February 1, 1900 to February 10, 1904, 55, Bancroft Library, G-B Box 42, v.3.

37. *Estate of Adolph Sutro, Deceased Appraised by A.S. Baldwin, March-April-May, 1910*. Estate of Adolph Sutro Album, San Francisco History Center, San Francisco Public Library.

38. *San Francisco Call,* January 5, 1911.

39. *Estate of Adolph Sutro, Deceased Appraised by A.S. Baldwin, March-April-May, 1910*. Estate of Adolph Sutro Album, San Francisco History Center, San Francisco Public Library.

40. *Ibid.*

41. Hospitalhttps://www.nps.gov/nr/travel/wwIIbayarea/mil.htm.

42. *San Francisco Call*, December 16, 1912.

43. *San Francisco Chronicle,* January 9,1920.

44. *Estate of Adolph Sutro, Deceased Appraised by A.S. Baldwin, March-April-May, 1910*. Estate of Adolph Sutro Album, San Francisco History Center, San Francisco Public Library.

45. *San Francisco Call*, February 24, 1898.

46. It is not known what work McLaren did on this project.

47. *San Francisco Chronicle,* May 11, 1912.

48. *San Francisco Chronicle*, January 31, 1911.

49. *San Francisco Call*, October 10, 1912.

50. $1,417,877/825 acres = $1,719 per acre.

51. http://opensfhistory.org/news/2017/08/14/westwood-park-a-closer-look/#1.

52. Kathleen O. Beitiks, *Westwood Park: Building a Bungalow Neighborhood in San Francisco* (San Francisco: K.O. Beitiks, 2017), ISBN 978-0-692-84435-0.

53. San Francisco Planning Department, *Landmark Recommendation Resolutions for Theodore Roosevelt Middle School, George Washington High School, and Sunshine School*, December 6, 2017, Case Number: 2017-000965.

54. *San Francisco Chronicle*, June 12,1920.

55. *San Francisco Chronicle*, June 5, 1920.

56. Carolyn S. Loeb, *Entrepreneurial Vernacular: Developers' Subdivisions in the 1920s* (Baltimore: Johns Hopkins University Press, 2001).

57. http://www.50justin.com/stmaryspark.htm.

58. Archives of the San Francisco Catholic Archdiocese.

59. *San Francisco Chronicle*, April 25, 1914.

60. *San Francisco Chronicle*, February 22, 1914.

61. *San Francisco Chronicle*, January 17, 1925.

62. *San Francisco Chronicle*, June 27, 1925; *San Francisco Chronicle*, November 8, 1927.

63. Declaration of Conditions, Covenants and Agreements Affecting Title, Declaration by the Roman Catholic Archbishop of San Francisco,

March 21, 1924. Archives of the Archdiocese of San Francisco.

Chapter 6

1. Werner Hegemann and Elbert Peets, *The American Vitruvius: An Architect's Handbook of Civic Art* (New York: The Architecture Book Publishing Co, 1922; revised edition edited by Thomas C. Meyers, Jr., De Facto Publishing, 2008), 151, 166. Hegemann and McDuffie were friends. Hegemann worked on city plans for Berkeley and Oakland in the mid–1910s. See Christine Crasemann Collins, *Werner Hegemann and the Search for Universal Urbanism* (New York: W.W. Norton, 2005), 141.

2. Mel Scott, *The San Francisco Bay Area, a Metropolis in Perspective* (Berkeley: University of California Press, 1959), 168.

3. Mitchell Schwarzer, *San Francisco, Architecture of the San Francisco Bay Area* (San Francisco: William Stout Publishers, 2007), 26.

4. Sally B. Woodbridge, et. al., *San Francisco Architecture: The Illustrative Guide to Over 1,000 of the Best Buildings, Parks, and Public Artworks in the Bay Area* (San Francisco: Chronicle Books, 1992), 172.

5. Susan Dinkelspiel Cerny, *Architectural Guidebook to San Francisco and the Bay Area* (Layton, UT: Gibbs Smith Publisher, 2007), 98.

6. Richard Brandi, *St. Francis Wood* (San Francisco: Outside Lands Media, 2012).

7. Greg Gaar and Ryder W. Miller, *San Francisco: A Natural History* (Charleston, SC: Arcadia Publishing, 2006), 76.

8. Robert E. Stewart, Jr., and Mary Frances Stewart, *Adolph Sutro: A Biography* (Berkeley, CA: Howell-North, 1962), 171. See also Mae Silver, *Rancho San Miguel* (San Francisco: Ord Street Press, 2001), 59–76.

9. Richard Brandi, "Farms, Fire and Forest: Adolph Sutro and Development 'West of Twin Peaks,'" *The Argonaut: Journal of the San Francisco Museum and Historical Society*, 14:1, Summer 2003.

10. In a speech given in 1932, Duncan McDuffie said that he scouted the property with Louis Titus, C.C. Young, Perry T. Tompkins, and Elmer I. Rowell in March 1912. He credited the group with the concept for St. Francis Wood.

11. Written by Duncan McDuffie December 11, 1932.

12. *Claremont Country Houses and Their Gardens*, Berkeley Architectural Heritage Association, 2000.

13. Marc A. Weiss, *The Rise of the Community Builders: The American Real Estate Industry and Urban Land Planning* (Washington, DC: BeardBooks, 2002; reprinted by Columbia University Press, 1987), 1–5, 58.

14. Joan Draper, "John Galen Howard" in Robert Winter, *Toward a Simpler Way of Life: The Arts and Crafts Architects of California* (Berkeley: University of California Press, 1991), 38.

15. "Largest Deal in Home Lands, Sutro Property All Acquired by Company That Plans for Great Residence Park," *San Francisco Chronicle*, May 4, 1912; advertisement, *San Francisco Chronicle,* October 12, 1912.

16. Letter from Duncan McDuffie to Olmsted Bothers, April 6, 1914, 0037 Library of Congress.

17. Sally B. Woodbridge, *John Galen Howard and the University of California: The Design of a Great Public University Campus* (Berkeley: University of California Press, 2002), 19.

18. Joan Draper, "John Galen Howard" in Robert Winter, *Toward a Simpler Way of Life: The Arts and Crafts Architects of California* (Berkeley: University of California Press, 1991), 32.

19. *San Francisco Chronicle*, January 25, 1913.

20. *San Francisco Chronicle*, March 20, 1921.

21. Interview with Nancy Mettier, May 13, 2011.

22. Conversation with Arleyn Levee, January 18, 2012.

23. Elmer I. Rowell notes to Duncan McDuffie 1932; Bancroft Library holdings.

24. Correspondence between Duncan McDuffie and the Olmsted brothers, March 8, 1916, Library of Congress Olmsted Associates Records, MSS52571, January 29, 1917.

25. Letter to Duncan McDuffie from Olmsted Brothers, dated April 18, 1914, referencing plans 99, 100, and 101.

26. Letter to Olmsted Brothers from Duncan McDuffie, dated June 19, 1916; Rachel Gordon, "St. Francis Circle's Intricate Traffic Ballet," *San Francisco Chronicle*, February 2, 2009.

27. *San Francisco Chronicle,* December 20, 1913.

28. *San Francisco Chronicle,* September 18, 1915. The ad does not mention the address or any details about the houses.

29. From data provided by St. Francis Wood Home Association. Does not include lot sales where no house was constructed.

30. *San Francisco Chronicle*, September 11, 1919.

31. *Architect & Engineer,* June 1919, page 50.

32. *San Francisco Chronicle*, September 25, 1920. At the same time, Mason-Duffie advertised a house for sale in the older section for $16,000. (*San Francisco Chronicle,* August 20,1920.) The house was at 24 San Benito Way. It's not clear if this was a resale or new house.

33. *San Francisco Chronicle*, January 28, 1922; *San Francisco Chronicle*, February 11, 1922.

34. "St. Francis Wood Homes," undated brochure in Bancroft Library, Mason-McDuffie collection, Banc Mss 89/12, box 22.

35. *San Francisco Chronicle*, May 6, 1922.

36. *San Francisco Chronicle*, March 25, 1922.

37. *San Francisco Chronicle*, October 12, 1912.

38. Virginia and Lee McAlister, *A Field Guide to American Houses* (New York: Alfred A. Knopf, 2005), 397.

39. This grouping was featured in *American Vitruvius: An Architect's Handbook Of Civic Art* by Werner Hegemann and Elbert Peets in 1922.

40. Robert M. Fogelson, *Bourgeois Nightmares: Suburbia 1870–1930* (New Haven: Yale University Press, 2005), 16.

41. The St. Francis Wood data sheet dated 2005 shows 561 properties.

42. "Procedure of the Approval of Plans," St. Francis Wood Home Association, undated.

43. www.outsidelands.org/gutterson.php.

44. Robert Winter, *Toward a Simpler Way of Life: The Arts & Crafts Architects of California* (Berkeley: University of California Press, 1997), 73.

45. *Ibid.*

46. Sally Woodbridge, 1988, *Bay Area Houses* (Layton, UT: Gibbs Smith, 1988), 10.

47. St. Francis Wood records attribute the design of 70 Terrace Drive to Ballantine (spelled with an "a"). Globlentz helped design 65 San Benito Way, 75 San Lorenzo Way, 60 Santa Monica Way, 70 Santa Monica Way, and 33 Santa Monica Way.

48. In Inge Schaefer Horton's book, *Early Women Architects of the San Francisco Bay Area* (Jefferson, NC: McFarland, 2010), 60, she quotes Dorothy Wormser Goblentz, who worked in Gutterson's office during 1917–18 and 1947–53.

49. Comfort is credited with the designs of 25 St. Francis Blvd, 150 San Fernando Way, 30 San Leandro Way, 70 Santa Monica, 1651 Portola (not extant), and 45 Terrace Drive.

50. In 1925 they designed the Hezlett's Silk Store Building in Berkeley, under contract to Mason-McDuffie for the client, Harry Spiro. Source: Berkeley Architectural Heritage website, www.berkeleyheritage.com accessed April 30, 2011.

51. *Architect & Engineer*, December 26, 1926.

52. Richard W. Longstreth, *Julia Morgan, Architect* (Berkeley Architectural Heritage Association, 1977), 9.

53. "Street Planting at St. Francis Wood," Olmsted Brothers, Landscape Architects, November 15, 1916, National Park Service, Frederick Law Olmsted National Historic Site.

54. Monthly letter to St. Francis Wood residents by Herbert B. Holt, president, July 24, 1933.

55. *Map Showing the Widening of Portola Drive from West Portal Ave to Sydney Way*, July 1963, City and County of San Francisco, Department of Public Works, Bureau of Engineering, Division of Surveys and Mapping.

56. *Capital Improvement Program for Fiscal Years 1953/1954 to 1958/1959* (San Francisco Department of City Planning, 1953), 44.

57. Interview with Carolyn Squeri, April 23, 2011; interview with Phyllis Charlton, May 6, 2011.

58. *San Francisco Chronicle*, February 7, 2004.

Chapter 7

1. *San Francisco Chronicle*, January 4, 1921.

2. *San Francisco Chronicle*, June 21, 1904; *San Francisco Chronicle*, January 14, 1906.

3. Daniella Thompson, "Mark Daniels Excelled in Developing and Marketing Scenic Beauty," Berkeley Heritage website. http://berkeleyheritage.com/eastbay_then-now/mark_daniels.html.

4. *San Francisco Call*, September 14, 1912.

5. *San Francisco Call*, September 18, 1912.

6. *San Francisco Call*, November 16, 1912.

7. *San Francisco Call*, September 21, 1912; *San Francisco Call*, November 16, 1912.

8. *Building and Engineering News*, 17:1, March 1917, 16.

9. www.askart.com/artist/Orestes_Stefano_Sarsi/11006798/Orestes_Stefano_Sarsi.aspx.

10. *San Francisco Call*, July 13, 1912.

11. *Homes & Grounds* (San Francisco: J.A. Drummond, Publisher), March 1916.

12. *San Francisco Chronicle*, May 29, 1915.

13. Undated brochure, c. 1913 by Newell-Murdoch Co., 30 Montgomery, San Francisco; *San Francisco Call*, October 19, 1912.

14. Newell-Murdoch Co., Undated brochure.

15. *San Francisco Chronicle*, September 27, 1913.

16. *Homes & Grounds* (San Francisco: J.A. Drummond, Publisher), March 1916.

17. *San Francisco Chronicle*, March 8, 1919. Eventually, the city took responsibility for the sewers, and the Pacific Gas & Electric Company took over the street light system.

18. *San Francisco Chronicle*, April 3, 1920; April 24, 1926.

19. *San Francisco Chronicle*, January 8, 1921; *San Francisco Chronicle*, March 1, 1921; *San Francisco Chronicle*, May 15, 1963.

20. California Historical Society *San Francisco Chronicle* clipping files.

21. California Historical Society *San Francisco Chronicle* clipping files; *San Francisco Chronicle*, October 30, 1920; September 20, 1924; April 2, 1926; July 12, 1930; and April 1, 1949; City of San Francisco Planning Department, *Sunset District Residential Builders, 1925–50*, Historic Context Statement, 2013, 62.

22. 275 Pacheco (APN 2862-003) is not attributed to Bernard Maybeck in standard architectural guidebooks, but the building permit filed July 7, 1917, shows the architect as "Maybeck and White, Lick Building." The builder was John M. Bartlett, 565 16th Street, Oakland; and the owner was Mrs. Dahlia H. Loeb, 639 Masonic Avenue, San Francisco. The same information is contained in *Building and Engineering News*, July 11, 1917, 18.

23. *San Francisco Examiner*, January 11, 1971 repeats the legend.

24. Forest Hill Association Minutes May 5, 1919; July 2, 1919; July 7, 1919; February 2, 1920; February 23, 1920, courtesy Will Connolly and Harold A. Wright.

25. Jacqueline Proctor, *Bay Area Beauty: The Artistry of Harold G. Stoner, Architect* (San Francisco: Blurb Inc., 2011), 28.

26. *San Francisco Call*, May 11, 1912, 20.

27. *San Francisco Chronicle*, June 5, 1932.

28. *San Francisco Call*, October 10, 1912.

29. *San Francisco Chronicle*, May 4, 1918.

30. *San Francisco Chronicle*, October 30, 1920.

31. *San Francisco Chronicle*, August 2, 1924.

32. *San Francisco Chronicle*, April 11,1921.

33. *San Francisco Chronicle*, March 1, 1922.

34. *San Francisco Chronicle,* May 19, 1965.

35. *San Francisco Chronicle*, August 2, 1924; *San Francisco Examiner*, August 21, 1924.

36. *Homes and Grounds*, October 1926.

37. Jacqueline Proctor, *Bay Area Beauty: The Artistry of Harold G. Stoner, Architect* (San Francisco: Blurb Inc., 2011), 158.

38. http://mtdavidson.org/great-depression/ Accessed February 2, 2015.

39. Western Neighborhoods Project website: http://www.outsidelands.org/commodore-sloat.php, accessed February 2, 2015.

40. http://www.outsidelands.org/commodore-sloat.php.

41. Susan Cerny Dinkelspiel, *An Architectural Guidebook to San Francisco and the Bay Area* (Salt Lake City: Gibbs Smith, 2007), 99.

Chapter 8

1. "Bank Acts as Santa Claus," *Coast Banker and Pacific Banker and California Banker*, Vol. 12, 1914; "Bank Control Sold," *Insurance and Investment News*, Vols. 13–14, 1914.

2. *San Francisco Chronicle*, February 7, 1915.

3. *San Francisco Call*, November 27, 1906.

4. *San Francisco Chronicle*, October 15, 1915; *San Francisco Blue Book*, 1913.

5. Frank Morton Todd, "The Story of the Exposition: Being the Official History…" Vol. 1. (New York: G.P. Putman's Sons, 1921) https://archive.org/details/storyofexpositio02todd/page/n13/mode/2up

6. *San Francisco Chronicle*, March 17, 1918.

7. *San Francisco Call*, January 10, 1898.

8. *San Francisco Chronicle,* May 28, 1911.

9. *San Francisco Chronicle,* December 29,1911.

10. *San Francisco Chronicle*, December 31, 1910; *San Francisco Chronicle*, September 30, 1916.

11. *San Francisco Chronicle,* September 1, 1910; *San Francisco Chronicle,* April 12, 1911.

12. *San Francisco Chronicle*, March 4, 1916.

13. *Army Register*, 1947, https://www.fold3.com/image/312834340?terms=%22emile%20p.%20antonovich%22.

14. Bridget Maley, "Classically Inspired-and Connected," *New Fillmore* Magazine, October 30, 2015, http://newfillmore.com/2016/11/30/an-architects-classic-but-understated-homes/.

15. *San Francisco Chronicle*, May 6, 1916.

16. *San Francisco Chronicle*, August 8,1916.

17. *San Francisco Chronicle*, November 17, 1918; *Building and Engineering News*, Vol. 19.

18. *San Francisco Chronicle*, March 18, 1923; *Oakland Chronicle*, September 26, 1925.

19. https://search.ancestry.co.uk/cgi-bin/sse.doperty.

20. files.usgwarchives.net/ca/yolo/bios/merritt600gbs.txt.

21. J. M Guinn, *History of the State of California*

Biographical Record of the Sacramento Valley (Chicago: Chapman Publishing Co, 1906), 1645.

22. *Coast Banker* magazine, July 1914.

23. *San Francisco Chronicle,* January 31, 1927.

24. *San Francisco Chronicle,* May 2, 1925.

25. Undated written account by Anne Hawkins Cotton, transcript of oral history by Sidney Hawkins William, March 15, 1987. Box 1, Charles Hawkins files at the San Francisco History Center, San Francisco Public Library, uncatalogued.

26. *Ibid.*

27. *Ibid.*

28. *San Francisco Chronicle*, June 27, 1914.

29. *San Francisco Chronicle*, June 20, 1914.

30. Charles Hawkins files at the San Francisco History Center, San Francisco Public Library, Box 1, uncatalogued.

31. The 1915 Sanborn maps show no streets or buildings between Vasquez and Portola.

32. *San Francisco Call*, February 20, 1916.

33. *Ibid.*

34. Charles Hawkins files at the San Francisco History Center, San Francisco Public Library, Box 1, uncatalogued.

35. *San Francisco Chronicle,* November 29, 1942; www.naval-history.net/WW2UScasaaDB-USMCbyNameR.htm

36. Bernard Maybeck collection, Environmental Design Archives, University of California, Berkeley, 1965-1, Box 4/Folder III, 12 "Correspondence Office, 1922–1946."

37. *San Francisco Chronicle,* March 27, 1902; *San Francisco Chronicle,* March 10, 1930; *San Francisco Chronicle,* November 11, 1930; and *San Francisco Chronicle,* February 6, 1937; Mrs. John A. Logan, *The Part Taken by Women in American History* (Wilmington, Delaware: The Perry-Nalle Publishing Company, 1912); https://www.ahgp.org/women/elizabeth_gerberding_1857_1902.html.

38. *San Francisco Chronicle*, March 26, 1932.

39. Charles Hawkins files at the San Francisco History Center, San Francisco Public Library, Box 1, uncatalogued.

Chapter 9

1. https://www.geni.com/people/Harry-Allen/6000000000544338531.

2. *Railroad Gazetteer*, 19:6, 1881; H.B. Allen, "How Allen and Company Have Developed 'Sea Cliff'" in *National Real Estate Journal*, Vol. 23, 1922.

3. Windsor Terrace ad, *San Francisco Chronicle*, January 25, 1915.

4. *San Francisco Chronicle*, March 28, 1914.

5. According to David Parry, Farr designed 1634, 1648, and 1651 Eighth Avenue. Some of the houses on Eighth and Ninth avenues are similar in style; Farr may have also designed 1683, 1684, and 1692 Eighth Avenue and 1636, 1650, 1660, and 1680 Ninth Avenue. Another respected architect, Henry A. Schulze of Oakland, may have designed at least five houses.

6. *San Francisco Chronicle*, February 24, 1914.

7. Windsor Terrace ad, *San Francisco Chronicle*, October 25, 1914.

8. Real estate agents and historian David Parry, "Pacific Heights Architects #23—Albert Farr," September 2004. https://www.classicsfproperties.com/Pages/Architecture.aspx.

9. According to Sanborn maps.

10. The size of a Spanish league varied, but 1 league is a little more than about 4,000 acres. Sutro's Rancho San Miguel was originally 1 league.

11. Paul W. Gates, "The Land Business of Thomas O. Larkin," *California Historical Quarterly*, 54:4 (Winter 1975), 323–44, published by University of California Press in association with the California Historical Society.

12. ICF International. *Historical Resources Evaluation for 726 El Camino Del Mar, San Francisco* (ICF 0211.14), prepared for the City of San Francisco Planning Department, March 2014.

13. California Historical Society, *San Francisco Chronicle* clipping file collection: *San Francisco Chronicle*, August 30, 1895; *San Francisco Chronicle*, October 1, 1904; November 26, 1905; August 6, 1908; October 29, 1909; April 5, 1913; and September 26, 1914.

14. *Homes and Grounds,* October 1916, 293–313.

15. *San Francisco Chronicle*, September 27, 1912.

16. Sea Cliff is sometimes spelled as one word, Seacliff.

17. *Homes and Grounds,* October 1916, 293–313.

18. *San Francisco Examiner,* November 6, 1926.

19. *San Francisco Chronicle*, September 20, 1922.

20. *Homes and Grounds,* October 1916, 293–313.

21. Marlea Graham, "Mark Daniels: Engineer & Architect, Part II," *Eden: Journal of the California Garden & Landscape Historic Society,* 10:1, Spring 2007, 5.

22. www.nps.gov/goga/learn/historyculture/upload/Property_El_Camino_del_Mar_sr_2014_v2.pdf.

23. *San Francisco Chronicle,* September 27, 1912.

24. *Architect and Engineer,* April 1918, Vol. 53, 108.

25. *Homes and Grounds,* October 1916, 293–313.

26. https://www.nps.gov/goga/learn/historyculture/vestiges-china-beach.htm.

27. *San Francisco Chronicle*, June 25, 1921.

28. *The Building Review* XXI:3, March 1922, 32.

29. H.B. Allen, "How Allen and Company Have Developed 'Sea Cliff,'" *The National Real Estate Journal,* Vol. 23, 1922.

30. "The Belvedere Land Company—Celebrating 125 Years," *Marin County Historical Society Newsletter,* October 1980, 42:2, Fall 2015.

31. California Historical Society, *San Francisco Chronicle* clipping file collection.

Chapter 10

1. *San Francisco Chronicle*, January 16, 1909.

2. *San Francisco Chronicle*, January 8, 1897.

3. Lewis Francis Byington, *The History of San Francisco* (Chicago: S.J. Clarke Publishing, 1931), 389.

4. *San Francisco Chronicle*, September 30, 1910.

5. *San Francisco Chronicle*, September 21,1937.

6. *San Francisco Chronicle*, April 13, 1907.

7. *San Francisco Chronicle*, April 20, 1929; "Report of Marsden Manson to the Mayor and Committee on Reconstruction on the Improvements Now Necessary to Execute and an Estimate of the Cost of the Same," 1906: https://oac.cdlib.org/view?docId=hb929006xs&brand=oac4&doc.view=entire_text.

8. "San Mateo County State Road Assured," *San Francisco Call,* February 23, 1913.

9. *San Francisco Chronicle*, August 8, 1905.

10. Joanne Garrison, *Burlingame Centennial 1908–2008* (Burlingame, CA: Burlingame Historical Society, 2007), 28.

11. *San Francisco Chronicle*, October 6, 1910.

12. *San Francisco Chronicle*, December 22, 1914.

13. "*San Francisco Chronicle*, April 20, 1929; Nion Tucker Estate Sold," *San Mateo Times*, March 14, 1951.

14. *San Mateo Times*, April 13, 1929.

15. *San Francisco Chronicle*, April 21, 1929.

16. History of the Berkeley Schools...1918: https://books.google.com/books?id=A3hEAQAAMAAJ&pg=PA142&lpg=PA142&dq=berkeley+%22walter+hoag%22&source=bl&ots=FJ77z9WLmr&sig=aKw4qs4eA3YJ47andGqMkVFzInc&hl=en&sa=X&ved=2ahUKEwidobP8tYTfAhXIlFQKHeKFB3YQ6AEwAHoECAcQAQ#v=onepage&q=berkeley%20%22walter%20hoag%22&f=false.

17. *Spring Valley Water Co. V. City of San Francisco*: https://archive.org/stream/springvalleywate01spri/springvalleywate01spri_djvu.txt.

18. *San Francisco Chronicle*, July 22, 1905.

19. *San Francisco Call*, June 22, 1906.

20. *Spring Valley Water Co. V. City of San Francisco*: https://archive.org/stream/springvalleywate01spri/springvalleywate01spri_djvu.txt.

21. *U.C. Register*, 1899: https://books.google.com/books?id=PhVJAQAAMAAJ&pg=PA350&lpg=PA350&dq=san+francisco+%22william+am+hoag%22&source=bl&ots=WLN0Mu63XV&sig=Mnf49vf2pRPqc7CPqswuCvPnfyA&hl=en&sa=X&ved=2ahUKEwjFneuOjt3eAhUHh1QKHWauDPgQ6AEwAXoECAEQAQ#v=onepage&q=san%20francisco%20%22william%20burnham%20hoag%22&f=false.

22. "Wanted," *Mining and Scientific Press*, June 24, 1899: https://books.google.com/books?id=H5Q5AQAAMAAJ&pg=PA673&lpg=PA673&dq=san+francisco+%22w.+b.+hoag%22&source=bl&ots=CLFFJHj7j_&sig=mBq1j7h3zVjzh6Jo5Wf7f4L7GFc&hl=en&sa=X&ved=2ahUKEwiTgtD7x_3eAhWoHzQIHdkUB9AQ6AEwDnoECAgQAQ#v=onepage&q=san%20francisco%20%22w.%20b.%20hoag%22&f=false.

23. "William B. Hoag" obituary, *San Francisco Chronicle*, July 21, 1955.

24. *San Francisco Call*, April 7, 1912.

25. *San Francisco Chronicle*, June 22, 1912.

26. Aptos Beach and County Club ad, May 17, 1925; *San Francisco Chronicle*, December 4, 1920; *San Francisco Chronicle*, November 21, 1925.

27. *San Francisco Chronicle*, April 16, 1927.

28. At that time, it was called Bakers Beach; now it is Baker Beach.

29. *San Francisco Examiner*, March 27, 1910; *San Francisco Examiner*, January 5, 1910.

30. The author found no information about the Boston Investment Company, except that it was created by Lyon & Hoag.

31. www.foundsf.org/index.php?title=Work_on_Land_%26_Water,_1880-1920: Archives of the West ORBIS Cascade Alliance: archiveswest.orbiscascade.org/ark:/80444/xv14450#IDMHB2ANMLXV1EMSBIUR4LJCVZOI31TWIWRRJQ5ERGOT4LCMUOB2P.

32. *San Francisco Call*, April 23, 1910.

33. *San Francisco Examiner*, April 14, 1910.

34. *San Francisco Chronicle*, January 7, 1911.

35. Patrick McGrew, "Neighborhoods and Innovators: An Architect's View of San Francisco's Subdivisions Before 1915," *The Argonaut: Journal of the San Francisco Museum and Historical Society*. 15:2 (Winter 2004).

36. "Real Estate Transactions," *San Francisco Call*, May 26, 1901.

37. *San Francisco Chronicle*, October 7, 1903.

38. *San Francisco Chronicle*, January 6, 1906.

39. *San Francisco Chronicle*, October 25, 1903.

40. *San Francisco Chronicle*, April 30, 1910.

41. Ansel Adams and Mary Street Alinder, *Ansel Adams: An Autobiography* (Oxford: Oxford University Press, 1985).

42. *Homes and Grounds*, March 1916.

43. Philip W. Alexander and Charles P. Hamm, *History of San Mateo County* (Burlingame, CA: Press of Burlingame Pub. Co., 1916), 73–74.

44. *San Francisco Call*, June 8, 1912.

45. Ashbury Terrace is situated at the confluence of the Flint Tract Homestead, Park Lane Tract, and the Western Addition. It is just north of the boundary of Rancho San Miguel.

46. *San Francisco Call*, July 28, 1898; *San Francisco Chronicle*, June 18, 1914.

47. Patrick McGrew, "Neighborhoods and Innovators: An Architect's View of San Francisco's Subdivisions Before 1915," *The Argonaut: Journal of The San Francisco Museum and Historical Society*, 15:2 (Winter 2004).

48. *San Francisco Chronicle*, January 31, 1914.

49. *San Francisco Chronicle*, January 25, 1913.

50. https://www.nps.gov/goga/learn/historyculture/vestiges-lincoln-park.htm.

51. *San Francisco Chronicle*, February 7, 1914.

52. David Perry, "Theo S. Boehm Architect 1889–1948," real estate fact sheet, June 2016, www.classicsfproperties.com/Pages/Architecture.aspx.

53. *San Francisco Chronicle*, March 28, 1914.

54. *San Francisco Chronicle*, April 10, 1914.

55. *San Francisco Chronicle*, October 21, 1916.

56. *San Francisco Chronicle*, January 15, 1919.

57. Inge Schaefer Horton, *Early Women Architects of the San Francisco Bay Area* (Jefferson, NC: McFarland, 2010), 298.

58. *San Francisco Chronicle*, November 16, 1918.

59. *San Francisco Chronicle*, December 3, 1921.

60. *San Francisco Chronicle*, March 22, 1924.

61. *San Francisco Chronicle*, November 28, 1931.

62. *San Francisco Chronicle*, December 5, 1931.

63. *San Francisco Chronicle*, April 2, 1932.

64. *San Francisco Chronicle*, March 19, 1932.

65. Mary Brown, *Sunset District Residential Builders, 1925–1950 Historic Context Statement*, San Francisco Planning Department, April 3, 2013.

66. *San Francisco Chronicle*, June 3, 1933.

67. Mary Brown, *Sunset District Residential Builders, 1925–1950* Historic Context Statement. San Francisco Planning Department, April 3, 2013.

68. *San Francisco Examiner*, September 30, 1939.

Chapter 11

1. The streets have been renamed several times: Palm Avenue was originally Mears Street, then Michigan Avenue, and finally Palm Avenue. Jordan Avenue was once Merrifield Street, Commonwealth was Chase Street, and Euclid Street was Richmond Avenue.

2. *San Francisco Chronicle*, November 14, 1890; *San Francisco Chronicle*, January 1, 1891.

3. *Daily Alta California*, June 2, 1891.

4. *San Francisco Chronicle*, June 22, 1895.

5. Advertisement in the 1894 Handy block book.

6. *San Francisco Chronicle*, April 9, 1914; communication with John Freeman, August 20, 2014.

7. *San Francisco Chronicle*, October 29, 1904; *San Francisco Chronicle*, April 10, 1906.

8. *San Francisco Chronicle*, April 8, 1905.

9. *San Francisco Chronicle*, September 28, 1907; *San Francisco Chronicle*, October 6, 1907.

10. Woodruff Minor, *A Home in Alameda* (Alameda, CA: Alameda Museum, 2009).

11. www.findagrave.com/cgi-bin/fg.cgi?page=gr&GRid=52963598; John Henry Brown, *History of Dallas County, Texas from 1837 to 1887* (Dallas: Milligan, Cornett & Farnham, 1887); Greta Dutcher and Stephen Rowland, *Images of America: Alameda* (Charleston, SC: Arcadia Publishing, 2009), 26. Helen O'Brien-Sheehan, "Old Vedanta Temple," *Guidelines: Newsletter for San Francisco City Guides and Sponsors*; "Report of Department E—Lands and Buildings," *Preliminary Report Concerning the Financial Operations by the San Francisco Relief and Red Cross*, March, 19, 1907, 70.

12. *San Francisco Chronicle*, October 6, 1907.

13. *San Francisco Chronicle*, September 28, 1907; *San Francisco Chronicle*, October 6, 1907.

14. *San Francisco Call*, May 6, 1910.

15. *San Francisco Chronicle*, November 29, 1919.

16. *San Francisco Call*, March 29, 1908; *San Francisco Call*, April 19, 1908; *San Francisco Chronicle*, March 4, 1909; *San Francisco Call*, March 6, 1909; *San Francisco Call*, January 13, 1911.

17. *San Francisco Call,* December 11, 1910.

18. *San Francisco Chronicle,* May 20, 1911; *San Francisco Chronicle,* December 7, 1912.

19. *San Francisco Chronicle,* September 8, 1910.

20. *San Francisco Chronicle,* March 7, 1914.

21. *San Francisco Chronicle,* June 13, 1914, *San Francisco Chronicle*; September 11, 1915.

22. *San Francisco Call,* March 18, 1911.

23. *San Francisco Chronicle* March 14, 1952; *San Francisco Examiner,* March 14, 1954.

24. https://stgregorysf.org/about-st-gregory-2/.

25. *San Francisco Call,* October 16, 1909.

26. Conversation with John Freeman, December 2019.

27. *San Francisco Examiner,* January 22, 1910; *San Francisco Call,* November 11, 1911.

28. *San Francisco Call,* December 19, 1910.

29. Much of this section is based on Woody LaBounty, *Ingleside Terraces: San Francisco Racetrack to Residence Park* (San Francisco: Outside Lands Media, 2012).

30. *San Francisco Chronicle,* January 28, 1910.

31. *San Francisco Call,* November 11, 1911.

32. The Forest Hill and St. Francis Wood residence parks were filed after Ingleside Terraces.

33. City engineer O'Shaughnessy would have undoubtedly approved this design, but he was not appointed until September 1912.

34. *San Francisco Chronicle,* November 4, 1906; City Directory, 1912; *San Francisco Chronicle,* April 19, 1939.

35. *San Francisco Call,* May 25, 1912.

36. Woody LaBounty, *Ingleside Terraces; San Francisco Racetrack to Residence Park* (San Francisco: Outside Lands Media, 2011), 70.

37. *San Francisco Call,* February 23, 1913; *San Francisco Chronicle,* August 31, 1913.

38. Woody LaBounty, *Ingleside Terraces; San Francisco Racetrack to Residence Park* (San Francisco: Outside Lands Media, 2011).

39. Charles Henry Holt," *San Francisco Bay Region,* Vol. 3, 1924.

40. *Ukiah Republican Press,* November 15, 1922; *Ukiah Republican Press,* February 21, 1923.

41. *Ukiah Dispatch Democrat,* September 10, 1926.

42. *San Francisco Chronicle* October 14, 1916.

43. *San Francisco News,* January 3,1952.

44. Transcript of an Interview with George R. Nelson, Penny de Paoli, Judith Waldhorn, Gary Kray, and Mrs. George Nelson, Victorian Architectural Collection compiled by Judith Lynch Waldhorn, Ephemera Collection, San Francisco History Center, San Francisco Public Library, August 31, 1974.

45. Judith Waldhorn Lynch, "Draft Notes: Interview with George Nelson," October 8, 1974. (Notes on file at San Francisco Architectural Heritage, Fernando Nelson file.)

46. Transcript of an Interview with George R. Nelson, Penny de Paoli, Judith Waldhorn, Gary Kray, and Mrs. George Nelson, Victorian Architectural Collection compiled by Judith Lynch

Waldhorn, Ephemera Collection, San Francisco History Center, San Francisco Public Library, August 31, 1974.

47. John Freeman, Fernando Nelson Builder, *Western Neighborhoods Project Member Newsletter,* Summer 2007.

48. Richard Brandi interview with William A. Nelson Jr. (born 1925), son of William A. Nelson, and grandson of Fernando Nelson, January 20, 2007, in the home of William Nelson, Novato CA.

49. Draft transcript of an interview with George R. Nelson, Penny de Paoli, Judith Waldhorn, Gary Kray, Mrs. George Nelson, Victorian Architectural Collection compiled by Judith Lynch Waldhorn, Ephemera Collection, San Francisco History Center, San Francisco Public Library, August 31, 1974.

50. *San Francisco Call,* December 3, 1897; *San Francisco Chronicle,* April 26,1913.

51. Much of this section comes from Inge Horton, "Fernando Nelson and the Creation of Parkway Terrace" www.outsidelands.org/parkway_terrace_jewel.php.

52. Communication with architectural historian James Russiello, 2019.

53. *San Francisco Chronicle,* February 19, 1916.

54. *San Francisco Examiner,* June 4, 1916.

55. Interview on January 20, 2007 with William A. Nelson Jr. (born 1925), son of William A. Nelson and grandson of Fernando Nelson. Interview with Richard Brandi held in the home of William Nelson, Novato CA.

Chapter 12

1. The macadamized road was an early attempt at paving, named after its inventor, Scottish engineer John Loudon McAdam. Anita Day Hubbard, *Cities Within the City*, typescript of *San Francisco Bulletin* columns at the San Francisco History Archives, San Francisco Public Library, August to November 1924, 63; Jean Kortum, *The West Side of Twin Peaks*, unpublished manuscript, 1994; Gladys Hansen, *San Francisco Almanac* (San Francisco: Chronicle Books, 1995), 380.

2. *Daily Alta California*, February 25, 1867.

3. Michael Corbett, *Corbett Heights (Western Part of Eureka Valley) Historic Context Statement,* May 11, 2017. *San Francisco Chronicle,* October 27, 1902.

4. *San Francisco Chronicle,* March 6, 1909.

5. *San Francisco Chronicle,* May 24, 1908.

6. *San Francisco Chronicle,* October 9, 1909.

7. *San Francisco Call,* June, 28, 1913.

8. *San Francisco Examiner,* March 29, 1914.

9. *San Francisco Examiner,* July 28, 1928.

10. City Directory 1928; *San Francisco Chronicle,* February 14, 1928; *San Francisco Chronicle,* February 3, 1929.

11. *San Francisco Chronicle,* September 14, 1913.

12. *San Francisco Examiner,* December 21, 1913.

13. *San Francisco Chronicle,* August 15, 1914.

Chapter 13

1. Marlea Graham, "Mark Roy Daniels (1881–1952), Engineer & Architect (Part I–IV)" in *Eden: Journal of the California Garden & Landscape History Society,* Winter 2006–Fall 2007 issues.

2. *San Francisco Call* January 25, 1913.

3. *San Francisco Examiner*, October 13, 1912.

4. *San Francisco Call,* February 19, 1916.

5. *San Francisco Chronicle,* January 6, 1912.

6. *San Francisco Chronicle*, June 12, 1915.

7. *San Francisco Chronicle*, March 17, 1917.

8. https://www.history.com/news/americas-patriotic-victory-gardens.

9. *San Francisco Chronicle* June 1,1919.

10. Ethan Carr, *Wilderness by Design: Landscape Architecture and the National Park Service* (Lincoln, NE: University of Nebraska Press, 1998), 73–74; R. Bryce Workman, *National Park Service Uniforms: In Search of an Identity, 1872–1920* (Harpers Ferry, WV [U.S. Dept. of the Interior]: National Park Service History Collection, 1994), 29–32.

11. De Haro came to California in 1821. He was comandante of the Presidio and the first alcalde of Yerba Buena (now San Francisco). He died intestate on January 1, 1849, leaving seven heirs who proceeded to sell their fractional holdings, leading to confused titles and lawsuits. See also Jean Kortum, "The West Side of Twin Peaks," unpublished manuscript, 1994, 19. From the collection of Richard Brandi.

12. Laurence H. Shoup and Suzanne Baker, *Cultural Resource Overview Lake Merced Transport*, San Francisco Water Management Program, January 1981, 14.

13. *Cultural Resource Overview Lake Merced Transport*, quoting Dwinelle.

14. *Ibid.*, 32.

15. *Ibid.*, 31.

16. *Ibid.*, 52.

17. Eden: *Journal of the California Garden & Landscape History Society,* 10:1, Spring 2007.

18. Mark Daniels, "A Residence Park on the Site of the Panama-Pacific Exposition," *The Journal of the American Institute of Architects*, V:4, April 1917.

19. Marc A. Weiss, "The Real Estate Industry and the Politics of Zoning in San Francisco, 1914–1928" in *Planning Perspectives*, 3 (1988), 311–24.

20. Mark Daniels, "A Residence Park on the Site of the Panama-Pacific Exposition" *The Journal of the American Institute of Architects*, V:4, April 1917.

21. *Ibid.*

22. *Ibid.*

23. *Los Angeles Herald*, November 3, 1916.

24. *San Francisco Examiner*, October 22, 1916.

25. *San Francisco Examiner*, March 31, 1917.

26. Mark Daniels, "A Residence Park on the Site of the Panama-Pacific Exposition," *The Journal of the American Institute of Architects*, V:4, April 1917.

27. *San Francisco Examiner,* April 19, 1917; *San Francisco Chronicle*, April 19, 1917; *San Francisco Chronicle*, October 31, 1918.

28. Neal Hotelling, "The Forgotten Landscape Engineer of Pebble Beach," Del Monte Forest Property Owners website. www.dmfpo.org/stories/dmf_origins5_engineer.pdf.

29. *Santa Cruz Sentinel,* January 20, 1952, 6.

30. *San Francisco Chronicle*, January 17, 1925.

31. Stephen Tobriner, *Bracing for Disaster: Earthquake-Resistant Architecture and Engineering in San Francisco, 1838–1933* (Berkeley, CA: Heyday Books, 2006), 268.

32. Melvin H. Schuelz, *A Chesley Bonestell Space Art Chronology* (Parkland, FL: Universal Publishers/uPublish.com, 1999).

33. www.lib.berkeley.edu/news_events/bridge/up032.html.

Bibliography

Akimoto, Fukuo. "California Garden Suburbs: St. Francis Wood and Palos Verdes." *Journal of Urban Design*. 12:1 (February 2007): 43–72.

Akimoto, Fukuo, and Charles H. Cheney. In *Planning Perspectives*. (July 18, 2003): 253–75.

Alexander, James Beach, and James Lee Height. *San Francisco: Building the Dream City*. San Francisco: Scottwall Associates, 2002.

Alexander, Philip W., and Charles P. Hamm. *History of San Mateo County*. Burlingame, CA: Press of Burlingame Pub. Co. (1916).

Archer, John. "Country and City in the American Romantic Suburb." *Journal of the Society of Architectural Historians* 42:2 (May 1983): 139–56.

Beitiks, Katherine O. *Westwood Park: Building a Bungalow Neighborhood in San Francisco.* (self-published 2017), ISBN 978-0-692-84435-0.

Blackford, Mansel G. *The Lost Dream: Businessmen and City Planning on the Pacific Coast, 1890–1920*. Columbus: Ohio State University Press, 1993.

Brandi, Richard. "Farms, Fire and Forest: Adolph Sutro and Development West of Twin Peaks." *The Argonaut: Journal of the San Francisco Museum and Historical Society* 14:1 (Summer 2003).

_____. *San Francisco's St. Francis Wood*. San Francisco: Outside Lands Media, 2012.

_____. *San Francisco's West Portal Neighborhoods*. Charleston, SC: Arcadia Books, 2005.

Brandi, Richard, and Woody LaBounty. *San Francisco's Parkside District: 1905–1957* Historic Context Statement, 2008.

Burnham, Daniel, with Edward H. Bennett. *Report on a Plan for San Francisco*. Berkeley: Urban Books (1971) (originally written 1905).

Cerny, Susan Dinkelspiel. *Architectural Guidebook to San Francisco and the Bay Area*. Layton, UT: Gibbs Smith Publisher, 2007.

"Charles Henry Holt." *San Francisco Bay Region* 3 (1924).

"Claremont Country Houses and Their Gardens." Berkeley Architectural Heritage Association (2000).

Collins, Christine Crasemann. *Werner Hegemann and the Search for Universal Urbanism*. New York: W. W. Norton, 2005.

Corbett, Michael. *Corbett Heights (Western Part of Eureka Valley)* Historic Context Statement (May 11, 2017).

Daniels, Mark. "Forest Hill—A Residence Park." *Homes & Grounds* 1:3 (March 1916).

Delehanty, Randolph. *In the Victorian Style*. San Francisco: Chronicle Books, 1991.

Dewart, Marion Louis Stireman. "South San Francisco 75th Anniversary." *Soroptimist International of Northern San Mateo County* (1983).

Dinkelspiel, Susan Cerny. *An Architectural Guidebook to San Francisco and the Bay Area*. Salt Lake City, UT: Gibbs Smith, 2007.

Draper, Joan. "John Galen Howard." In Robert Winter, *Toward a Simpler Way of Life: The Arts and Crafts Architects of California*. Berkeley: University of California Press, 1991.

Fogelson, Robert M. *Bourgeois Nightmares, Suburbia 1870–1930*. New Haven: Yale University Press, 2005.

Foundation for San Francisco's Architectural Heritage, The. *Splendid Survivors: San Francisco's Downtown Architectural Heritage*. San Francisco: California Living Books, 1979.

Freeman, Richard, et al. *Domestic Architecture of the San Francisco Bay Region*. San Francisco: San Francisco Museum of Art, 1949.

Gaar, Greg, and Miller, Ryder W. *San Francisco: A Natural History*. Charleston, SC: Arcadia Publishing, 2006.

Garrison, Joanne. *Burlingame Centennial 1908–2008*. Burlingame, CA: Burlingame Historical Society, 2007.

Gebhard, David, et al. *Architecture in San Francisco and Northern California*. Salt Lake City: Gibbs-Smith Publisher, 1985.

Gowans, Alan. *The Comfortable House: North American Suburban Architecture, 1890–1930*. Cambridge: MIT Press, 1986.

Graham, Marlea. "Mark Roy Daniels (1881–1952). Engineer & Architect (Parts I–IV)." *Eden: Journal of the California Garden & Landscape History Society* (Winter 2006–Fall 2007).

Gregory, Daniel. *Be It Ever So Humble: The Impact of the Merchant Builder-Land Developer on the Evolution of Housing in the Bay Area 1850–1979*. Berkeley: University of California, 1979.

Gumina, Deanna P. *The Italians of San Francisco 1850–1930*. New York: The Center for Migration Studies of New York, 1978.

Gutterson, Henry H. *The Building Review* XX (August 1921): 24.

Hegemann, Walter, and Elbert Peets. *The American Vitruvius: An Architect's Handbook of Civic Art.* New York: Architecture Book Publishing Co, 1922. (Revised edition, Meyers Jr., Thomas, ed. De Facto Publishing, 2008.)

Hines, Thomas S. *Burnham of Chicago: Architect and Planner.* New York: Oxford University Press, 1974, 174–96.

History of Public Transit in San Francisco 1850–1948. Transportation Technical Committee of the Departments of Public Works, Public Utilities, Police and City Planning, City and County of San Francisco, June 1948.

Horiuchi, Lynne. "Object Lessons in Home Building: Racialized Real Estate Marketing in San Francisco." *Landscape Journal* 26:1 (2007): 61–82.

Horton, Inge Schaefer. *Early Women Architects of the San Francisco Bay Area.* Jefferson, NC: McFarland, 2010.

_____. "A Jewel Restored: Fernando Nelson's House in Parkway Terrace." www.outsidelands.org/parkway_terrace_jewel.php.

Hynding, Alan. *From Frontier to Suburb: The Story of the San Mateo Peninsula.* Belmont, CA: Star Publishing Company, 1894.

Issel, William, and Robert W. Cherny. *San Francisco 1865–1932: Politics, Power and Urban Development.* Berkeley: University of California Press, 1986.

Kahn, Judd. *Imperial San Francisco, Politics and Planning in an American City 1897–1906.* Lincoln: University of Nebraska Press, 1979.

Kirker, Harold. *California's Architectural Frontier.* San Marino, CA: The Henry E. Huntington Library and Art Gallery, 1960. (Reissued 1970 by Russell & Russel, New York.)

Klaus, Susan L. *A Modern Arcadia: Frederick Law Olmsted, Jr., and the Plan for Forest Hills Gardens.* Amherst: University of Massachusetts Press, 2002.

LaBounty, Woody. *Ingleside Terraces: San Francisco Racetrack to Residence Park.* San Francisco: Outside Lands Media, 2012.

Lampl, Elizabeth Jo, and Kimberly P. Williams. *Chevy Chase, a Home in the Nation's Capital.* Crownsville, MD: Maryland Historical Trust Press, 1998, 92–94.

Lieber, Robert, and Sarah Lau, ed. *The Last Great World's Fair: San Francisco's Panama-Pacific International Exposition 1915.* San Francisco: Golden Gate Parks Conservatory, 2004, 20.

Loeb, Carolyn S. *Entrepreneurial Vernacular: Developers' Subdivisions in the 1920s.* Baltimore: Johns Hopkins University Press, 2001.

Longstreth, Richard W. *Julia Morgan, Architect.* Berkeley Architectural Heritage Association, 1977.

_____. *On the Edge of the World: Four Architects in San Francisco at the Turn of the Century.* Cambridge: MIT Press, 1983.

Lotchin, Roger W. "The Darwinian City: The Politics of Urbanization in San Francisco Between the World Wars." *Pacific Historical Review* 48:3 (August 1979).

McAlister, Virginia, and Lee McAlester. *A Field Guide to American Houses.* New York: Alfred A. Knopf, 2005.

McClelland, Linda Flint, et al. *Historic Residential Suburbs in the United States, 1830–1960.* National Park Service, September 2002.

McDuffie, Duncan. "St. Francis Wood," A speech delivered to the residents of St. Francis Wood on December 11, 1932.

McGrew, Patrick. *The Historic Houses of Presidio Terrace.* San Francisco: Friends of Presidio Terrace Association, 1995.

_____. "Neighborhoods and Innovators: An Architect's View of San Francisco's Subdivisions Before 1915." *The Argonaut: Journal of San Francisco Museum and Historical Society.* 15:2 (Winter 2004): 62–79.

Miller, Mervyn. *English Garden Cities: An Introduction.* Swindon, UK: English Heritage, 2010.

Minor, Woodruff. *A Home in Alameda.* Alameda, CA: Alameda Museum, 2009.

Neighborhood Commercial Buildings, 1865–1965 Historic Context Statement, February 17, 2016.

Olmsted, Roger, and T. H. Watkins. *Here Today: San Francisco's Architectural Heritage.* San Francisco: Chronicle Books, 1968.

Oscar, Lewis, *Annals of San Francisco, The.* Berkeley: Howell-North Books, 1966.

_____. *San Francisco: Mission to Metropolis.* Berkeley, CA: Howell-North Books, 1966, 163.

Perles, Anthony. *Inside Muni, Operations of the Municipal Railway.* Glendale, CA: Interurban Press, 1982.

_____. *The People's Railway: The History of the Municipal Railway of San Francisco.* Glendale, CA: Interurban Press, 1981.

Proctor, Jacquie. *Bay Area Beauty: The Artistry of Harold G. Stoner, Architect.* San Francisco: Blurb, 2010.

Ring, Vincent D. "Tunnels and Residential Growth in San Francisco, 1910–38." Master's thesis. University of San Francisco, 1971.

Ryder, David Warren. *Great Citizen: A Biography of William H. Crocker.* San Francisco: Historical Publications, 1962.

San Francisco City and County Department of Public Works, Bureau of Engineering, Division of Surveys and Mapping. *Map Showing the Widening of Portola Drive from West Portal Ave to Sydney Way* (July 1963).

Savage, Charles C. *Architecture of the Private Streets of St Louis: The Architects and the Houses They Designed.* Columbia: University of Missouri Press, 1987.

Schuelz, Melvin H. *A Chesley Bonestell Space Art Chronology.* Parkland, FL: Universal Publishers/uPublish.com, 1999.

Schwarzer, Mitchell. *San Francisco: Architecture of the San Francisco Bay Area: History and Guide.* San Francisco: William Stout Publishers, 2007.

Scott, Mel. *San Francisco Bay Area, The: A Metropolis in Perspective.* Berkeley: University of California Press, 1959.

Shoup, Laurence H., and Suzanne Baker. *Cultural*

Resource Overview Lake Merced Transport. San Francisco Water Management Program (January 1981): 14.

Shumate, Albert. *Rincon Hill and South Park: San Francisco's Early Fashionable Neighborhoods.* Sausalito, CA: Wingate Press, 1988.

Silver, Mae. *Rancho San Miguel.* San Francisco: Ord Street Press, 2001.

Stern, Robert A.M., and John Montague Massengale. *The Anglo American Suburb.* New York: St. Martin's Press, 1981.

Stern, Robert A.M., et al. *Paradise Planned: The Garden Suburb and the Modern City.* New York: The Monacelli Press, 2013, 48.

Stewart, Robert E., Jr., and Mary F. Stewart. *Adolph Sutro: A Biography.* Berkeley, CA: Howell-North, 1962.

Thompson, Daniella. "Mark Daniels Excelled in Developing and Marketing Scenic Beauty." Berkeley Heritage website, http://berkeleyheritage. com/eastbay_then-now/mark_daniels.html.

Tobriner, Stephen. *Bracing for Disaster: Earthquake-Resistant Architecture and Engineering in San Francisco, 1838–1933.* Berkeley, CA: Heyday Books, 2006.

Walker, Richard. "Classy City: Residential Realms of the Bay Region." Online, http://geog.berkeley. edu/PeopleHistory/faculty/R_Walker/ClassCity. pdf.

_____. "Industry Builds Out the City: The Suburbanization of Manufacturing in San Francisco, 1850–1940." (Originally written in 2005 for *The Manufactured Metropolis,* Robert Lewis, ed. Philadelphia: Temple University Press.)

Weiss, Marc A. "The Real Estate Industry and the Politics of Zoning in San Francisco, 1914–1928." *Planning Perspectives* 3 (September 1988).

_____. *The Rise of the Community Builders.* New York: Columbia University Press, 1987.

"Wellesley Park." Historic American Landscape Survey HALS CA-44, 2005.

Wiley, Peter B. *National Trust Guide/San Francisco.* New York: John Wiley and Sons, 2000.

Wilson, William H. *The City Beautiful Movement.* Baltimore: John Hopkins Press, 1989.

Winter, Robert. *Toward a Simpler Way of Life: The Arts and Crafts Architects of California.* Berkeley: University of California Press, 1997.

Woodbridge, Sally. *Bay Area Houses.* Layton, UT: Gibbs Smith, 1988.

_____. *John Galen Howard and the University of California: The Design of a Great Public University Campus.* Berkeley: University of California Press, 2002.

Woodbridge, Sally, et al. *San Francisco Architecture.* Berkeley, CA: Ten Speed Press, 2005.

_____. *San Francisco Architecture: The Illustrative Guide to Over 1,000 of the Best Buildings, Parks, and Public Artworks in the Bay Area.* San Francisco: Chronicle Books, 1992.

Wright, Gwendolyn. *Building the Dream: A Social History of Housing.* New York: Pantheon Books, 1981.

Young, Terence. *Building San Francisco's Parks 1850–1930.* Baltimore: Johns Hopkins University Press, 2004.

Collections

Archives of the San Francisco Catholic Archdiocese.

Baldwin & Howell Records, 1891–1974. San Francisco History Center, San Francisco Public Library.

Charles Cherney papers. Bancroft Library, University of California, Berkeley; and California State Library, Sacramento.

Charles Hawkins files at the San Francisco History Center, San Francisco Public Library, uncatalogued.

James Phelan papers. Bancroft Library, University of California, Berkeley.

James Rolph papers. California Historical Society, North Baker Library, San Francisco.

M. M. (Maurice, Michael) O'Shaughnessy papers. Bancroft Library, University of California, Berkeley.

Mason-McDuffie collection, Bancroft Library, University of California, Berkeley.

San Francisco Historical Photograph Collection, San Francisco History Center. San Francisco Public Library.

Index

Numbers in *bold italics* indicate pages with illustrations